IP Multicasting:

THE COMPLETE GUIDE TO INTERACTIVE CORPORATE NETWORKS

DAVE KOSIUR

WILEY COMPUTER PUBLISHING

John Wiley & Sons, Inc.
New York • Chichester • Weinheim • Brisbane • Singapore • Toronto

ıobotka

Managing Editor: Micheline Frederick

Text Design & Composition: North Market Street Graphics

Designations used by companies to distinguish their products are often claimed as trademarks. In all instances where John Wiley & Sons, Inc., is aware of a claim, the product names appear in initial capital or ALL CAPITAL LETTERS. Readers, however, should contact the appropriate companies for more complete information regarding trademarks and registration.

This book is printed on acid-free paper. ∞

Published by John Wiley & Sons, Inc.

Published simultaneously in Canada.

This publication is designed to provide accurate and authoritative information in regard to the subject matter covered. It is sold with the understanding that the publisher is not engaged in professional services. If professional advice or other expert assistance is required, the services of a competent professional person should be sought.

Library of Congress Cataloging-in-Publication Data:
Kosiur, David R.
     IP multicasting : the complete guide to interactive corporate
networks / Dave Kosiur.
          p.   cm.
     "Wiley computer publishing."
     Includes index.
     ISBN 0-471-24359-0 (paper : alk. paper)
     1. Interactive multimedia.   2. Intranets (Computer networks)
3. Local area networks (Computer networks)   I. Title.
QA76.76.I59K67   1998
004.6'6—dc21   97-43990
                                                                CIP

Printed in the United States of America.

10 9 8 7 6 5 4 3 2 1

A C K N O W L E D G M E N T S

This book started out from a passing remark that I made on the phone one day to Carol Long at John Wiley & Sons. Little did I realize then that it would lead to this book. It's been quite an experience tracking developments in the fast moving technology of IP Multicasting as they occur.

I owe a lot to both Carol and my friend Eric Siegel, who proved good sounding boards as the conception and organization of this project got off the ground. Eric particularly helped me get my hands around the issues of multicasting and pointed out the differences between the forest and the trees.

I also owe a lot to my wife, Sue. It's almost an automatic response that I have to thank her for her understanding and patience as I spent days and nights writing this book. But, even more so, I could not have gotten this book done without her, since she created all the graphics for the book.

Other individuals also helped me get additional information or screen shots that I needed to finish this project. Thanks go to William Carrico and Scott Relth (Precept Software, Inc.), Albert Chen (GlobalCast, Inc.), Ross Finlayson (Live Networks, Inc.), and Peter Parnes (Lulea University of Technology, Sweden).

C O N T E N T S

1

Introduction

The world's largest network of networks, the Internet, has displayed remarkable flexibility as it's evolved from a research-oriented network to one with a myriad number of commercial applications. This flexibility owes much of its success to the dedicated engineers who are constantly looking for ways to offer new applications and improve the bandwidth and services offered on the Internet.

Today's Internet faces a series of serious challenges that were largely nonexistent at its inception. Not only is the number of users of the Internet growing exponentially, but so too are the number of networks comprising the Internet, and thus the number of devices used to interconnect these networks (i.e., routers).

This unprecedented growth is accompanied by the multiplication of new applications. Many applications previously available only to limited numbers of power users with high-end workstations are starting to become mainstream applications in the PC world—videoconferencing, video broadcasts, collaborative applications, and push technologies, for example. And these new applications bring with them new types of data—

video and audio, for example—which make new demands on a network's response and ability to deliver the data.

In the past, there were well-defined distinctions between the types of networks and the types of data they carried—telephone networks carried analog voice data while IP (Internet Protocol), IPX (Internet Packet Exchange), and SNA (Systems Network Architecture) networks dealt with digital data from computers. But that's all changed as every type of data imaginable has become digital, leading designers to figure out ways to handle the vastly different transmission requirements of each data type without compromising the networks or the data. Network designers are now faced with the challenge of supporting the timely and reliable delivery of any kind of data, especially real-time and multimedia data, to any user.

In addition to the new requirements for real-time data, applications are quickly evolving from one-to-one communications to one-to-many and many-to-many communications. Many of the new applications aim to link together multiple users, either as collaborators (designing a new product with a shared whiteboard application, for example) or simply as recipients of the same information (stock quotes or multimedia concerts, for instance). Widespread use of these applications can easily overload existing networks when the same bits of information have to be transmitted to different users at the same time. But new technologies using more intelligence distributed across the network make it possible to reduce unnecessary duplication of bits and relieve some of the network load. This book focuses on one of the newer technologies that's rapidly growing in use—IP multicasting.

Multipoint Communications

The fundamental method of network communications is between two host computers, or unicasting. These one-to-one sessions can offer a great deal of control of the data traffic between the source and receiver, allowing for acknowledgment of receipt, requests for retransmission of data, changes in transmission rate, and so on.

But many Internet applications involve one-to-many or many-to-many (*multipoint*) communications, where one or more sources are sending data to multiple receivers. It's possible to provide transmissions to multiple receivers in three different ways—*unicast*, where a separate copy of the data is delivered to each recipient; *broadcast*, where a data packet is forwarded to all portions of the network even if only a few of the destinations are intended recipients; and *multicast*, where a single packet is addressed to all intended recipients and the network replicates packets only as needed.

Unicasting

In multipoint unicasting, a source sends an individual copy of a message to each recipient (Figure 1.1); in such cases, the number of receivers is limited by the sender's bandwidth. For example, if we chose to set up a videoconference over 10-Mbps Ethernet and the data stream required 500 Kbps for each participant, we'd only be able to set up simultaneous point-to-point sessions among five people (a total of 20 connections is required for each person to communicate with the other four; see Figure 1.2) before we'd saturate the network.

> NOTE   For the sake of simplicity, I'm ignoring the effects of collisions on an Ethernet LAN (local area network), which would reduce the available bandwidth by as much as one-third.

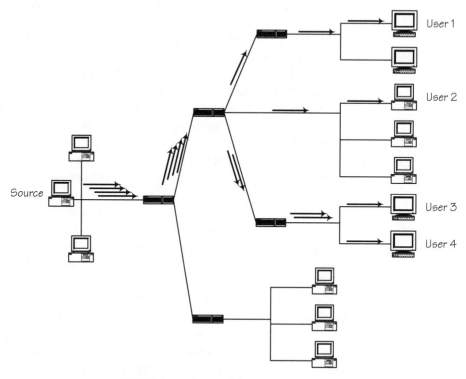

FIGURE 1.1   Flow of data in unicasting.

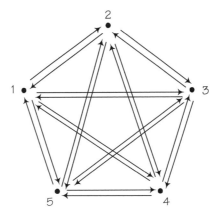

FIGURE 1.2 Number of links in a five-party session.

Transferring a file from an FTP (File Transfer Protocol) file server to your computer is an example of unicasting; the data in the file is sent over the network from the server only to your computer. But if five other people in your workgroup want to copy the same file to their own computers at the same time using FTP, the FTP server would have to send the file to each of the five recipients separately, using five times as much bandwidth as your single transfer. Some newer services, like Pointcast and similar push technologies, have to maintain separate unicast sessions for each user; although the raw data on the server is the same, each user has his or her own custom profile and has to be treated as an individual.

Unicasting is quite suitable for many applications on the Internet today, mainly because these applications involve one-to-one communications; client/server applications, for example, are almost exclusively unicast applications. Unicasting offers certain advantages in communication sessions, such as allowing the sender and receiver to control the flow between themselves and providing the recipient a way to acknowledge receipt of data or ask for retransmission of missing packets.

Even when the same data must be sent to more than one recipient at the same time, unicasting works well as long as the number of recipients is small. But when unicast protocols are used for data distribution and replication, there are real limits to how many parallel sessions a single server, such as an FTP server or a video server, can support. For a hundred simultaneous unicast sessions, a high-performance, dedicated server would typically be required. Data replication via parallel unicasting to multiple clients requires large amounts of server processing and large buffering overheads to maintain the state of sessions. It also uses excessive amounts of network bandwidth. If you've ever tried to download the latest version of Netscape Navigator or Microsoft's Internet Explorer just after it's been released, you've probably run across these bottlenecks.

Broadcasting

Broadcasting is at the other end of the network spectrum, so to speak. Under certain circumstances, it can be more efficient to transmit one copy of a message to all network nodes and let the receiving nodes decide if they want the message. Distributing the task of duplicating the packets among the network hosts rather than focussing the task at the sender's host machine is a definite advantage to the sender.

There are many network hardware technologies that include mechanisms to send packets to multiple destinations at the same time. On a bus technology like Ethernet, broadcast delivery can be accomplished with a single packet transmission on the wire.

For example, on an Ethernet LAN, the hardware interface on each host computer attached to the Ethernet cable monitors the net for packets bearing a broadcast address and accepts these packets. But other software running on the host must make the decision whether the broadcast data are actually of interest to the host, wasting the host's computing resources if the data are of no use. As long as broadcasts do not make up a significant portion of the net's traffic, though, this host process of filtering the broadcast is a suitable compromise between using network resources and host resources.

WAN (wide area network)-based broadcasting has to depend on network devices like routers to duplicate packets and distribute them among the subnets compromising the WAN or internetwork. Once on a LAN, these systems depend on the LAN's broadcast technologies (like the Ethernet example just described) to deliver the packets to each host computer.

Broadcasting on a wide area network is often used for maintaining or diagnosing the state of the internetwork. There are two primary types of broadcasts used for these functions—those that ask questions about network component status or availability and those that advertise this type of information. An example of broadcasts that ask questions are IP ARP (Address Resolution Protocol packets), which typically flood the entire subnet and have the target respond directly to the broadcast. Broadcasts that advertise information are generated by routing protocols such as RIP (Routing Information Protocol), OSPF (Open Shortest Path First), and

IGRP (Interior Gateway Routing Protocol). (We'll see in later chapters that the routing protocols used for multicasting may also use broadcasting to communicate.)

Broadcast traffic can quickly grow out of control at larger sites (e.g., greater than 300 or more networked devices) and reduce the bandwidth available to support mission-critical applications (and even general-purpose traffic). In worst-case scenarios, broadcast storms can effectively shut down the network, since the broadcasts may monopolize all of the available bandwidth.

It's often necessary to restrict such broadcasts to a single subnet to prevent broadcasts from crowding out other traffic and overwhelming the entire network. On the downside, broadcasting places an unwanted computational burden on workstations that are not interested in receiving the message that's been broadcast, since they have to process at least part of the message to determine if it's something of interest (Figure 1.3). Broadcast data that no one accepts, as shown in the lower half of Figure 1.3, simply wastes network and computational resources.

One significant feature that broadcasting (and multicasting) offers is relieving the source from the task of duplicating any packet that's destined for multiple recipients. The source transmits a single copy of the packet to the appropriate broadcast address and the network devices (routers, switches) take over, duplicating the packet as needed to cover the network.

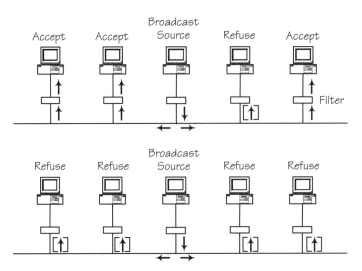

FIGURE 1.3 Filtering and accepting data from a network broadcast.

Multicasting

Like broadcasting, multicasting is natively supported on many LAN technologies. In Ethernet, for example, a series of multicast addresses are defined that workstations can monitor to receive data, much like their monitor broadcast addresses.

Multicasting falls between unicasting and broadcasting. Rather than send data to a single host (unicasting) or to all hosts on a network (broadcasting), multicasting aims to deliver data to a select group of hosts, called the *host group*. The host group is defined by a specified multicast address.

On a LAN, each host's net interface monitors the LAN and accepts packets addressed to the multicast address defining the host group to which it belongs. Unlike broadcasting, multicasting allows each host to choose whether it wants to participate in a multicast.

Multicasting on a WAN has some similarities to LAN multicasting. Host groups are essentially the same, since the concept of host groups is fundamental to any type of multicasting. But now membership information concerning host groups has to be maintained across the entire WAN or internetwork. Procedures for joining a host group and maintaining a host group differ from the LAN case since routers have to get involved, passing group information among themselves to maintain the fabric of the multicast internetwork.

Once a host group is set up and the sender starts transmitting packets to the host group address, the network infrastructure takes on the responsibility for delivering the necessary data streams to all members of the group. Only one copy of a multicast message passes over any link (such as a router) in the network; copies of the message are only made when paths diverge at a router (e.g., the message is supposed to be passed on to another router as well as to a workstation attached to the current router), helping to conserve bandwidth (Figure 1.4).

A multicast datagram is delivered to destination group members with the same best-effort reliability as a standard unicast IP datagram. This means that multicast datagrams are not guaranteed to reach all members of the group, nor to arrive in the same order as they were transmitted.

In multicasting, as in broadcasting, the source of a message usually has no idea of its recipients or the state of delivery of the data. Other methods have to be invoked to provide feedback, usually involving unicast traffic. This contrasts with protocols like TCP (Transmission Control Protocol), where some form of flow control or positive acknowledgment of packet receipt can be used to control a session between the sender and recipient. The initial implementations of WAN multicasting systems are

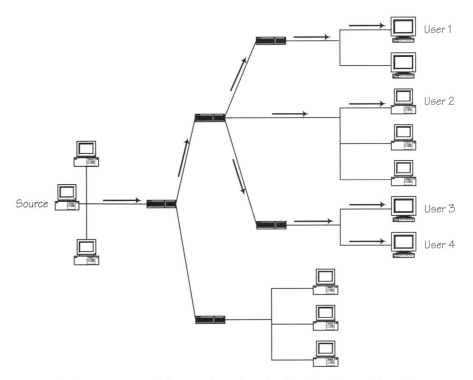

FIGURE 1.4 Flow of data and packet duplication in multicasting.

thus usually termed unreliable, since they rely on IP's best-effort delivery to transmit packets. We'll see in Chapter 6 what is being done to make multicasting a reliable transmission service.

IP multicasting isn't meant for every application found on the Internet. The protocols involved don't offer any advantages to Web browsing, sending e-mail, or running TELNET for remote access to a host computer, for instance. But they do make a difference for applications that focus on group activities, such as webcasting applications, file transfers, electronic software distribution, and groupware applications like video-conferencing and shared whiteboards. If more than two or three people are sharing common data in a given application, then IP multicasting can help reduce the demand on network bandwidth.

It's not always possible, or logical, to keep on adding higher-speed services to your network in order to accommodate more users and more applications. Rather than depend only on these brute-force solutions, you should also be looking to use clever solutions that can alleviate network congestion. One such solution is IP multicasting.

The Basic Components of Multicasting

Like other WAN multicasting systems, IP multicasting depends on three components: protocols for establishing and controlling multicast groups, a router infrastructure for distribution of multicast traffic, and application protocols and APIs (Application Programming Interfaces) that enable desktop computers and workstations to put multicasting to good use. I'll cover each of these components in detail throughout the remainder of this book.

Group membership is handled via IGMP (Internet Group Management Protocol), which handles communications between routers and the LANs (and attached hosts) they serve.

Key among the routing protocols that are covered in depth in Chapter 5 are Distance-Vector Multicast Routing Protocol (DVRMP), Multicast Open Shortest Path First (MOSPF), and Protocol-Independent Multicast (PIM).

Just as routing protocols are important for defining the infrastructure for transmitting data to multicast groups, application protocols are required to control multicast sessions and coordinate traffic among groups as needed. Among the crucial application protocols are Real-Time Transport Protocol (RTP), Real-Time Control Protocol (RTCP), and Resource Reservation Protocol (RSVP), which are the focus of Chapters 6 and 7. RSVP allows network administrators to specify particular service requirements for various applications, enabling the network to reserve end-to-end QoS (Quality of Service). RTP works alongside TCP to transport streaming data across networks and synchronize multiple streams. RTP inserts timing and sequencing information into each packet to minimize latency and jitter, enabling audio and video streams to be played smoothly despite occasional dropped packets. Feedback on network conditions and reception quality is provided by RTCP. With the information provided by RTCP, problems can be isolated to the desktop or the network.

IP multicasting owes its heritage to an experimental service on the Internet called the MBone, or Multicast Backbone. A virtual network layered atop sections of the physical Internet, the MBone was designed to create a semipermanent IP Multicast testbed without waiting for the deployment of multicast-capable routers throughout the entire Internet (Figure 1.5). Many of the protocols previously mentioned were developed to make the MBone work and are applicable to any multicasting WAN.

Although the MBone is an important resource and testbed, it has some limits in performance and scalability that will keep it from becoming a truly enterprise-class multicast service. Many of the industry's leading

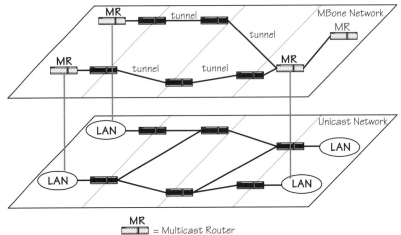

FIGURE 1.5 Sample MBone network overlay.

protocol designers are hard at work on standards for multicast routing protocols that can sustain scalable architectures.

Even as designers and service providers look to commercial support of IP multicasting, there are significant issues that remain to be solved. The MBone has already exhibited the scalability problems that can occur as the multicasting network grows—not only do the participating routers have to deal with the dynamic topological changes common to internetworks, but they also have to deal with the dynamics of host groups as members join and leave the groups. Group distribution is also changing as more members join a multicast session. A wider variety of media bandwidth is being used and members may be more widely distributed, with a lower density, than in the original MBone sessions. Much of this will be covered in Chapter 5.

The first implementations of IP multicasting have depended on the traditional best-effort delivery methods of IP, which renders delivery unreliable. Efforts are under way to define protocols for reliable delivery of multicast traffic, with some already in use. A variety of protocols have been proposed, since thus far no single reliable multicast protocol is capable of handling the wide variety of group distributions, amount of feedback required, or the various types of data involved (see Chapter 6).

As we move to commercial deployment of IP multicasting, the issue of secure sessions also becomes more important. Much of this work is piggybacking on the IETF's (Internet Engineering Task Force) work on secure unicast IP transmissions (the IPSec Working Group), but multicasting poses special problems, especially when the distribution of cryptographic keys have to be taken into account, as we'll see later in the book.

Last, but certainly not least, Quality of Service (QoS) for multicast traffic is an important issue. Although I'm jumping the gun slightly, multicasting will be of immense importance to the distribution of multimedia and real-time data on the Internet. But many types of multimedia have special timing and delay requirements which have to be guaranteed by the network if the delivered data is to be useful. Combining QoS reservations with multicasting is still an active area of research as network developers seek to combine multicasting with multimedia data distribution on IP networks.

Applications for Multicasting

Many different kinds of applications have already been developed to use IP multicasting, with more on the way. Many of these can be categorized according to whether they're real-time applications and use only single media data or multimedia (Figure 1.6). Here are some examples.

Streaming multimedia, particularly audio, video, or combined audio and video, can be distributed to a multicasting group. Using products like Progressive Networks' RealAudio and RealVideo, which are designed to use multicasting when it's available, recordings of conference sessions, concerts, and interviews have been multicast over the Internet.

	Real-time	Non-real-time
Multimedia	• Video server • Videoconferencing • Internet audio • Graphics & audio	• Replication • Video & Web servers • Kiosks • Content delivery • Intranet & Internet
Data-only	• Stock quotes • News feeds • Whiteboarding • Interactive gaming	• Information delivery • Server-server • Server-desktop • Database replication • Software distribution

FIGURE 1.6 Categorizing multicast applications.

Similarly, recordings of a company's annual meeting and CEO's speeches can be multicast on intranets to employees who ordinarily wouldn't receive the video and audio. Scheduled replays of important speeches can also be multicast over the intranets.

In education, class lectures can be recorded in advance and then multicast to students located in their homes or a special classroom, making distance learning more of a reality. Interactive videoconferencing using White Pine Software's CU-SeeMe or Intel's ProShare can take advantage of multicasting to reduce the bandwidth requirements for student discussions.

Recently, *push technologies* have become a popular way to distribute identical data to multiple receivers. These data might be news, stock quotes, or other timely information that's of common interest to a large number of people. But many of the first push systems do not use multicast to distribute the data. Instead, they unicast the data separately to each recipient and use proxy or caching servers to distribute the load. But that approach is changing; for real-time *push* of mission-critical data such as stock data to brokerage houses, for example, Tibco's Information Bus system uses multicasting to prevent saturation of the available bandwidth.

Some companies have also used multicasting to electronically distribute important files and software updates over a corporate network. For example, Toys "Я" Us has been able to use multicasting over a satellite network to transmit 1-Mbyte software updates to 250 of its stores, turning what had been a 6¼-hour transmission into one that now takes only 3 minutes and 4 seconds. Similarly, General Motors distributes inventory data and software to their dealers across the nation by multicasting over a satellite network.

Remember that multicasting is not a panacea (i.e., it doesn't work for one-to-one sessions or when different users must access the same information or file at different times). But, once you've finished this book, you should have a good idea of when multicasting is applicable, either immediately or when new protocols are implemented.

Interactive Applications and Multicasting

Even though multicasting has already been used for distribution of static data like stock quotes and other financial or news data to users, networked multimedia has become one of the major driving forces behind the interest in multicasting.

Today's networks have been rapidly evolving from their initial stages of supporting primarily text-based data and a limited number of users.

More business users are now wired and often use more than one network device—desktop computers, laptops, PDAs, and even special pagers. But more importantly than supporting more users and devices, network administrators and network designers are faced with the task of supporting a wider variety of data types, particularly with the increasing popularity of multimedia.

Thus, not only is more network bandwidth required to support the ever-increasing number of users, but network designers also have to look for new ways to contain and allocate bandwidth consumption per user. If not immediately, the typical business network will soon have to be capable of supporting not only numeric and textual data, but also ordinary as well as interactive (or real-time) multimedia.

A wide variety of applications run on networks (Figure 1.7). Interactive applications can range from a terminal emulator that requires typing in a command on a keyboard to control a remote host computer or using a Web browser to view pages on another site to the interactive play between players in multiplayer network games and the even faster interactions required for transaction processing of on-line orders. But one of the biggest changes to networked applications over the past few years has been the increasing interest in multimedia.

What Is Multimedia?

For our purposes, it is a mixture of text, graphics, pictures, audio, and video, all in digitized form. Not all of these forms need to be included in a single application to make it a multimedia application, but at least any two of these forms of data are required to fit the definition.

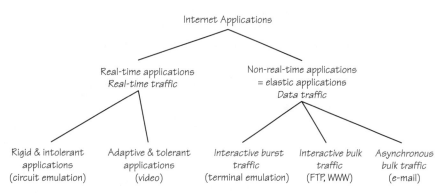

FIGURE 1.7 Categories of multimedia applications (examples given in parentheses).

Just as nature abhors a vacuum, users will always find ways to use any available bandwidth on a network. Even as new technologies like Gigabit Ethernet make it easier to provide more bandwidth, applications are gobbling up more bandwidth and placing restrictive demands on such data delivery parameters as network latency and jitter. Thus real-time data (which we'll see includes more than just multimedia data) requires some kind of bandwidth reservation based on quality of service as well as priorities related to mission-criticality. And if this real-time data is provided to a group of users, efficient methods for distributing the data (ones which don't unduly multiply the copies of the data) are required to avoid overloading network bandwidth (Table 1.1).

Let's take a brief look at some of the requirements for running multimedia and other real-time data on networks (more details will be provided in Chapter 7).

Some of the simpler multimedia data, such as text combined with graphics, or animation files, do not pose special transmission problems on networks. These files may be larger than the norm, but they don't require synchronization of different parts of the data. But more complex multimedia data, such as that used in interactive applications—videoconferencing and streaming video, for example—impose special restrictions on networks beyond demands for more bandwidth (Table 1.2 and Figure 1.8).

Such multimedia data are very dependent on both consistent bandwidth availability and consistent network delay (or latency).

While bandwidth is the crucial factor when precise amounts of data must be delivered within a certain time period, latency affects the response time between clients and servers. Latency is the minimum time that elapses between requesting and receiving data. It can be affected by many different factors, including bandwidth, an internetwork's infrastructure, routing techniques, and transfer protocols.

Real-time interactive applications such as desktop videoconferencing are sensitive to accumulated delays, usually less than 0.2 seconds end-to-

TABLE 1.1 Network Requirements and Possible Solutions

Requirement	*Solution*
Increased network bandwidth	Gigabit Ethernet, ATM
Bandwidth-efficient group delivery of information	IP multicasting
Delivery of real-time data, including synchronized multimedia	QoS (using RSVP, for example)

TABLE 1.2 Sample Data Rates for Multimedia Applications

Application	*Bandwidth*
Telephone-quality audio	64 Kbps
Simple application sharing	100 Kbps
Videoconferencing	128 Kbps–1 Mbps
MPEG video	1.54 Mbps
Imaging	8–100 Mbps
Virtual reality	>100 Mbps

end (which must include any processing, such as compression/decompression, by the sending and receiving computers). Interactive traffic (such as a TELNET terminal session) can stand slightly longer latencies, of the order of 1 second or less. Bulk transfer traffic (an FTP file transfer, for example) can deal with any latency since the services have built-in measures for dealing with acknowledgment of lost packets, rearranging packet sequences, and so on, but are not time-dependent.

As previously mentioned, traditional internetwork protocols like IP provide what is termed *best-effort delivery,* treating every message independently. In an IP network, a source may transmit a packet to a destination without any prior negotiation or communication. Furthermore, the network has no information that a particular packet belongs to a suite of packets, such as a file transfer or a video stream. The network will do its best to deliver each of these packets independently. This approach often introduces considerable latency and variability of delay in end-to-end paths, which aren't compatible with much of the data generated by the newer applications seen on networks, such as videoconferencing and streaming multimedia that depend on known delays and little, if any, data loss.

Some crucial network traffic relies on short response times, high bandwidth, or other characteristics. These properties can be impacted by low-priority traffic or by poorly designed applications that abuse the network. Technologies to provide quality of service attempt to provide a method for categorizing and prioritizing traffic to ensure that traffic that's crucial to the enterprise will always flow across the internetwork in a timely manner, regardless of competing demands for bandwidth by less-important applications.

With the move to multimedia, applications now require control over the quality of service they receive from the networks. To support the different latency and bandwidth requirements of multimedia and other real-time

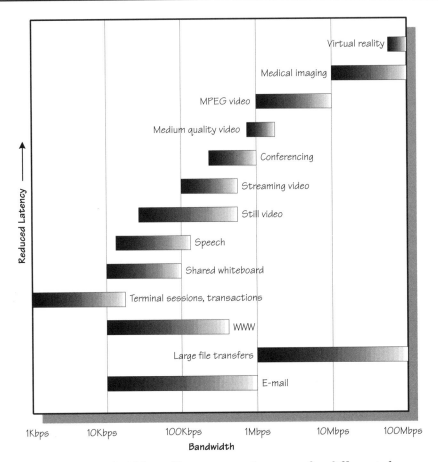

FIGURE 1.8 Bandwidth and latency requirements for different classes of applications.

applications, networks can use QoS parameters to accept an application's network traffic and prioritize it relative to other QoS requests from other applications. QoS provides network services that are differentiated by their bandwidth, latency, jitter (i.e., the variation in latency), and error rates.

An application can request a service based on its QoS requirements. The network, in turn, must determine if it's capable of providing the required services. If not, the connection can be refused or the QoS renegotiated.

Even when networks support bandwidth allocation and latency guarantees using quality-of-service requests, transmitting the same data to multiple recipients can overload a network. This is when IP multicasting can be used to your advantage—combine multicasting with QoS-based resource reservations and you've got a potential winner.

Who Should Read This Book

This book is aimed at IS managers, system administrators, and network managers who are looking to understand what multicasting is and how it can be used for applications on intranets and the Internet. The goal is to provide the reader with enough background to understand the protocols and systems associated with multicasting so he or she can plan for using multicasting applications and modify his or her networks accordingly.

When finished with the book, the reader will have an understanding of the differences between unicasting and multicasting, how multicasting works, and how it can be used for business applications, such as multimedia, push technologies, and videoconferencing.

In writing this book, I've assumed that readers are already somewhat familiar with TCP/IP protocols and internetworks. If you're new to TCP/IP protocols, Chapter 2 will serve as an introduction to these protocols. Readers experienced with these protocols can either use Chapter 2 as a quick refresher or skip it entirely.

Overview of the Book

The bulk of this book explains the technical details of IP multicasting and how to prepare your network for using it. Chapter 2 is a brief introduction to protocols and the basics of TCP/IP and routing; it can be easily skipped by more technical readers.

Chapter 3 expands on the concepts of multicasting mentioned earlier in this chapter, discussing the different types of multicasting protocols, how IP multicast addresses are selected and used for multicast sessions, and how multicast groups are formed.

Chapter 4 starts with a discussion of basic routing issues for unicasting, then proceeds to discuss the issues surrounding multicast routing, such as tree construction and scalability.

Chapter 5 discusses the many types of routing protocols that have been proposed for handling multicast traffic. The five main routing protocols, each of which is best for certain networks, will be discussed in this chapter.

Chapter 6 gets to the meat of how data can be transported utilizing multicasting. It covers RTP (Real-Time Transport Protocol), RTCP (Real-Time Transport Control Protocol), RTSP (Real-Time Streaming Protocol), and the various protocols that have been proposed for reliable multicasting.

Chapter 7 discusses the requirements that new applications put on multiservice networks. It also discusses various approaches to Quality of Service (QoS), what protocols are developed for use with QoS, and how it can be managed to provide appropriate bandwidth and network response for interactive applications.

Chapter 8 covers the protocols and procedures that are being developed to simplify how multicast sessions are announced on the Internet. This includes providing such information as bandwidth and computer requirements for a session, the different types of data available for selection by the receiver, and broadcaster information. Issues surrounding private, secure multicast sessions are also discussed.

Chapter 9 attempts to provide an overview of the available IP multicasting software, grouped according to different classes of applications, specifically multimedia, groupware, videoconferencing, push technologies, distance learning, and file transfers.

Chapter 10 offers a brief historical perspective and overview of the MBone, the Internet's experimental network for testing multicasting applications, which led to the creation of many of the protocols and commercial applications now showing up for multicasting. The chapter also includes a look at some of the current commercial networks for multicasting.

Chapter 11 covers the details of planning networks for multicasting, discussing satellite nets, frame relay, SMDS (Switched Multimegabit Data Service), ATM (Asychronous Transfer Mode), dial-up connections, as well as ISDN (Integrated Services Digital Network). Strategies for transitioning from restricted subnets with multicast support to full multicast networks are also included.

Chapter 12 is my attempt to cover some of the remaining issues that need to be resolved for multicasting to become more commonplace on the Internet and within intranets.

Read on!

Networks and Protocols

The basic function of any network is the delivery of data from a source to one or more receivers. A myriad number of technologies have been developed to accomplish this task, including a wide variety of physical media for transmitting data, different ways for organizing network devices to cope with increasing network complexity, and many protocols to govern how everything fits together to form a functioning whole.

It can take more than a single book to cover all of these aspects of networking, so I won't be covering all the details of networking here. In order to set the stage for understanding how IP multicasting works and how networks and applications need to be configured to use IP multicasting, this chapter will concentrate on the TCP/IP protocols and how networks are built using these protocols. If you're already familiar with TCP/IP protocols and routing, feel free to skip this chapter.

Networks

Networks come in all shapes and sizes, ranging from simple ones meant to connect a few PCs and a printer together to international nets encompassing thousands of computing devices scattered across the planet. There are many different ways to build a network, such as Ethernet, Token Ring, and wireless, just to mention some common media, as well as IP versus IPX versus SNA protocols and so on.

Let's take a brief look at how networks are categorized and organized before we move on to the bulk of the chapter, which focuses on protocols. A network is most often categorized by how data are routed within the network and under what conditions data are accepted by the network devices. Networks are usually called either circuit-switched networks or packet-switched networks. Circuit-switched networks can also be called connection-oriented networks, while packet-switched networks are often called connectionless networks.

In the early days of electrical communications, *circuit switching* actually meant switching between physical circuits through electromechanical exchanges to establish a call between two systems (such as two telephones). Today, in a fully electronic network, a circuit is a connection which behaves as if it were a physical circuit. This *virtual wire* is not shared with any other users or communications. Once set up to accept a given rate of bits per second, this bit rate is guaranteed for the duration of the connection. ATM (Asynchronous Transfer Mode) networks are a good example of circuit-switched networks. ATM has become an increasingly important network technology in the last few years and often figures in the design of many integrated services networks these days. I'll be covering some of the details of ATM and how it relates to IP multicasting in Chapter 11.

In circuit-switched networks like the telephone network, the source and the destination must establish a connection to exchange data. For example, on a telephone network, you have to dial your party's phone number and he has to answer the phone before you can start a conversation. Networks operating in a circuit-switched mode are aware of communications between the sending and receiving systems, but not that the two systems have agreed to communicate.

The advantage of a circuit-switched network is its guaranteed capacity; once a circuit is established, no other network activity decreases the circuit's capacity. One disadvantage of circuit switching is the cost—the cost of a circuit is fixed, independent of the traffic that flows on it. For instance, you pay a fixed rate for a phone call, even when there are silences in your conversation.

The alternative network style, *packet switching*, focuses on the ability to share transmission systems between two or more data streams. In packet switching, data between two end-systems is not sent as a continuous stream of bits. Instead, it is divided into small units called packets that are sent one at a time. These packets are multiplexed, or allocated different time slots for transmission. More than one source can inject packets over the same wires into packet networks, so that when one source is not transmitting, network resources are available for use by other sources. To allow the network to sort out these multiple flows of data, each packet carries an identifier of its destination. Thus, logical paths instead of physical circuits exist between communicating end-systems.

The main advantage of packet switching is that multiple communications among computers can occur concurrently. The disadvantage is that, as network activity increases, a given pair of communicating computers receives less of the network capacity.

Packet-switched networks like the Internet and other IP-based networks provide what is termed *best-effort delivery*, treating every message independently. In a packet-switched network, a source may transmit a packet to a destination without any prior negotiation or communication. Other means of feedback have to be employed to deliver information on a message's delivery status (e.g., was it successfully received or is a retransmission required?). Furthermore, the network has no information that a particular packet belongs to a suite of packets, such as a file transfer or a video stream. The network will do its best to deliver each of these packets independently, whereas in connection-oriented mode the network may ensure at set-up time that the required resources are allocated to guarantee a certain performance. We'll see in Chapter 7 how some of the concepts behind circuit switching are being applied to IP networks to provide better allocation and control of bandwidth and guaranteed delivery.

Even though the network views each message independently, packet-switched services allow users to interact with each other. However, the users' applications must assume the responsibility for that interaction, such as not sending another file until receipt of the first one has been acknowledged.

Some examples of circuit-switched or connection-oriented networks are the telephone system, ISDN, and X.25. Networks that operate as packet-switched or connectionless networks include Ethernet, Token Ring, and IP networks.

Network Addresses

In order to forward data to the appropriate destination(s), network protocols need some kind of addressing scheme for the hosts that are to receive the data. Likewise, data sources require network addresses as well in case network protocols have to inform the source host of a change in the network, undeliverable messages, or other problems. Much like the physical network addresses found in frames (in Ethernet, for example), TCP/IP uses a 32-bit integer called the IP address for each host on an internetwork.

> NOTE   The latest version of the IP protocol, IPv6, provides 128 bits for addresses.

Each IP address is actually the combination of network identifier (netid) and a host identifier (hostid) (Figure 2.1). Every host on an internetwork has a single unique IP address. Routers, on the other hand, usually have more than one network address, since they support multiple interfaces to the internetwork (one for Ethernet and another for Token Ring, for instance).

The designers of TCP/IP and the Internet chose to create different classes of networks to accommodate address allocation among networks of different sizes. Why allocate over 16,000 possible addresses to a company when it only has 128 network devices, for example?

IPv4 addresses are divided into three major classes: A, B, and C (see Table 2.1). A fourth class, D, will be mentioned frequently throughout this book—it's reserved for special uses such as multicasting. Each address consists of four octets, or sets of eight binary digits, which are separated by decimals in the customary notation (known as the dotted decimal notation). The first 1 to 4 digits in the first octet determine which class the IP address is in. Since each address class supports different numbers of networks and hosts within a class, the partitioning of the octets between the netid and the hostid changes from class to class (Figure 2.2). Class A addresses use the last three octets to specify IP nodes, while Class B addresses use the last two octets for this purpose, and Class C addresses use the last octet.

Although the IP address specifies a network connection, we'll see shortly that further information is required to ensure that the data are delivered to the proper application on the host. TCP/IP protocols insert a

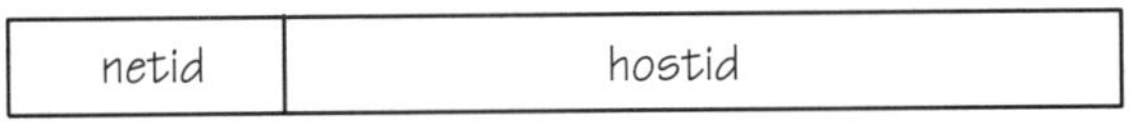

netid	hostid

FIGURE 2.1   A generic IP address.

TABLE 2.1   Address Classes and Numbers of Nets and Hosts

Class	*Network ID*	*# Unique Networks*	*Host Address ID*	*# Unique Hosts*
A	7 bits	128	24 bits	16,777,216
B	14 bits	>16,000	16 bits	65,536
C	21 bits	>2 million	8 bits	256

number known as a *port* or *port number* into each packet so they can identify data from different applications (Figure 2.3). Each application uses a
different port number to identify itself, enabling a transport protocol to
decide which application should receive a packet's data. But ports merely
identify application protocols (such as FTP or DNS, see later in this chapter) and not the applications that are actually running on a given computer. Another number, called the *socket,* is therefore calculated by
combining a port number with the computer's network address. The
socket is then used to identify one end of a network conversation.

In addition to classifying IP addresses according to the network class,
TCP/IP supports three different types of network addresses: unicast, broadcast, and multicast.

> NOTE   IPv6 does not define a broadcast address; it does define a new address type, the
> *anycast* address. To achieve the same effect as a broadcast address, IPv6 uses a multicast
> address, with a group defined as all interfaces. An anycast address refers to one of a set of
> interfaces.

Unicast addresses are the most straightforward, referring to traffic
that's directed to a single network interface, such as the Ethernet card in
your PC. A broadcast address is one that refers to all the interfaces

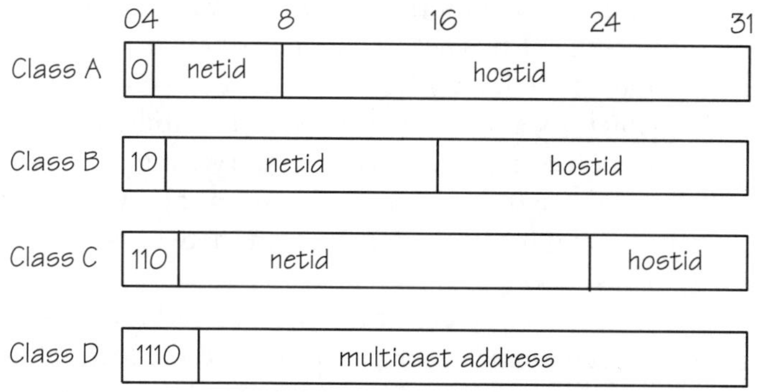

FIGURE 2.2   IP address classes.

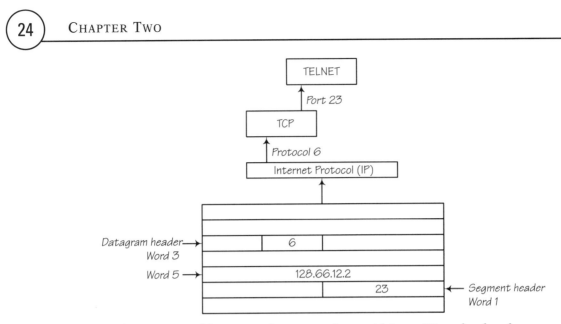

FIGURE 2.3 Addresses and port numbers within an IP packet header.

attached to a network; in this case, a message sent to a broadcast address is delivered to all computers attached to the LAN or network. Lastly, a multicast address identifies a group of interfaces found on the network. When a message is directed to a multicast address, the network will attempt to deliver it to all of the interfaces that are part of the multicast group and no other computers. In such cases, the original message is generated once and that message is duplicated as necessary by routers in the network to deliver it to the interfaces of the group.

Internetworks

Although computers can perform useful tasks on a simple network, such as a single Ethernet LAN, today's networks are more complex than the small office LAN using a few cables to connect together a few PCs and a printer. Even though users want the ability to communicate between any two points, regardless of the intervening technologies, the inability of a single type of network hardware to satisfy all communications constraints necessitates connecting different networks together to create internetworks.

In order to create an internetwork, some software has to be inserted between applications programs and the technology-dependent communications systems to hide the low-level details and make the collection of connected networks appear as a single large network to users. In addition, special computers have to be included that interconnect two networks and pass packets from one to the other (translating the packets as required by the network technologies). These special computers are called routers. We'll see later in this chapter how routers handle these network interconnections and maintain information about the composition of the internetwork.

Before we delve any further into internetworks, it's worth reviewing some of the network terminology that will appear in this chapter and occasionally through other parts of this book. Since we're focusing on TCP/IP networks in this book, much of the terminology is specific to TCP/IP nets (Figure 2.4).

First, computing systems using TCP/IP protocols may act as hosts or as routers. Systems that actually send or receive messages are *hosts,* while systems that relay those messages across networks are *routers.*

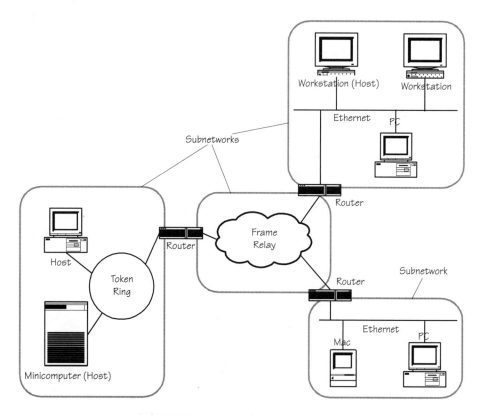

FIGURE 2.4 A sample internetwork.

A *subnetwork* consists of all systems that can directly communicate using homogeneous technologies. For example, a single frame relay network forms a subnetwork. When TCP/IP joins several subnetworks together, the resulting connection is an internetwork, or internet for short.

ROUTING VERSUS SWITCHING

Routers and switches are decision points in a network—deciding where on the network they should forward the packets they receive. The difference between the two types of devices is what part of a packet they scan to make a forwarding decision. Switches look at MAC (Media Access Control) addresses in layer 2 (the Data Link Layer) of a protocol stack (see the next section for more on protocol layers and stacks). Routers review network addresses found in layer 3, the Network Layer (Figure 2.5).

Every router has two basic functions: route calculation and frame forwarding. Since routers are responsible for determining the topology of the network, they have to identify the viable paths through the network infrastructure; this is called route calculation. The routing protocol provides a way for routers to communicate and build a map of the network. A second component of route calculation is the application of filters (e.g., restrictions, priority criteria) to traffic. These filters are applied to each packet in a particular traffic flow between two points.

Frame forwarding is the processing of inbound traffic and the subsequent forwarding of this traffic to the appropriate outbound destination link. Routers evaluate an incoming packet's layer 3 contents to determine the source and destination addresses for forwarding decisions.

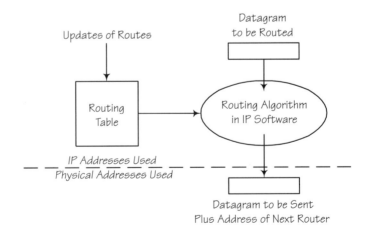

FIGURE 2.5 Basic operations in a router.

Routers have always been relied on to offer four basic functions that switches do not perform. First, routers can filter traffic to reduce contention for limited WAN bandwidth much better than layer 2 switches. Second, broadcast storms, such as those generated by TCP/IP ARP messages and NetWare SAP (Service Advertisement Protocol) messages, can be controlled by routers. Third, by breaking a network into subnets, routers can be used to create separate administrative network domains, helping to scale the network for management purposes. Lastly, routers are routinely used as security firewalls between corporate net sites and the public Internet.

Routers are not without their downside, however. While switches are largely *plug and play,* network administrators have to determine and specify a relatively large set of configuration parameters to make each router work in their network. Configuration errors can make entire networks unusable. Routers have also offered less performance in forwarding packets than switches and usually cost more per port than switches.

Routers use the destination network, not the destination host, when routing a packet. Since routing is based on networks, the amount of information that a router needs to store is proportional to the number of networks forming the internetwork, not the number of computers. Typically, a routing table contains a pair of addresses: the IP address of a destination network N and the IP address of the next router along the path to network N. This router is called the *next hop* and the concept of using a routing table to store a next hop for each destination is called next-hop routing.

While routers can be used to limit broadcast traffic to their attached subnets, in a switch-only network, all workstations and servers attached to the network are forced to decode all broadcast frames. Processing the added broadcast traffic requires additional CPU (central processing unit) interrupts and can degrade application performance on each of the hosts, even if the broadcast is of no interest to them.

Protocol Structure

Simply stated, protocols are the rules that determine everything about the way a network operates. Protocols have two important roles. First, they describe the *semantics* of messages; that is, the meaning associated with the bits transmitted between two entities. For instance, protocols define which part of a message contains the raw data and which part might be derived from the data—say a checksum that's been calculated to guard against data corruption.

Second, protocols also define the *actions* taken upon receipt of a message. In keeping with the previous example, a receiver of the message would be expected to compute the checksum of the data in the received message and match it with the one it received to determine if the data had been corrupted during transmission.

Two important principles are at the heart of protocol development: protocol layering and peer communications.

Layering protocols provides three advantages. First, it allows a complex problem to be broken into smaller, more manageable pieces. Since each layer solves only a part of the problem, it is easier to write and debug the software for a single layer than a monolithic application trying to solve the whole problem.

The OSI (Open Systems Interconnection) Reference Model (Figure 2.6) is one example of how network protocols can be layered. In an effort to standardize a way of looking at, and comparing, network protocols, the International Standards Organization (ISO) created the 7-layer OSI model that defines the basic network functions. Each layer in the model corresponds to one level of network functionality.

A second advantage in using layers for designing protocol suites is that it simplifies substituting one protocol for another. When protocols are designed, specifications set forth how a protocol exchanges data with a pro-

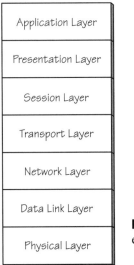

FIGURE 2.6 The OSI Reference Model.

tocol layered above or below it. As long as a developer follows these specifications, he or she can substitute a new, better protocol for the one currently in the suite without affecting the general behavior of the network.

A NOTE ON NOMENCLATURE   The interface between adjoining layers is known as the *service boundary.* Data that is transmitted from one layer to another through the service boundary is defined by the lower layer's service definition.

Third, layering allows us to reuse functionality. The functionality provided by a lower layer protocol can be shared and used in different ways by different protocols in overlying layers. For example, in Figure 2.7, a datagram received by the IP protocol may be directed to either the **ICMP** (Internet Control Message Protocol), UDP (User Datagram Protocol), TCP, or EGP (Exterior Gateway Protocol) protocol in the transport layer; similarly, any of those protocols could generate data for transmission by the IP protocol.

The other fundamental concept in protocol design is that of *peer communications.* Consider a situation in which a number of services are required to communicate with someone—delivering a letter via the post office is a good example. If I wish to send a letter to someone in a foreign country, I'll deliver the letter to a postal worker at my local post office, who will then forward it to a distribution center and eventually to the foreign country where my correspondent resides. In this simple example, my foreign correspondent and I are peers—we've settled on a common language and format for the letter. The postal worker in my post office and another postal worker in the foreign post office are also peers of each other, since

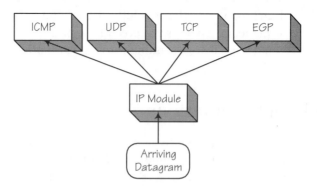

FIGURE 2.7 Multiple protocols using a layer's functionality.

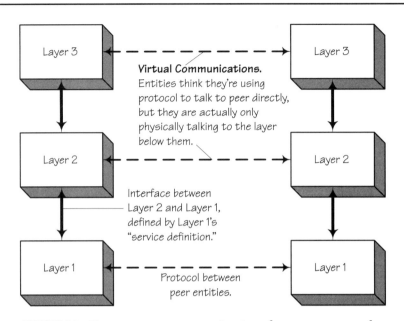

FIGURE 2.8   Peer-to-peer communications between protocols.

they follow similar rules for sorting and distributing the mail. If you're looking for a definition of peers, here's one: Parties communicating at the same level in a hierarchy of communications services are called peers.

In other words, peer communications governed by protocols in a given layer take place as if no other protocols are involved (Figure 2.8). The peers communicate using their rules without worrying if other protocols need to add to the message's data in order to transmit it between two computers, for instance. When I wrote the letter in the previous example, I didn't worry whether my letter was going to be transmitted by truck, boat, or plane, or whether the post office had specific rules for sorting and bagging letters before sending it to its destination.

Protocol Implementations

While there are many network protocols (such as NetWare's IPX/SPX and IBM's SNA, for example), we'll only be concerned with the protocols collectively known as the IP or TCP/IP protocols.

The TCP/IP protocols that form the basis of the Internet and intranets define how data are subdivided into packets for transmission across a network, as well as how applications can transfer files and send electronic mail. While the TCP/IP protocols don't neatly fit into all seven layers of the OSI Reference Model, they do provide all the necessary functionality for productive networking (Figure 2.9).

The applications protocols at the top of the *stack,* as the layered protocols are often called, organize the data that networks will transfer. Beneath the application protocols is the transport layer, which is responsible for delivering the applications' information to the destination. Transport protocols in turn rely on the protocols found in the network (or internetwork) layer, which bear the responsibility of understanding the topology of the network and forwarding information through the network to its destination. The lowest layers describe the network technology itself, including descriptions of the physical media and electrical signals.

TCP/IP

It's much easier to understand TCP/IP by lumping together the protocols found in the network and transport layers, since these protocols work together very closely. These are the protocols that give the TCP/IP protocol suite its name, even though there are many other protocols within the suite.

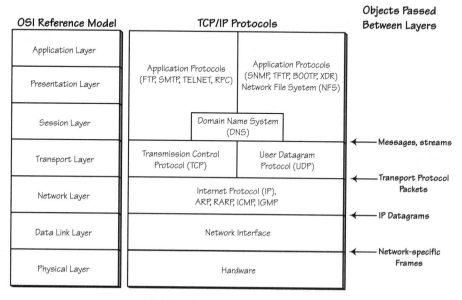

FIGURE 2.9 TCP/IP protocols.

TCP/IP and the Lower OSI Layers

The bottom two layers of the OSI model are often treated as one, the network technology layer, since specifications for the link layer are strongly linked with the specs for the physical layer. The bottom layer in the OSI Reference Model, the Physical Layer, pertains strictly to network technology itself—where systems connect to each other and what type of electrical (or other) signals are used to exchange information. Typical network media range from twisted-pair copper wires, dial-up modems, and high-speed fiber optic cables, to satellites, for example.

Each network technology defines an addressing mechanism to specify the destination for each packet of data. The hardware specifies how computers are assigned addresses, for example, the number of bits that comprise an address, and where the destination address field is located in a data packet.

Data Link Layer protocols determine how a computing system is interfaced to the network hardware. For example, the basic unit of information that Ethernet transfers is called a frame and its format is included as part of the IEEE Ethernet specs. Similarly, other protocols define the frame structures for Token Ring and ISDN network media. TCP/IP was designed to be independent of the network media involved and thus interface with just about any protocol defining OSI layers 1 and 2. This openness or media-independence is one of the advantages of using TCP/IP for networking. The TCP/IP protocols do not include specific definitions for the Physical Layer and Data Link Layer. We'll see in Chapter 3 that IP multicasting depends on the multicasting capabilities of the LAN's Data Link Layer to "go the final mile" (i.e., deliver multicast data to the host on its locally attached LAN).

IP AND ASSOCIATED PROTOCOLS

The protocols found in the network layer have the responsibility for forwarding packets across all the interfaces that make up an internetwork (which is one reason why IP is called the *Internet* Protocol). Thus, the network layer specifications include rules not only for forwarding packets, but also for host addresses and protocols for delivering diagnostic information about the internetwork.

IP, or the Internet Protocol, is a connectionless protocol which defines the basic unit of data transfer used throughout a TCP/IP internetwork, choosing a path over which the data is sent (Figure 2.10).

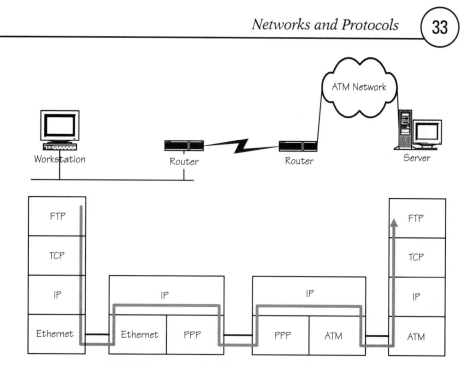

FIGURE 2.10 IP and forwarding data traffic.

By convention, the packets that IP transfers are called *datagrams*. They consist of a datagram header and the data area. In addition to containing the network addresses of the source and destination of the datagram, the IP or datagram header includes options that can be used to define a type of service, route options, a timestamp, and fragment processing options, for example. The IPv6 header has changed significantly, doing away with the options field and using pointers to header extensions which follow the initial header in IPv6 datagrams (Figure 2.11).

One important field in the IPv4 header is the Time to Live, or TTL, field. The TTL field specifies how long, in seconds, the datagram is allowed to remain on an internetwork. Routers and hosts that process datagrams decrement the TTL field as time passes and remove the datagram from the internetwork when its time expires. This helps keep errant datagrams from continuing to travel on an internetwork if routing tables become corrupt and form routing loops. We'll see in later chapters that TTL values can be used to help control multicast traffic.

NOTE In IPv6, the TTL field has been renamed to the Hop Limit field, which is more descriptive of the real world. In practice, very few routers decrement the TTL field by a non-integral number less than 1. Thus, a TTL value of *N* allows the packet to traverse *N*-1 routers

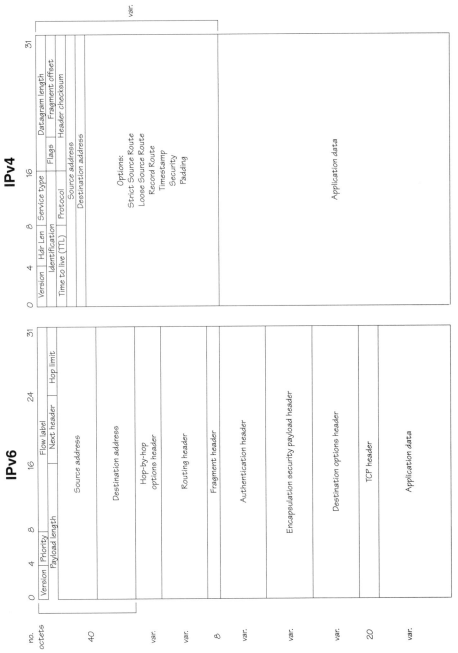

FIGURE 2.11 IPv4 and IPv6 packet headers.

34

> # IPv4 versus IPv6
>
> Version 4 of IP (IPv4) has been used to provide the basic communication mechanisms of TCP/IP and the Internet for around 20 years. But, as new applications for networks were introduced and internetworks were greatly expanded (both in size and number), it became more obvious that a new version of IP was required. The proposed new version is called IPv6.
>
> Conceptually, IPv6 differs little from IPv4. But many details have changed; for example, IPv6 provides larger addresses and IPv6 replaces the IPv4 variable-length options field with a series of fixed-format headers (which leads to faster processing).
>
> The major changes in IPv6 are: Addresses are now 128 bits long instead of 32 bits; a new flexible header format uses a fixed-format header with a set of optional headers; network resources can be preallocated instead of using IPv4's type-of-service specification; IPv6 can more easily accommodate future extensions than IPv4.
>
> I'll point out the significant differences between IPv4 and IPv6 in the appropriate sections throughout this book.

or make *N*-1 hops. The Hop Limit field thus reflects the fact that the field limits the number of hops a packet can make, not the number of seconds it will remain on the network.

Aside from moving data from its source to its destination, the protocols in the network layer coordinate functions such as discovering neighbors, controlling address assignments, and managing group memberships. Neighbor discovery lets a system identify other hosts and routers on its link. Hosts have to learn of at least one router so they can forward datagrams to systems not on their link.

IPv4 relies on a separate protocol for resolving addresses, the Address Resolution Protocol (ARP). ARP, which is another protocol that's a part of the network layer, is used to help network devices determine an IP address. ARP translates IP addresses into physical network addresses; for example, ARP converts a 32-bit IPv4 address into an Ethernet MAC address for transmission on an Ethernet LAN. ARP has two functions: The first function maps an IP address to a physical address when sending a packet and the second function answers requests from other machines. A related protocol, RARP, does the opposite, converting physical network addresses into IP addresses.

ICMP, or the Internet Control Message Protocol, provides communications among routers as well as between routers and hosts. ICMPs are primarily used for three major actions on a network: retarding the transmission rate, changing a host's routing table, and helping hosts determine whether a destination can be reached. If a router is unable to forward an IP datagram, for example, it uses ICMP to inform the sender that there's a problem. Additionally, with IPv6, ARP's functions have been incorporated into ICMP.

IGMP, or the Internet Group Management Protocol, is an important protocol for multicasting because it's the protocol used to inform routers that a member of a multicast group is on the subnet connected to the router. This membership information is also forwarded to the multicast source via IGMP. (Chapter 3 contains more details on how IGMP is used in multicasting.)

TCP AND UDP

While IP and related protocols in the network layer are responsible for moving data from a source to its destination, the transport protocols (TCP and UDP) have the responsibility of distinguishing between traffic from different applications within the system and compensating for IP's lack of reliability. (Recall that IP is designed for best-effort delivery and is therefore classified as an unreliable protocol.)

Since unreliable links mean that some datagrams do not arrive at the destination, other methods are needed to provide reliability. In a process called *end-to-end verification* within the transport layer, the source and destination systems detect datagram losses and attempt to recover lost datagrams. The end-to-end software located within the transport layer uses checksums, acknowledgments, and timeouts to control transmission of datagrams.

Located above IP in the TCP/IP stack, either TCP (Transmission Control Protocol) or UDP (User Datagram Protocol) can be used to determine the maximum transmission that can be used (that is, the packet size) and fine-tune transmissions accordingly (Figure 2.12).

The simplest level of service is datagram delivery, which does not guarantee delivery and does not protect against datagram corruption. UDP provides a best-effort delivery; it does its best to transfer datagrams for its applications, but UDP makes no guarantees. Datagrams may get reordered or lost in transit and the applications using UDP must be prepared for such events. While the IP layer is responsible for transferring data between

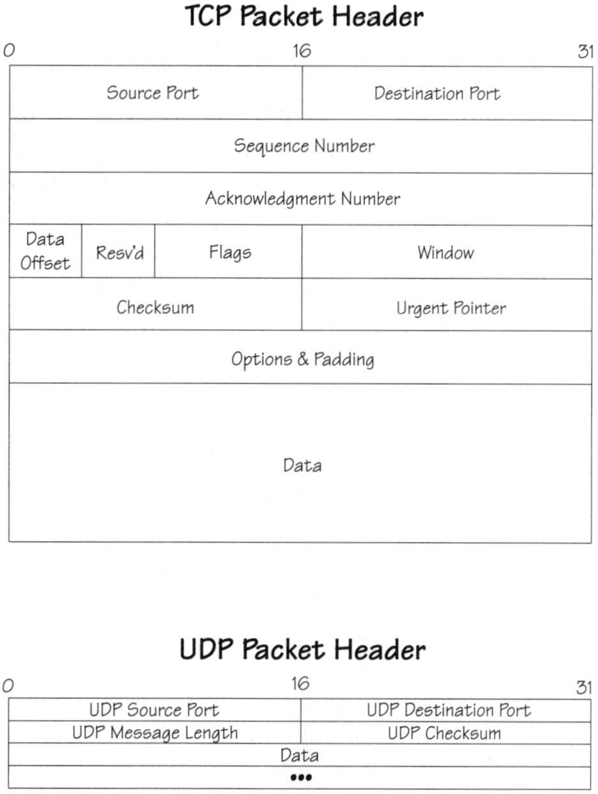

TCP Packet Header

0	16	31

Source Port	Destination Port
Sequence Number	
Acknowledgment Number	

Data Offset	Resv'd	Flags	Window
Checksum		Urgent Pointer
Options & Padding			
Data			

UDP Packet Header

0	16	31

UDP Source Port	UDP Destination Port
UDP Message Length	UDP Checksum
Data	
•••	

FIGURE 2.12 TCP and UDP packet headers.

a pair of hosts (as identified by their IP addresses) on an internetwork, UDP must be able to differentiate among multiple sources or destinations within one host.

Why use UDP? Since UDP is connectionless, it's a simpler protocol to implement and applications do not have to establish or clear connections (as they do with TCP). When an application has data to send, it just sends it. This approach makes things simpler for the application, and it can eliminate a substantial delay in a communication (as with multimedia or interactive applications). Many of the protocols used in IP multicasting run on top of UDP.

On the other hand, to achieve reliability, TCP uses a connection-oriented service. TCP relies on socket pairs to identify individual connections. TCP's reliable delivery service offers error-free delivery, assured delivery, sequenced packets, and no duplication of packets.

As part of its operation, TCP divides a data stream into chunks called *TCP segments* and transmits them using IP. In most cases, each TCP segment is sent in a single IP datagram. If necessary, TCP will split segments into multiple IP datagrams that are compatible with the physical data frames that carry bits between hosts on a network. TCP reassembles the TCP segments at the other end to form an uninterrupted data stream.

In connection-oriented protocols, the sender and the receiver must establish a connection to exchange data. TCP transmits data in segments encased in IP datagrams, along with checksums used to detect data corruption and sequence numbers to ensure an ordered byte stream. TCP is considered a reliable transport mechanism because it requires the receiving computer to acknowledge not only the receipt of data, but also its completeness and sequence.

In order to provide reliable transfers over the underlying IP system, which only can offer unreliable packet delivery, TCP uses a technique known as *positive acknowledgment with retransmission.* In short, the technique requires that a recipient send an acknowledgment (ACK) message back to the source as it receives data. The sender keeps a record of each packet sent and waits for an acknowledgment before sending the next packet. The sender can also retransmit a packet if it does not receive an acknowledgment within a specified period of time.

Unfortunately, simple positive acknowledgment, can waste quite a bit of network bandwidth because the system must delay sending any packets until it receives an acknowledgment for the previous packet. A refinement of the method, which is used by TCP, is called the *sliding window technique.* While this technique also relies on positive acknowledgments and retransmissions of missing packets, it's a more complex procedure. Since the sliding window technique can transmit multiple packets before waiting for an acknowledgment, it provides for more effective use of the network's bandwidth.

To see how the sliding window technique works, consider a sequence of packets as shown in Figure 2.13. In this example, we've set the window size to eight packets, allowing the sender to transmit eight packets before it receives a acknowledgment. When it receives an acknowledgment for the first packet in the sequence (ACK 1 in the figure), the sender slides the window forward one packet and sends the next packet. As other acknowledgments are received (ACK 2 and ACK 3, for example), the sender continues sliding the window forward through the sequence, transmitting the next packet and so on, as long as it continues to receive acknowledgments. This way, some packets are already on their way to the receiver as the sender waits for acknowledgments of earlier packets.

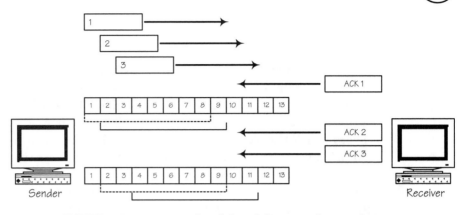

FIGURE 2.13　An example of the sliding window technique.

The performance of a sender using the sliding window technique depends on two variables: the window size and the speed at which the network accepts packets. By increasing the window size, it's possible to eliminate the network's idle time entirely, with the sender transmitting packets as quickly as the network can transfer them.

This requirement for acknowledgments can make TCP unsuited for the transmission of real-time data. Some types of data, such as voice and video, rely on proper sequencing of their data and do not want to have out-of-sequence packets retransmitted. Depending on the number of lost packets, both real-time audio and video sessions can continue without the missing packets rather than attempting to place any retransmitted packets back into sequence; in such cases, the quality may suffer, but most of the session's data would still be usable.

ROUTING PROTOCOLS

Although routing protocols are a part of the internetwork layer, they deserve a special section of their own. We've already mentioned the role of routers in internetworks; routers want to understand how the network is put together (what connects to what) so they can tell how to get from one point to another. Routing protocols help routers create a map of the network. The main difference between routing protocols is how they share information and compute routes.

Link-state routing protocols create the map in three phases: First, each router meets its neighbors (learn your neighborhood); then the routers share that information with other routers on the network (learn about other neighborhoods); finally, routers combine the information and calculate routes. Link-state protocols flood the network with link-state data, which can lead to unnecessary bandwidth usage; but this potential disadvantage is offset by the speed and efficiency of link-state routing. The best known link-state routing protocol is OSPF (Open Shortest Path First).

An alternate approach is to use a distance vector algorithm to compute routes. With link-state algorithms, routers share only the identity of their neighbors, but they flood the entire network with this information. Routers using distance vector algorithms adopt a different approach, periodically sharing their knowledge of the entire network, but only with their neighbors. As neighboring routers learn new information, they pass that information on to their neighbors and so on until, slowly but surely, the information makes its way across the entire network. The RIP (Routing Information Protocol) is the best known routing protocol that uses the distance vector algorithm. (Other routing protocols of importance to multicasting will be covered later in this book, in Chapter 5.)

As routers learn of the network topology, they store it in a table. The format of the table and their updates are determined by the routing protocol in use.

Application Layer Protocols

Unless something goes wrong with the network, everything that encompasses the network below the application layer is transparent to the computer user. The application layer is where the user gets to do something useful with the networks—sending e-mail, browsing a Web site, or transferring a file, for example.

Some of the important application protocols are FTP (File Transfer Protocol) for file transfers, HTTP (HyperText Transfer Protocol) for the World Wide Web, and SNMP (Simple Network Management Protocol) for controlling network devices. DNS (Domain Naming Services) is also useful because it's responsible for converting numeric IP addresses into names that can be more easily remembered by users. Many other protocols dealing with the finer details of applications can be included in the application layer. These include SMTP (Simple Mail Transport Protocol), POP (Post Office Protocol), IMAP (Internet Mail Access Protocol), and MIME (Multimedia Internet Mail Extensions) for e-mail.

There are occasions when it's necessary to retrieve files, such as applications or worksheets, from someone else's computer. On the Internet, you use the File Transfer Protocol (FTP) for file transfers between file servers and client computers like your PC. Depending on your software, you can select files one by one and upload or download them, or you can create a list of files and have them transfer as a batch.

Certainly the most visible interface to the Internet these days is the Web, which is based on a standard set of codes called HTML (HyperText Markup Language) and a technology known as HTTP (HyperText Transfer Protocol). The browser on the user's computer looks at HTML to determine how the text and graphics should be displayed. HTTP determines how a file (such as an HTML document) is transferred from server to client.

Although Web-related traffic on the Internet is the single largest component of Internet activity, there are actually more e-mail users than Web users on the Internet. E-mail is probably the most commonly used form of communication between people on the Internet. The Simple Mail Transport Protocol (SMTP) and Post Office Protocol (POP) are the two essential Internet protocols for e-mail. SMTP is used for transferring mail between servers, while POP and a newer protocol, Internet Mail Access Protocol (IMAP), are used to handle the retrieval of messages.

POP and IMAP were originally designed for text-only mail. MIME, which stands for Multimedia Internet Mail Extensions, extends the capabilities of e-mail messaging. MIME-compliant messages can consist of more than one part; these parts might be graphics, video or sound clips, or other types of multimedia.

Summary

In this day and age, it's important to be able to link together networks using different technologies into a single internetwork. Routers make that possible and the TCP/IP protocols are ideally suited to create networks since they accommodate a wide variety of network hardware technologies.

Even though IP internetworks are packet-switched, or connectionless, networks, the TCP/IP suite offers both connectionless and connection-oriented data transfer to applications, thanks to the UDP and TCP protocols, respectively.

Now it's time to turn our attention to the details of how multicasting works on IP internets.

3

The Basics of Multicasting

In Chapter 1, we saw that multicasting is a convenient way of distributing information to a group of select users without overly taxing a network's bandwidth. On a local area network like Ethernet, multicasting can be implemented rather simply. But, when we attempt to support multicasting on wide area networks like corporate intranets and the Internet, the situation becomes more complicated.

As Stephen Deering wrote in his Ph.D. thesis, "The multicast routing problem is how to arrange for routers to deliver one copy of a packet to every other subnetwork to which group members are attached, across an arbitrary topology of routers and subnetworks (represented by the 'cloud')."

With that in mind, let's take a look at the problems and procedures surrounding the set-up of a multicast session and distribution of multicast data on an internetwork.

The Components of Multicasting

There are four major processes behind a successful implementation of multicasting (Figure 3.1).

1. First, there's the definition of a multicast host group, which is handled on IP networks by specially coded addresses called multicast addresses. (These are the Class D addresses in IPv4; IPv6 doesn't yet have a similarly-named class, but a group of such addresses exists.)

2. Second, a mechanism is required for joining and leaving a host multicast group. This not only includes either sender- or receiver-based control of the group membership, but also the protocols used to transmit and manage the group membership information throughout the network, if necessary.

3. As we've already seen (Chapter 2), complex IP networks cannot forward data without the assistance of routers, which form the third component of a multicasting system. A series of routing protocols have been specifically formulated to support multicasting, both to handle the duplication of multicast traffic as needed and, more importantly, to handle issues surrounding group management.

4. Lastly, there are the application protocols for creating and managing the data that are distributed in a multicasting session.

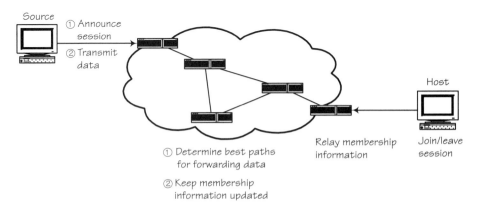

FIGURE 3.1 The components and processes of a multicasting system.

Fundamental Issues in Multicasting

Although multicasting is a good way of conserving bandwidth while transmitting data to multiple receivers, it still does have some problems and shortcomings that may need to be addressed, depending on your network design and the applications that you expect to use multicasting for. The successful deployment of multicasting on WANs requires that a number of these issues be resolved. At the present time, some of the issues do not have definitive solutions.

The rest of this section summarizes many of the issues surrounding WAN multicasting. Several of these issues can be categorized according to the breakdown of components previously mentioned, such as joining and leaving a group, efficient transmission of multicast traffic, and scalability. Other categories of problems include time-sensitive delivery of multicast traffic, guaranteed arrival of the traffic, and security.

Joining and Leaving a Group

Considering the distributed nature of the Internet and the lack of any centralized source of information on Internet activities, it shouldn't be surprising that there's no one, centralized way of learning what multicast sessions are currently available for reception or which sessions are planned for future transmission.

It's difficult to learn what multicast sessions are available on an internetwork. Developers on the MBone have been experimenting with applications that list multicast groups like a TV Guide publication. Many users depend on mailing lists for notification of new multicast sessions. No single standardized way of announcing a multicast session has yet been adopted. In a closed corporate environment, maintaining a Web page with scheduled multicasts or using e-mail to notify employees are both reasonable approaches.

One of the main features distinguishing multicasting from unicasting and broadcasting is its focus on a select group of hosts. Rather than transmit data to a single host, as in unicasting, or to every host on the net, as in broadcasting, multicast traffic is transmitted only to those hosts on the net that have chosen to join that particular multicast host group.

It's significant to note that, in IP Multicast and many other multicasting protocols, the sender has no idea which hosts have joined the host group. In fact, it's quite possible to have no one join a host group, but the transmission of data will go on!

This lack of knowledge of host group members on the part of the sender is a compromise that was introduced to prevent overwhelming the sender with traffic that was related to joining and leaving the group. If the sender had to take care of the bookkeeping associated with group membership, the sending host might well suffer serious degradations of performance that could keep it from actually transmitting the multicast data. This could be especially crucial in cases involving the transmission of real-time data.

Another group-related complication stems from the fact that multicast group membership should be dynamic. This makes it easier for users to come and go as they please, but it causes problems in tracking active members. As we'll see shortly, routers bear the responsibility of updating each other concerning group membership of the hosts they serve. Without a centralized list of group members (which some multicasting protocols do provide), this dynamic nature of group membership forces the routers to periodically poll their subnets to see which, if any, contain group members.

Dynamic group membership also can have a negative effect on network bandwidth, the very resource multicasting is trying to conserve. While the amount of traffic generated by routers and hosts to ascertain group membership is not large, the delays associated with leaving a host group can lead to *wasted* bandwidth.

It can take some time for information about hosts leaving a session to be passed from router to router in order to stop forwarding unwanted multicast traffic. During that time, the source is still transmitting its multicast data and that data is forwarded to the routers forming the tree, before an inactive branch is removed (the removal process is called pruning); thus routers which no longer are active members of the multicast tree (because they no longer have active host members on their subnets) may receive unwanted multicast traffic, wasting bandwidth.

LAN technology has made it convenient and inexpensive to multicast data. It is especially convenient for the transmitter, which can transmit a single copy of a packet and reach multiple recipients. However, multicast is not so inexpensive for the receivers. Since it is difficult for the hardware to do perfect filtering of many addresses, a receiver that wishes to receive any multicast addresses winds up processing software interrupts for wrong numbers (i.e., traffic with destination addresses it is not interested in receiving).

Efficient Transmission of Multicast Traffic

The concept of efficient use of network resources is certainly not a revolutionary one, but it's a concept that isn't always adhered to. Network managers pay closer attention to efficient use when they begin to tax their available network resources or are planning to accommodate new users and new applications. It's also considered a sign of good protocol design if efficient use of resources can be accommodated.

But, in the case of multicasting, it's difficult to decide which resources should be optimized and trade-offs are required. For example, what issue should be the predominant optimizing factor in the design of multicasting systems? Should it be efficient use of routers or perhaps fast setup and teardown of host groups and trees? Or should it be setting up optimal paths between the sources and their receivers?

Multicast traffic is routed along trees rather than along arbitrary paths to minimize transmission cost through link sharing; for continuous media such as video, the volume of data transferred makes this goal even more important. For real-time multimedia applications, there are two additional factors: delay constraints, particularly for interactive applications, and media heterogeneity.

Separate handling of media streams is essential if you want to use the most effective coding techniques for each stream. The question then arises whether you should use the same or separate distribution trees for each stream. Using the same distribution tree makes it easier to control the internetwork and helps guarantee delivery of related traffic, but it may tax the network's resources. On the other hand, using separate distribution trees allows separate quality-of-service requests for each and allows the receiver to selectively receive only one stream (such as an audio feed without the video feed) based on his or her network's capabilities. One problem with this approach is that the management overhead of multiple trees per source would be prohibitive.

The interaction of routing and resource reservations (and the related issues surrounding admission control) further complicates matters. Even in the simple case of static routing, success in building a multicast tree depends on having adequate resources at each router. Resource reservations can become even more problematic when coupled with the dynamics of changing group memberships and the accompanying router changes as multicast trees change.

Time-Sensitive Delivery of Multicast Traffic

As mentioned earlier in Chapters 1 and 2, the rising use of real-time data and multimedia poses special restrictions on the transmission capabilities of packet-switched networks like the Internet.

There are situations where data has to be delivered to all recipients simultaneously. Some data, such as stock quotes and other financial data, need to be delivered to all recipients at the same time, or at least within a narrow window of time. If the data didn't arrive simultaneously, some traders would be able to act on the data sooner than others, which would be construed as an unfair advantage.

A different type of time sensitivity relates to the temporal sequencing of the data, such as in video and audio data. Not only does the sequence of data have to be maintained during delivery (or at least be easily reconstructed by the receiving hosts), but issues of synchronization between different, but related, data streams arise. A typical session consisting of both video and audio utilizes different algorithms for compressing and later expanding the data, and some synchronization data has to be included to help reconstruct the original session. Since the Internet and most multicasting protocols treat each data stream independently of every other, it's likely that two related data streams (such as the audio and video streams previously mentioned) will travel from a source to a receiver by different paths. Even if a resource reservation protocol like RSVP is used to maintain a path with guaranteed quality of service, it is still likely that different paths will be chosen for the audio and video streams, since the audio stream can tolerate a lower QoS than the video stream. Maintaining links between related streams throughout a path of routers is still an unsolved problem on the Internet, for unicasting as well as multicasting.

Guaranteed Arrival of Multicast Traffic

Just as it may be important to deliver data to a series of hosts at a particular time, it may also be important to ensure that the data is, in fact, delivered. As mentioned earlier, IP multicasting's dependence on IP leads to best-effort delivery, which is unreliable.

Unreliable delivery also means that a reliable protocol has to be layered atop IP multicasting in order to accommodate applications such as financial transactions or file transfers, where any loss of data is unacceptable. There are many proposals for reliable multicast protocols currently under consideration by the IETF, and some of these have already been used in commercial products, so routine reliable multicasting is merely a matter of time (see Chapter 6).

Scalability

Any protocol that's used on the Internet to communicate between more than a few devices has to deal with the problems of scalability. The

Internet itself is a testimony to the fact that scalable protocols can be designed and work well, and that attention to protocol scalability is worthwhile.

Multicasting protocols have to deal with many scalability issues that other protocols do not. There are some common issues, of course—router updates are a scalability issue that has to be addressed by unicast routing protocols as well as multicast routing protocols, for instance, and broadcasting protocols have to deal with packet duplication in ways similar to multicasting. But some issues are unique to multicasting.

Feedback for error and flow control is conveniently handled in the unicasting case by TCP and other protocols, but multicasting protocols don't take advantage of TCP and need other procedures to be designed for feedback. One reason is that more sources of feedback can be expected from a multicast session than from a unicast session; using unicast-style methods would easily lead to *feedback implosions* at the source. We'll see in Chapter 6 some of the ways that multicast protocols are being developed to handle feedback and thereby improve reliability.

Another unique attribute of multicast scalability stems from the use of groups. As opposed to broadcasting, where every host on the network receives the packets, multicasting allows hosts to choose not to receive the data; therefore, entire subnets might not have any receivers. In most multicasting schemes, the routers have the responsibility of informing each other where participating hosts are. As a result, protocols have to be devised to construct this network topology and keep it updated. But, since the density of host group members distributed over the internetwork may vary widely from topologically dense groups to very sparse (i.e., widely spreadout) groupings, it is not a simple matter to keep the network infrastructure up to date.

It's a question not only of the density of these groups, but also of their number. As the number of receiver groups grows, the routers must store more information about the topology of the multicasting network. This additional stored information may lead to depletion of resources that the routers may need for other network duties, such as unicasting routing, QoS reservations, and so on.

A related issue is how to scale multicast routing for the commercial Internet, with its increasing numbers of Internet Service Providers (ISPs) and domains. The MBone was unique in the way it was created as an experimental network, but its design cannot be extrapolated to the current Internet for everyday use by anyone and everyone who is connected to the Net. Even as the MBone grew, it was obvious that the routing protocols designed for multicasting would not scale well. The current slate of multi-cast routing protocols (such as PIM, MOSPF, and DVMRP; see Chapter 5) are not designed for multiple autonomous systems that do not necessarily want to share all their routing information. The Border Gateway Protocol (BGP) works for the IP protocol, but there is no equivalent for IP multi-cast. Just as Internet routing has evolved to using hierarchical routing and interdomain routing protocols, so too will multicast routing; work is already underway to solve these problems (see Chapter 6).

The current multicast routing protocols attempt to accurately and rapidly maintain distribution trees that are as close as possible to the tree of shortest-path routes (as defined by unicast traffic) as possible. This means that the shape of a distribution tree can change rapidly. In addition, since distribution trees can be global, they can be subject to a high fre-quency of control traffic. In contrast, the design focus for the interdomain unicast routing environment is on minimizing routing traffic and control-ling stability. In order to support interdomain multicast routing, the over-head associated with protocol and router control must be reduced and some measure of stability introduced into the multicast trees. Without this approach, it will be difficult to scale multicasting to the entire Internet. (For more details on interdomain multicast routing, see the last section of Chapter 5.)

Security

Another outstanding unresolved issue in multicasting is that of securing multicast sessions. The protocols that have been developed thus far for securing packets on IP networks, particularly for IPv6, are aimed at any kind of traffic, but are more easily applied to unicasting than multicasting or broadcasting. One reason for this is the complexity surrounding the exchange of cryptographic keys between the sender and the receiver. Extending this exchange to large numbers of receivers and coping with the dynamic host group memberships associated with multicasting have not been adequately resolved.

As more commercial networks and intranets support multicasting, the need to create private multicast host groups and protect private multi-cast traffic from eavesdropping will grow. Businesses may well want to ensure that only certain departments receive particular corporate data and content providers using multicasting will want only their subscribers to receive the data they purchased, for instance. While session announce-ments may be distributed via a public channel, some added means to control group membership and the privacy of the data is required to ensure that the traffic associated with a private multicast host group is only transmitted to the members of that group and can only be decoded by those members.

Network security also poses another problem for multicasting. Since many multicasting protocols (and particularly IP Multicast) use UDP for transmitting packets, these schemes are at odds with most current firewall strategies. Since UDP is a connectionless protocol, it's often difficult to tell which end of a UDP connection is the server and which is the client. This makes it difficult to tell whether an incoming packet at a firewall is a valid response to a query or an attempt to subvert a server. Since it's extremely difficult to perform any sort of selective filtering on UDP traffic in an application gateway (a particular type of firewall and one of the most popular types), many sites choose to explicitly disallow all UDP traffic from crossing the firewall.

Sender-Based Multicasting

Although this book concentrates on the multicasting system known as IP Multicast, there are other approaches to multicasting, even on IP networks. For the sake of completeness, we'll review them briefly here.

The major difference between the approaches to multicasting is whether the sender or the receiver establishes the connections necessary for forming a multicast group (Figure 3.2). There are three sender-based approaches to multicasting: Stream protocol version II (ST-II), Xpress Transport Protocol (XTP), and Multicast Transport Protocol (MTP). Only the system called IP Multicast is a receiver-based multicasting protocol.

The sender-based approach works well for small groups, but scales poorly to large and dynamic groups, as every new group member has to notify every potential sender within the group to be added to the recipient list. One advantage of receiver-based multicasting is that the sender does not need to maintain a list of receivers. This also makes it easier to make groups dynamic, letting members (i.e., receivers) join and leave multicast sessions as they wish.

Stream Protocol Version II (ST-II)

Stream protocol version II is a protocol that provides support for continuous media streams over IP networks. It is actually a new network layer

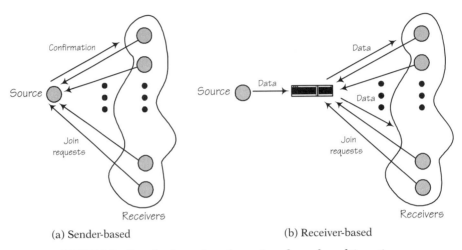

(a) Sender-based   (b) Receiver-based

FIGURE 3.2 Sender-based and receiver-based multicasting.

protocol that supports both multicasting and resource negotiations based on a sender-initiated approach, but it is more of a framework, with specific mechanisms expected to be provided externally. Although it uses some of IP's features, such as IP addresses for reaching hosts and other network devices, ST-II defines its own routing protocol and resource reservation scheme. The latest version of ST-II is defined in RFC 1190.

Unlike IP, ST-II is connection-oriented and defines a call setup facility in which hosts declare connections to the network before exchanging data. Call setup is used to define end-to-end virtual links between the source and the receiver. Part of this procedure consists of reserving network resources such as router buffers and network bandwidth. (Another resource reservation protocol, RSVP, works independently of ST-II and will be covered in detail in Chapter 7.) ST-II ensures end-to-end bandwidth and delay, so it doesn't need all the functionality of a lower-level transport protocol. Bandwidth reservations are stipulated for all participants in a multicast session.

The virtual link that ST-II defines is a fixed route (Figure 3.3). Once this virtual link between the source and a receiver is set up, the main data stream is transmitted along this link. But, rather than provide feedback from the receiver via this same virtual link, another link, the return channel, is defined to carry control messages in the other direction (i.e., from receiver to source). A separate return channel was chosen to reduce the possibility of degrading the delivery of the main data stream.

One drawback to the setup of a fixed-route link is ST-II's response when a link or node fails. ST-II suspends the connection between the source and receiver until the virtual link is re-established over an alternative route.

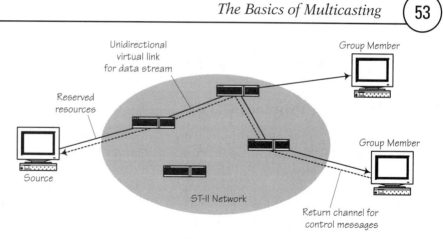

FIGURE 3.3 ST-II's setup of links for multicasting.

Being sender-based, most of the control of group membership in ST-II is centralized at the source. New recipients can be added by the source before initiation of data transmission or during the session. Each addition of a receiver requires an interaction with the data stream's source. When the source receives a request to join the session from a potential receiver, the source transmits a Connect message, which includes information on the session and its network requirements. As long as the requirements can be met by the receiver and its network, it can then join the session. If the receiver cannot meet the session's requirements, it will send back a Refuse message to the source. Since joining the group requires an acknowledgment by the source, no user can spontaneously join an ST-II session.

Leaving a session is not controlled by the source. Any receiver may leave the multicast session at any time by sending a Disconnect message.

Connect processing at each intermediate ST agent involves determining the set of next hop subnets required to reach all downstream receivers. If the actual resource allocation obtained along a subnet is less than the amount requested, then this is noted in the Connect packet by updating the flow specification.

Upon receiving a Connect indication, a receiver must determine whether it wishes to join the group, and return either an Accept or Refuse message to the stream source. During connection setup the stream source must wait for an Accept/Refuse reply from each initial receiver before beginning data transmission.

ST-II treats the entire stream as a homogeneous distribution path, requiring all group members to be capable of receiving the data stream. Whenever the source receives an Accept with a reduced flow specification, it must either adapt to the lower QoS for the entire stream or reject group participation for the specific receiver by sending it a Disconnect message.

Xpress Transport Protocol (XTP)

Unlike the other multicasting protocols we're discussing in this section, XTP (Xpress Transport Protocol) defines its own network- and transport-level protocols. But the use of XTP does not preclude the use of the regular IP protocols on the same network devices; rather it's designed to co-exist with them (Figure 3.4). XTP was designed to support a variety of applications, ranging from real-time embedded systems to multimedia distribution over WANs. The protocol provides all the functionality of TCP, UDP, and TP4, as well as services such as multicast transport, multicast group management, transport layer priorities, and traffic description for quality-of-service negotiation.

> NOTE   TP4 is a transport protocol that was designed by ISO. Its functionality is similar to TCP.

Like the other multicasting protocols mentioned in this book, XTP does not include any inherent address management scheme, depending on IP to handle device addressing. XTP also does not require any explicit setup processing between the sender and receivers, but it does require explicit handshaking between the sender and receivers that wish to join a multicast group. As is often the case with sender-receiver handshaking (or similar feedback mechanisms), XTP multicast does not scale well to large numbers of receivers.

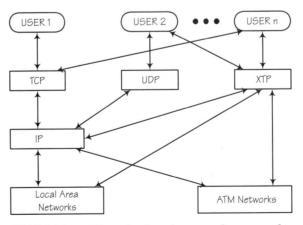

FIGURE 3.4   XTP and related network protocols.

The multicast group manager (MGM) has the responsibility of controlling group membership. Using the MGM, a user's application can selectively allow or deny the admission of any other user to the multicast group. Thus the MGM has the advantage of knowing its group membership at all times. This also allows better control of responses to failures in group membership. For example, if the failure of a group member destroys the integrity of the multicast group, the application controlling the MGM can choose to delete the failed member from the group and continue or abandon transmission entirely.

It's also possible to refine group control in other ways. For instance, one can define a group with three essential users that each receive all data reliably and an arbitrary number of other members who eavesdrop as they wish, without actively adding to the content. In such a case, the MGM would monitor and report failures of the three essential nodes, but would ignore the status of the eavesdropping members, since they're not considered essential to the group.

The specification allows the user to determine whether multicast transfers are unreliable or semireliable. In this case, semireliable transfers are defined to provide a "high probability of success" of delivery to all receivers, but reliability cannot be guaranteed.

XTP also has a built-in priority system to define the importance of the data. As long as the network supports priorities, the system can be used to bind end-to-end latencies to high-priority messages (Figure 3.5). The priority scheme is based on a static priority encoded in a 16-bit numeric field; the lower the numerical value, the higher the importance. This way, adding a delivery timestamp in the priority field automatically implements an earliest-deadline-first delivery policy.

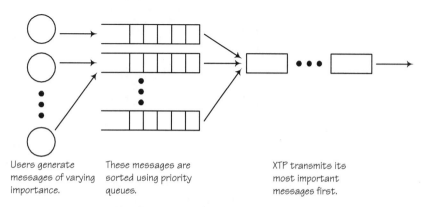

Users generate messages of varying importance.

These messages are sorted using priority queues.

XTP transmits its most important messages first.

FIGURE 3.5 XTP's priority system.

Multicast Transport Protocol (MTP)

MTP (Multicast Transport Protocol) is a transport-level protocol that's been designed to support reliable multicast transfers on top of existing protocols, such as IP multicasting (see the next section). It uses a multicast master to control all aspects of group communications.

As with other multicast protocols, MTP requires the use of an outside addressing authority to allocate a specific group address. Once the address is established, receivers issue a request to join the existing group using a unique connection identifier that is preassigned.

Within the framework of MTP, the multicast group, or *web* as it's now called (no relation to the World Wide Web), consists of three different types of members: *master, producers,* and *consumers.* The master is responsible for the ordering of messages for all web members and is responsible for rate control for any data transmissions. Rate control provides flow control within the protocol; members that cannot maintain a minimum flow are requested to leave the group. Much as the terms suggest, producers send the actual multicast data and consumers receive that data.

Before producers can send any data, they must first receive a token from the designated master (Figure 3.6). When the master receives a special request packet from the producer, it answers with a Confirm packet, which contains the sequence number for the new message. Producers then include this sequence number in every data packet belonging to the multicast data stream that they're transmitting. The sequencing of data streams by means of tokens leads to a global ordering of all streams; every con-

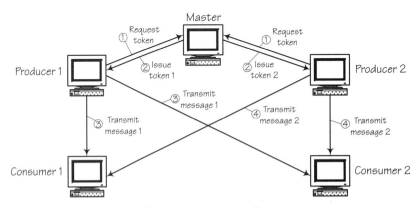

FIGURE 3.6 Sequence of communications between MTP master, producers, and consumers.

sumer receives the streams in the same order as the order in which they were sent, which is determined by the tokens issued.

Normally the master grants the token in the same order that the token requests are received. If there is a need to transmit some multicast data with a higher priority, applications can assign a priority to that data. This priority would be then be considered only when the master grants a token (i.e., the master would grant a token for high-priority traffic before granting tokens for lower-priority traffic, even if lower-priority requests had arrived at the master first). This has no effect on the transmission rate of any data; it is simply the sequencing of producers and their transmissions.

Consumers can request a retransmission of data packets when there is a gap in the packet sequence numbers of a message or no further packets are received for more than a given time period (called a *heartbeat*) while the message is still incomplete. In order to handle retransmissions, a producer keeps a copy of every data packet it sends. To limit the number of packets it stores, a producer will delete these copies after a special period of time set by the MTP system.

Users can join an MTP web by sending join packets to the multicast network address that was chosen by the original application. Each master in the web listens to this address and confirms the join if the parameters requested by the application are acceptable and are compatible with those requested by the members that have already joined. Dropping membership in a group is also coordinated through the master.

Initially every user tries to become a master itself. If a master already exists, the member is simply accepted into the web, but not as a master. If there is no answer from an existing member for that web, the new member becomes master of a new web.

One potential problem with MTP is the amount of overhead associated with the protocol, since virtually all control traffic has to flow through the master.

Receiver-Based Multicasting: IP Multicast

As an example of receiver-based multicasting, a major difference between IP Multicast and separately unicasting data to several destinations is best explained by the *host group model*. A host group is a set of network devices sharing a common identifying multicast address; they all receive any data packets addressed to this multicast address. The senders need not be members of the group and have no knowledge of the group's membership. From the sender's point of view, this model reduces the multicast service interface to a unicast one. This also implies that the network software has the task of managing the multicasts in a manner transparent to the users. From the network designer's point of view, this extra work is expected to result in a more efficient use of resources.

Specifying Group Addresses

The first step in setting up a multicast session is the selection of a host group address. The initiator, or source host, of a multicast session first has to select a destination address for the multicast data from the available IPv4 Class D (or equivalent IPv6) addresses. This destination address corresponds to an appropriate host group. The source host can then begin transmitting data packets on the internetwork using that group host address as the destination.

For others to receive the multicast data, they must be aware of the group address being used and join that multicast group. At the moment, there is no standardized procedure or application for maintaining a list of multicast group addresses. (See Chapter 8 for more details.) Some TV Guide-like applications have been written to maintain lists of scheduled multicasts. In other cases, potential participants in a multicast group are notified by e-mail.

We covered the basics of IP addressing and address classes in Chapter 2, so only a brief recap is needed here. In IPv4, the class D address (Figure 3.7) is used for controlling multicast sessions. Class D addresses start with 1110 as their high-order bits, which covers the range of host addresses from 224.0.0.0 to 239.255.255.255 (using the standard *dotted decimal* notation).

Class D addresses are subdivided into two types of group addresses—permanent and temporary. A range of addresses, from 224.0.0.0 to

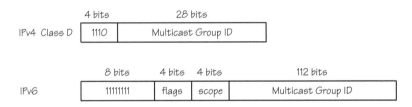

FIGURE 3.7 IPv4 and IPv6 multicast address formats.

224.0.0.255, is reserved for routing protocols and other low-level protocols that would be used to handle the discovery and maintenance of your network's topology. Permanent addresses include the 224.0.0.1 address, which is the *all-hosts group* that is used to address all of the multicast hosts that are directly connected to the same network as the source host (see Table 3.1). Another permanent address is 224.0.0.2, which addresses all routers on a subnet. Net news also depends on multicast addresses, using the range from 224.0.13.0 to 224.0.13.255. The official list of permanent multicast addresses can be found in RFC 1700, "Assigned Numbers."

In IPv6, a multicast address has a different format, due partly to the changed header format and partly to the increased length of IPv6 addresses (see the Sidebar on IPv6 addresses). An IPv6 multicast address consists of an 8-bit format field, which contains all ones (accounting for 1/256th of the total available addresses in IPv6), followed by a 4-bit flags field, a 4-bit scope field, then the 112-bit group ID.

Only the fourth bit of the Flags field has thus far been assigned a meaning. When the fourth bit equals 0, the address is a permanent one. If the fourth bit of the Flag field is set to 1, then the address is a transient one and will be available for re-assignment for other uses once the session is completed.

The Scope field determines the extent of the address, affecting the distribution of multicast messages through the internetwork's hierarchy. Table 3.2 lists assigned scope values; others will likely be assigned in the future. Although the group ID is independent of the scope field, the scope field still controls the distribution of the packet on the network, whether the address is permanent or temporary. For example, if the group of NTP (network time) servers is assigned a group ID of 43 (hex), then the IPv6 packet FF05:0:0:0:0:0:0:43 would be restricted to those NTP servers on the

TABLE 3.1 Some Registered IP Multicast Groups

Group	Description
224.0.0.0	Reserved
224.0.0.1	All systems on this subnet
224.0.0.2	All routers on this subnet
224.0.0.3	Unassigned
224.0.0.4	DVMRP routers
224.0.1.1	NTP network time protocol
224.0.1.2	SGI-Dogfight

IPv6 Addresses

IPv4's 32-bit addresses are subdivided into four 8-bit groupings called *octets*, which are then expressed in what's known as the dot notation— for example, 256.123.345.004. The designers of IPv6 have chosen a similar format composed of eight 16-bit integers separated by colons. Each integer is represented by four hexadecimal digits, as in FEDC:BA98:7654:3210:FEDE:BA98:7655:2130.

Some IPv6 addresses can be obtained by prepending 96 zero bits to an IPv4 address. These IPv4-compatible addresses are important if you're planning to tunnel IPv6 packets through an IPv4 network, since the prepended zeros can be easily added to, or removed from, the IPv4 address.

same site as the sender, but FF0E:0:0:0:0:0:0:43 would allow distribution to all NTP servers on the Internet.

Joining a Multicast Host Group

There are two different procedures for joining a host group, which differ primarily in who serves as the initiator. In the first case, a host initiates the membership request when it learns of the host group. In the second case, the router sends its periodic IGMP Host Membership Query to the subnet and the host that wishes to join the host group responds to that query.

If a host becomes aware of a multicast group and wishes to join the multicast session, the multicast application running on the workstation can direct the workstation to send a membership request to the local LAN router, if it's multicast-enabled. If the local router is not multicast-enabled,

TABLE 3.2   Multicast Address Scope Values

Value	Description
0	Reserved
1	Confined to a single system (node-local)
2	Confined to a single link (link-local)
5	Confined to a single site
8	Confined to a single organization
E	Global scope
F	Reserved

the membership request must be directed to the nearest local multicast-enabled router in the network.

The local multicast router then forwards the membership request to a multicast router that's the next level up in the hierarchy (Figure 3.8), and so on until a chain of multicast routers exists that can forward the multicast data from the source to the group member.

As these chains of routers form, requests to join the host group will eventually encounter a router that has already forwarded a membership request for the same host group. In these circumstances, the router does not generate another membership request to be passed up the hierarchy, but simply registers the fact that another router below it in the hierarchy must also receive the multicast traffic, creating what's called a *tree* of routers.

Multicast group membership requests are handled via the Internet Group Management Protocol (IGMP, see Figure 3.9). When a host first joins a group, it immediately transmits an IGMP Report for the group rather than waiting for the next IGMP Query from the router. This reduces what is known as the *join latency* for the host to join a given group on that subnet. If the group is already active on that subnet, then the join latency is unimportant; but if this is the first host on the subnet to join that particular multicast group, the join latency is more crucial. In the latter case, the time taken to forward the membership request to a router that's already

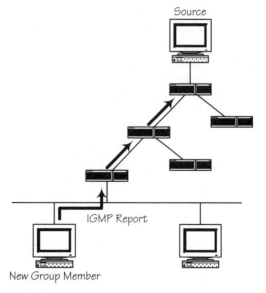

Source

IGMP Report

New Group Member

FIGURE 3.8 Joining a multicast session.

IGMP Version (4-bit)	IGMP Type (4-bit)	Unused (4-bit)	16-bit Checksum
Class D Multicast Group Address			

FIGURE 3.9   IGMP packet format.

part of the host group's tree may be excessive and could keep the member from receiving some of the multicast traffic for that session.

When a host attempts to join a multicast host group, the software driver on that computer creates a hardware multicast address (see Figure 3.10 and the Sidebar on Mapping to a Hardware Multicast Address). The network interface on the host then maps the IP host group address to a network address and updates its multicast reception filter so that it can receive LAN traffic corresponding to that host group address. Once the group membership request is relayed to the nearest multicast router and the corresponding hardware multicast address is calculated, the receiver's network interface starts filtering for the data-link layer address associated with the new multicast group address.

A second method for joining a host group is to simply have the host wait for an IGMP Host Membership Query, which is periodically issued by each multicast router. Since this is the same procedure for updating host group membership lists, the details of the procedure are covered in a later section on Group Membership Maintenance.

IGMP runs between hosts and their immediate neighboring multicast routers. If there is more than one IP multicast router on the LAN, one of the routers is elected to be the *interrogator* and assumes the responsibility of querying the LAN for the presence of any group members. Based on the group membership information learned via IGMP, a router is able to determine which, if any, multicast traffic should be forwarded to each of its leaf subnets.

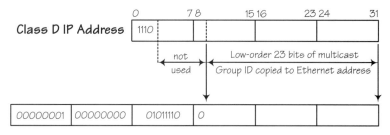

FIGURE 3.10   Mapping an IP multicast address to a hardware multicast address.

Mapping to a Hardware Multicast Address

Many network hardware technologies include a mechanism to send packets to multiple destinations simultaneously (broadcasting). With most hardware, the user specifies broadcast delivery by sending the packet to a special-reserved destination address called the broadcast address. Ethernet hardware addresses, for example, consist of 48-bit IDs, with one address reserved as the broadcast address. Similarly, Ethernet uses one bit in the address to indicate if the address is to be treated as a multicast address (the low-order bit in the high-order octet, i.e., 01.00.00.00.00.00). To map an IP multicast address to the corresponding Ethernet multicast address, the low-order 23 bits of the IP multicast address are placed into the low-order 23 bits of the special Ethernet multicast address, 01.00.5E.00.00.00 (see Figure 3.10). Note that this mapping is not unique, since IPv4 multicast addresses use 28 bits to identify a multicast group. Using only 23 bits in Ethernet to map the IP multicast address is a compromise. It's thought that the set of addresses is large enough that the chances of two groups choosing addresses with the same low-order 23 bits is small. The consequence of this design compromise is that some hosts may, in fact, receive multicast datagrams that are not destined for them.

IGMP Versions

IGMP version 1 was defined in RFC 1112 as part of IP multicasting. A newer version, 2.0, is an IETF draft and will most likely become the new standard before long; it's backward compatible with IGMP version 1. Another version, 3.0, is still in the early draft stages. Many of the differences revolve around options for leaving a group and reducing the leave latency, which we'll cover in more detail in a few pages.

Routers and Multicast Forwarding

In a receiver-based multicast approach like IP multicasting, routers not only bear the responsibility for managing group memberships, but they are also necessary to the forwarding of multicast data, deciding when to duplicate packets in order to reach group members when paths diverge (Figure 3.11). This, of course, is one of the advantages of multicasting that we've been mentioning all along (i.e., that packets are only duplicated as

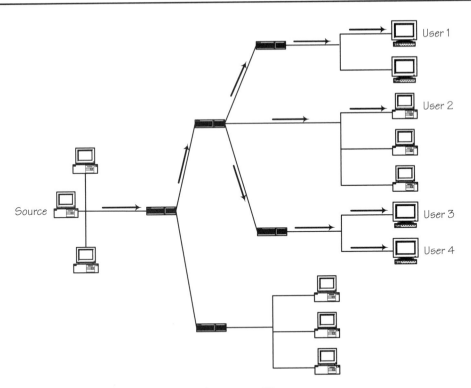

FIGURE 3.11   Multicast traffic over routers.

needed to reach all group members, thereby reducing the bandwidth requirements).

In order to forward multicast data to the appropriate receivers, multicast routing algorithms have to deal with many of the same issues as a unicast routing algorithm, such as learning the internetwork topology, detecting changes in the topology, and computing delivery paths on the topology.

WAN routers deliver the requested incoming multicast datagrams to the local LAN router. Then the local LAN router maps the host group address to its associated hardware address (Figure 3.10) and builds the message using that address for transmission on the LAN. Any hosts on the LAN which are filtering for the appropriate data-link layer address will be able to receive and process the multicast data.

As long as a router has a multicast group member *downstream* of it, it should forward any multicast packets. If it notes that it has group members on its local subnet as well as another router requiring the packet, then it duplicates the packet, transmitting one copy to its subnet and forwarding the other to the next router. But multicast packets might not always make it to all group members, especially if the members have many routers intervening between the source and destination. That's because each IP packet is assigned a value called the TTL, which controls how far a packet can be propagated over an internet.

The TTL (Time to Live) field of the IPv4 header controls the number of hops that an IP Multicast packet is allowed to propagate. Each time a router forwards a packet, its TTL is decremented by 1. If a multicast datagram has a TTL greater than 1, the multicast routers attached to the local network are responsible for forwarding the datagram on the internetwork. A multicast packet whose TTL is 0 is dropped without any error notification to the sender (Figure 3.12).

A multicast session can be easily restricted to the local subnet by setting the TTL field of the multicast packets to 1 (which is the default value). The local router will receive the multicast packets, decrement the TTL by 1, and therefore not forward the packets onto the rest of the internetwork.

The MBone, which we'll discuss in detail in Chapter 10, has a set of standard recommended settings for TTLs. They are: 1 for the local net, 15 for the local site, 63 for the region, and 127 for the world.

Group Membership Maintenance

As mentioned earlier in this section, IGMP is used to communicate host group memberships to neighboring routers, propagating the group information throughout the internetwork. Since IP multicasting group membership is dynamic and can change at any time, routers have to periodically poll their local group members to see if they're still part of the group.

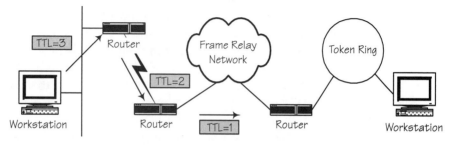

FIGURE 3.12 TTL changes across multiple hops.

IPv4's Time to Live versus IPv6's Hop Limit

In IPv6, the hop limit field has replaced the TTL field. The hop limit field is essentially treated the same as IPv4's TTL field. The name was changed to reflect the reality of how routers actually treat the TTL field. TTL values were supposed to be expressed in seconds to indicate how long a packet could remain on a network and routers were to decrement the value by the time spent in the router's queue (thought to be a value greater than 1 second). But the queueing time was usually measured in milliseconds and routers typically decremented the TTL value by 1. By renaming the field to hop limit, this IPv6 field is used to track how many routers the packet has crossed. (A *hop* has long been defined in internetworking as crossing a router from one subnet to another.) The IPv6 hop limit actually makes processing of a packet simpler than in IPv4, since the router does not have to determine the queueing time for the packet and simply decrements the count by 1 when it forwards the packet.

Multicast routers use IGMP to learn of the existence of host group members on their directly attached subnets. To accomplish this, they periodically send an IGMP Host Membership Query to the *all-hosts* group and have the IP hosts report their host group memberships. IGMP Query messages are addressed to the all-hosts group (i.e., IP address 224.0.0.1) and have an IP TTL set to 1. Thus, Query messages are not forwarded to any other multicast routers, but are restricted only to directly attached subnets.

Each host sends back one IGMP Host Membership Report message per host group (Figure 3.13), which is sent to the group address, so that all group members see it. Rather than congest the network by having all hosts report their membership at the same time, each host delays its report by a random interval if it has not seen a report for the same group from another host. As a result, only one membership report is sent in response for each active group address, even though many hosts may be members. One report is sent to each group of which the host is a member. Like IGMP Queries, IGMP Reports have a TTL of 1, restricting their transmission to the subnet.

NOTE Recall that IPv6 no longer includes a definition for IGMP, transferring all of IGMP's functions to ICMP; the procedures for sending queries and receiving reports are the same when using IPv6's ICMP.

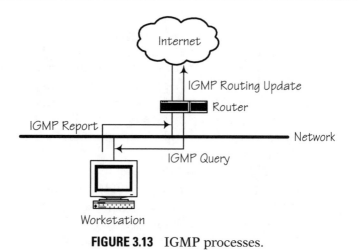

FIGURE 3.13 IGMP processes.

Multicast routers receive all multicast IP traffic in promiscuous mode. One advantage of this is that the routers do not have to be directly addressed when membership reports are submitted. Also, a router does not need to maintain a detailed list of which hosts belong to each multicast group; it is sufficient for the router to know that there is at least one group member on the given network interface.

If a router does not receive any Reports after a number of Queries, the router assumes that there are no group members present on that particular interface. If this is a leaf subnet, this interface will be removed from the delivery tree for the multicast group.

PRUNING AND GRAFTING

When a router no longer has any group members to service, it can attempt to remove itself from the tree of routers that have been defined for that group's multicast traffic. There are two different possible courses of action, depending on the router's location in the tree.

If the router is at an intermediate level in the tree—that is, it forwards multicast packets to other *downstream* routers—then it might have to remain a part of the tree. But it only has to forward packets, not duplicate them for its local subnet since it no longer has active group members on its subnet.

But, depending on the routing algorithm used to create and maintain the multicast tree of routers, the router may be able to disconnect itself from the tree (a process called *pruning*). The remaining routers will form a different tree with different paths between all the routers actively partici-

IGMP and Leave Latencies

IGMP version 2 lets a host inform a multicast router when it no longer wants to receive traffic for a given multicast group. Previously, in IGMP version 1 implementations, hosts could not explicitly exit a multicast group, but could only stop reporting interest in a given group. The length of time of membership was therefore determined by the polling frequency of the router.

IGMP version 2 defines a new procedure for electing the multicast querier on a LAN. Now, with IGMP version 2, the multicast router with the lowest IP address is always chosen as the querier.

IGMP version 2 also defines a new type of Query message, the Group-Specific Query. Group-Specific Query messages allow a router to transmit a Query to a specific multicast group rather than all groups that reside on a directly attached subnet.

Another message type, the Leave Group message, is defined in IGMP version 2 to lower the *leave latency*. Leave latency is measured from the router's perspective. In IGMP version 1, the leave latency was the time from a router's hearing the last report for a given group until the router aged out that interface from the delivery tree for that group. In IGMP version 2, by adding the Leave Group message, a group member can more quickly inform the router that it is one receiving traffic for a group. To determine if this is the last member of the group, the router quickly queries the subnet for other group members using the Group-Specific Query message. If no members send reports after several of these queries, the router can assume that the last member of the group has left the group. Lowering the leave latency can be especially beneficial if there's a high level of traffic, since a router can send prune messages upstream sooner, stopping the transmission of this unwanted traffic. IGMP version 3 enhances the Leave Group messages introduced in version 2 by supporting a Group-Source Leave message. This feature allows a host to leave an entire group or to specify the specific IP address of the (source, group) pair that it wishes to leave.

pating in the multicast session. (We'll see in Chapter 5 how the routing algorithms differ.)

In keeping with the tree terminology, leaves or branches which no longer contain members of a multicast group are removed, or pruned, from the tree (see Figure 3.14). This is usually done by the router attached

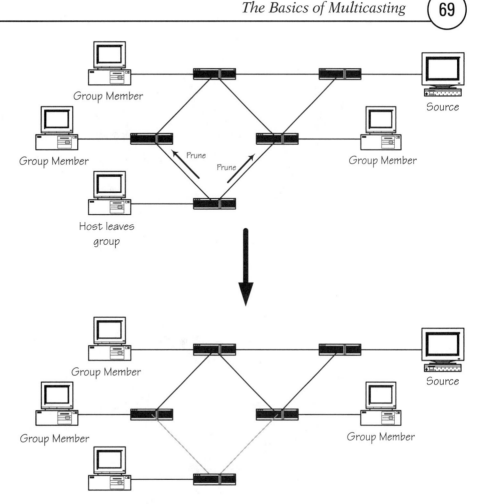

FIGURE 3.14 Example of pruning process.

to that leaf, once it determines that there are no active members of the group on the LAN it serves. The leaf router sends a message upstream to other routers in the multicast tree to remove it from the multicast tree.

Other upstream routers may also prune themselves from the tree as a result of this action, if all the intervening routers were a part of the multicast tree simply to forward datagrams to the leaf router which pruned itself.

Some multicast routing protocols (DVMRP, for example) have also made it easier for a group to rejoin a multicast tree by a process called *grafting* (Figure 3.15). The idea is to allow branches or leaves which had been pruned from a multicast tree to rejoin the tree with a minimum of effort, as quickly as possible (without waiting for the construction of an entirely new multicast tree). In such cases, a router that had previously

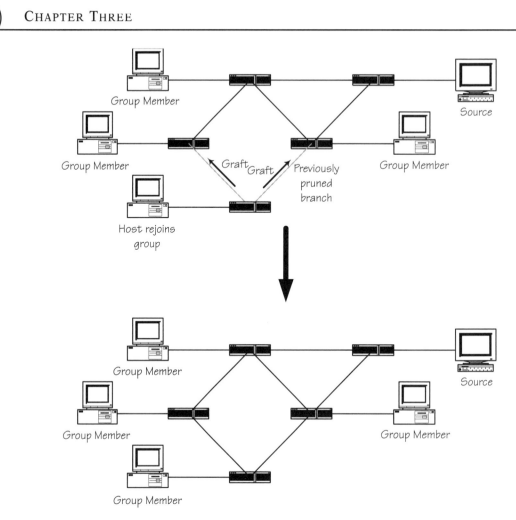

FIGURE 3.15 The grafting process.

issued a Prune message for the leaf it serves would forward a Graft message upstream and this would be repeated by upstream routers until the branch or leaf is reattached to the multicast tree. One reason grafting works is that there can be a considerable delay in processing prune messages; therefore, branches marked for pruning can be reattached before a new multicast tree is created throughout the network.

Summary

The design of a multicasting system faces a number of unique challenges, caused mainly by the distribution of host group members and the dynamic nature of group membership. Some sender-based multicasting protocols, such as ST-II, XTP, and MTP, solve some of the group membership problems by invoking sender-based control on sessions, but this limits their scalability and is not suitable for rapidly changing groups.

The system known as IP Multicast, which is receiver-based, is better suited to dynamic group memberships. Its design relies on routers using IGMP to determine which hosts are active members. In fact, an IP multicasting host does not know who the host group members are, nor does it receive feedback on the receipt of multicast data by the group members. Improving the feedback and reliability of multicast transmissions is the subject of another set of protocols, which we'll cover in another chapter (after we discuss the details of multicast routing protocols).

Multicast Routing Concepts

As I've mentioned in previous chapters, a major step in running a multicast session is the actual transmission of the data over a network of multicast routers. Since multicast data isn't transmitted to all parts of an internetwork, the multicast routers must be relied upon to define which subnets of the network contain group members who expect to receive the data. Plus all of this has to be handled in a dynamic fashion, since group members should be allowed the freedom of joining or leaving the multicast session at will. Thus, routers are extremely crucial to the success of IP multicasting.

As we've seen in Chapter 3, IGMP is only concerned with creation of multicast groups and the forwarding of multicast traffic from a router to group members on its directly attached subnets. Therefore, it's necessary to define multicast routing protocols which are responsible for the construction of multicast delivery trees and enabling multicast packet forwarding.

Before we discuss many of the concepts and issues surrounding multicast routing, let's take a brief look at some of the pertinent features of unicast routers.

Routing Basics and Issues

Routing is the process of finding a path from a source to every destination in the network. Routers comprising an **IP** internet form a cooperative, interconnected structure; datagrams pass from router to router until they reach a router that can deliver the datagram directly to the receiver.

In order to help routers determine delivery paths, routing protocols establish mutually consistent routing tables in every router that's a part of the network. The routing table consists of at least two columns—the address of a destination endpoint (either a host or a network) and the address of the network element that is the next hop in the *best* path to this destination (Figure 4.1). Whenever the IP routing software in a host or router needs to transmit a datagram, it consults the routing table to decide where to send the datagram.

Each router makes a local routing choice, but the choice depends on the global topology of the internetwork. Thus any routing protocol must communicate information about the global topology of the internetwork to each router in order to allow the router to make local routing decisions.

Partly to reduce memory and bandwidth requirements, routers are designed to use the destination network and not the destination host when routing a packet. As long as routing is based on networks rather than hosts, the amount of information that a router needs to store is propor-

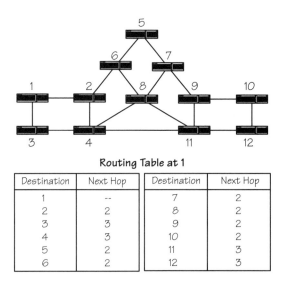

Routing Table at 1

Destination	Next Hop	Destination	Next Hop
1	--	7	2
2	2	8	2
3	3	9	2
4	3	10	2
5	2	11	3
6	2	12	3

FIGURE 4.1 Example network and routing table.

tional to the number of subnets forming the internetwork, not the number of computers.

A routing protocol must try to satisfy several mutually opposing requirements:

1. First, it should minimize routing table space; this impacts the RAM requirements of routers and hosts as well as network bandwidth, since the larger the tables, the greater the overhead in exchanging routing tables.
2. Second, the protocol should use a minimum of control messages to keep the overhead for system operation to a minimum.
3. Third, the protocol must be robust. This involves preventing misrouting of packets and minimizing, or avoiding entirely, potential problems such as routing loops and oscillations as routing information changes.
4. Lastly, the routing protocol should be designed to use an optimal path. This varies from protocol to protocol, since different network managers and situations use different metrics for defining what's optimal. Some examples include minimal delay, most secure links, or lowest monetary cost.

Routing Algorithms

There are a number of different unicast routing algorithms currently employed on datagram internets, each suited to different circumstances such as the size of the internet, the protocol layer at which routing is performed, or the relative scarcity of resources (processing power, memory, bandwidth, etc.).

Although there's a wide variety of routing protocols in use on the Internet, there are two fundamental routing algorithms in packet-switched networks: the distance-vector and link-state algorithms. Both algorithms assume that a router knows the address of each neighboring router and the cost of reaching each neighbor; the cost might be based on link capacity, queueing delay, per-packet charge, or some other net-related factor.

Generally speaking, in a distance-vector algorithm, a node tells its neighbors the distance from it to every other node in the network (Figure 4.2). In a link-state algorithm, a node tells every other node in the network its distance to its neighbors.

The distance-vector algorithm works well if nodes and links are always up, but it runs into many problems when links change state (i.e.,

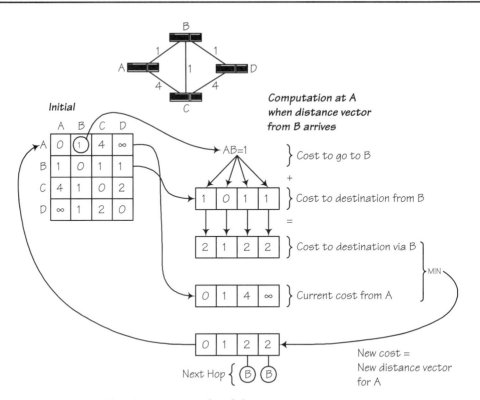

FIGURE 4.2   Example of distance-vector routing.

are broken or restored). The main disadvantage of distance-vector algorithms is that they do not scale well. Not only do the distance-vector algorithms respond slowly to changes, but the algorithms also require exchanges of large messages, requiring more bandwidth to operate. Because the routing update messages contain an entry for every possible network, the message size is proportional to the total number of networks in an internetwork.

Rather than follow the example of the distance-vector algorithm and send messages that contain lists of destinations, the philosophy in link-state routing is to distribute the topology of the network and cost of each link to all routers (Figure 4.3). Each router independently computes optimal paths to every destination. If each router sees the same cost for each link and uses the same algorithm to compute the best path, the routes are further guaranteed to be loop free. (Special measures have to be taken in the distance-vector algorithm to prevent the formation of loops.)

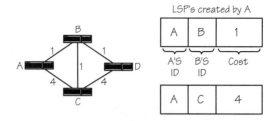

FIGURE 4.3 Example of link-state routing, showing two link-state records at router A.

In link-state routing, each router keeps the other routers informed of changes by periodically broadcasting a message that lists the status of each of its links. This *Link Status message* does not specify routes—it simply reports whether communication is possible between pairs of routers. Whenever a Link Status message arrives, a router uses the information to update its map of the internetwork, marking links as *up* or *down.* Whenever a link's status changes, the router recomputes routes by applying the well-known *Dijkstra shortest-path algorithm* to the resulting graph. Dijkstra's algorithm computes the shortest paths to all destinations from a single source.

One of the chief advantages of the link-state algorithm is that each router computes routes independently using the same original status data; the routers do not depend on the computations of intermediate machines. Also, because Link Status messages only carry information about the direct connections from a single router, the size does not depend on the number of networks in the internetwork. Thus, link-state algorithms scale better than distance-vector algorithms.

Scalability Issues

The computation and storage requirements of a routing protocol become excessive when the number of subnets on an internetwork is large. One solution is to use hierarchical routing to control the routing costs. In the Internet, there are three levels of routing, where each level can use a different routing protocol (Figure 4.4). The highest level is the Internet backbone, which interconnects multiple Autonomous Systems (ASs). Routing between autonomous systems uses an Exterior Gateway Protocol (EGP). The protocol that the gateway spoke to routers within a campus (and now, within an AS) is called an Interior Gateway Protocol (IGP).

An autonomous system can be defined as a group of networks and routers controlled by a single administrative authority (Figure 4.5). Since

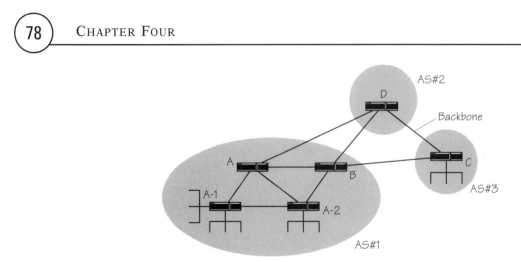

FIGURE 4.4 Hierarchical routing on the Internet.

an AS uses a different routing protocol than the Internet backbone, the routing information within the AS is hidden from the backbone routing protocols. Thus, to make networks that are hidden inside ASs reachable throughout the Internet, each autonomous system must agree to advertise network reachability information to other ASs, such as through the router running EGP in Figure 4.5. One major problem in interconnecting exterior and interior routing protocols is that they may use different routing techniques and different ways to decide link costs.

Just as autonomous systems hierarchically partition the Internet at the top level, interior routing protocols typically hierarchically partition

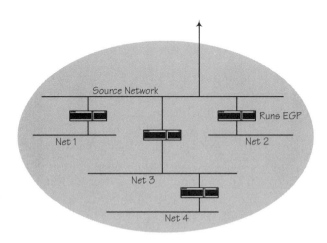

FIGURE 4.5 Example of an autonomous system.

each AS into areas. However, unlike autonomous systems, the same interior protocol routes packets both within and among areas.

Multicast Routing Issues

As we saw in Chapter 3, IGMP is concerned only with the creation of multicast groups and the forwarding of multicast traffic from a router to group members on its directly attached subnetworks. Since unicast routing protocols are designed to deliver packets from a source to a single destination and have no provisions for duplicating packets for multiple destinations, other routing protocols had to be designed to determine and maintain paths from a source to multiple destinations and enable multicast packet-forwarding.

Like unicast routers, multicast routers have to be concerned with the data they exchange with each other to ensure the forwarding of network traffic, learning the internet topology, detecting changes in the topology, and computing delivery paths on the topology. But multicast routers have a variety of other problems to solve as well. These issues stem from the construction of multicast delivery trees and the dynamics of group membership. For instance, since IP Multicasting allows group members to join and leave a host group at any time, the topology of the group's multicast delivery tree can change much more rapidly and more frequently than the topology of a regular IP internet dealing with unicast traffic.

Thus, although multicast routers need to deal with table sizes and the frequency and size of control message traffic, a primary focus of their design has been how the delivery trees are formed and maintained, the distribution and concentration of host group members, and the latencies associated with group members leaving the host group. Only recently have multicast routing designers sought to attack the scalability problems of multicasting in ways that parallel the solutions used for unicast routing (i.e., by defining hierarchies and proposing interdomain multicast routing protocols).

One of the fundamental tasks of a multicast routing protocol is to construct a multicast delivery tree to enable packet-forwarding. Multicast routing protocols establish or help establish the delivery tree for a given group, which enables multicast forwarding of packets addressed to the group. In the case of unicast traffic, routing protocols are also used to build a *forwarding table* (more commonly called a *routing table*).

As I pointed out earlier in this chapter, unicast destinations in the routing table are associated with a cost metric and a next-hop router in the path towards the destination. The key difference between unicast forwarding and multicast forwarding is that multicast packets must always be forwarded away from their source. If a packet is ever forwarded back toward its source, a forwarding loop could form, leading to a possible multicast *storm* where packets are duplicated without limit (or nearly so) and introduce undue amounts of excess traffic on the network that could prevent transmission of other traffic.

Each routing protocol constructs a forwarding table in its own way; the forwarding table tells each router that for a certain source, or for a given source sending to a certain group (called a (source, group) pair), packets are expected to arrive on a certain *inbound* or *upstream* interface and must be copied to a certain set of *outbound* or *downstream* interfaces in order to reach all known subnetworks with group members. The set of subnets and routers through which a multicast packet is forwarded forms a delivery tree, rooted at the source of the packet (Figure 4.6); copies of the multicast packet are generated only at the points where the tree branches.

Pruning

Since membership in IP Multicasting sessions is expected to be dynamic, one of the major issues multicast routing protocols have to deal with is maintaining the state of the delivery trees for multicast datagrams. The routing protocols accomplish this by a mechanism known as pruning.

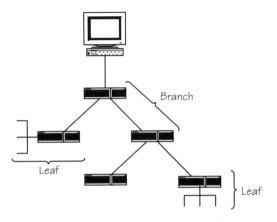

FIGURE 4.6   Delivery tree nomenclature.

In keeping with the tree terminology, leaves or branches which no longer contain members of a multicast group are removed, or pruned, from the tree. This is usually done by the router attached to that leaf, once it determines that there are no active members of the group on the LAN it serves (usually by sending IGMP queries; see Chapter 3). The leaf router sends a message upstream to other routers in the multicast tree to remove it from the multicast tree (see Figure 4.7).

Other upstream routers may also prune themselves from the tree as a result of this action, if all the intervening routers were a part of the multicast tree simply to forward datagrams to the leaf router which pruned itself.

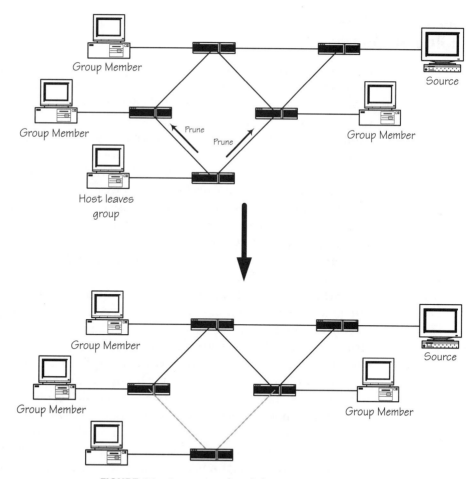

FIGURE 4.7 An example of the pruning process.

Pruning is important to the maintenance of multicast delivery trees because it helps reduce the demand on network resources by preventing the transmission of unwanted traffic to inactive group members and their subnets. But, since pruning is not instantaneous, formerly active subnets and routers belonging to the delivery tree may still receive multicast traffic before the pruning of the branch or leaf is accomplished. This *leave latency,* as it's called, varies among tree setup algorithms and is also affected by the size and structure of the delivery tree. In some cases, the amount of unwanted data may not pose problems, but when it's a full video stream, for instance, the impact on network resources can be more negative.

Dense-Mode versus Sparse-Mode Multicast Routing

As IP multicasting has evolved, new challenges have presented themselves to network engineers striving to efficiently distribute multicast data to group members. One continuing challenge has been how to efficiently route data to group members across widely varying network topologies. In some cases, many of an internetwork's subnets may contain at least one group member; thus, the group members are densely distributed across the network. Protocols designed to handle these situations are classified as dense-mode routing protocols. A different extreme is to consider that the group members are widely dispersed across the Internet, in what is referred to as *sparse-mode routing* (Figure 4.8). Note that this doesn't mean that the group has only a few members, but that the number of networks with group members is significantly smaller than the number of networks in the region as a whole.

While dense-mode protocols use a data-driven approach (*flood and prune*) to construct multicast distribution trees, sparse-mode protocols use a receiver-initiated process. That is, a router becomes involved in the construction of a multicast distribution tree only when one of the hosts on its subnet requests membership in a particular multicast group.

In addition to assuming that the group members are sparsely distributed throughout the network, sparse-mode protocols assume that bandwidth is not necessarily widely available. In these topologies, flooding would waste network bandwidth and could cause performance problems.

While dense-mode routing sends and stores explicit prune states in response to unwanted data packets, sparse-mode routing requires explicit joining. In sparse mode, the default action is not to send datagrams where

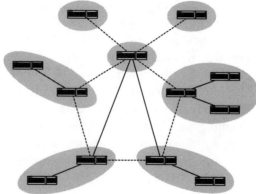

Dense Group

Sparse Group

Dashed line indicates unused links.

FIGURE 4.8 Dense and sparse group memberships.

they have not been requested. Thus, the cost of using a dense-mode routing protocol is the default broadcast behavior (to start building trees) and maintaining the prune state, whereas the cost of sparse-mode routing is the need to use shared trees (called rendezvous points or RPs) via which receivers hear of multicast sources and maintaining the tree state of RPs for idle groups.

Scalability

Another issue is how to scale multicast routing for the commercial Internet, with its increasing numbers of Internet Service Providers (ISPs) and domains. The MBone was unique in the way it was created as an experimental network, but its design cannot be extrapolated to the current Internet for everyday use by anyone and everyone who are connected to the Net. Even as the MBone grew, it was obvious that the routing protocols designed for multicasting would not scale well. The current slate of multicast routing protocols (such as PIM, MOSPF, and DVMRP; see Chapter 5) are not designed for multiple autonomous systems that do not necessarily want to share all their routing information. A unicast routing protocol, the Border Gateway Protocol (BGP), works for the IP protocol, but there is not yet an equivalent for IP Multicast. Just as Internet routing has evolved to using hierarchical routing and interdomain routing protocols, so too will multicast routing; work is already under way to solve these problems (see Chapter 5 for details).

The current multicast routing protocols attempt to accurately and rapidly maintain distribution trees that are as close as possible to the tree of shortest-path routes (as defined by unicast traffic) as possible. This means that the shape of a distribution tree can change rapidly. In addition, since distribution trees can be global, they can be subject to a high frequency of control traffic. In contrast, the design focus for the inter-domain unicast routing environment is on minimizing routing traffic and controlling stability. In order to support inter-domain multicast routing, the overhead associated with protocol and router control must be reduced and some measure of stability introduced into the multicast trees. Without this approach, it will be difficult to scale multicasting to the entire Internet.

Quality of Service

As I've mentioned earlier in this book, the increasing use of new networked applications such as interactive multimedia and time-sensitive delivery of data (*push* technologies) requires some kind of Quality of Service (QoS) support. Multicast protocols like ST-II include specifications of QoS as part of their link setup, but the more common protocols, like those used in IP multicasting, don't include such options.

Even considering the heterogeneity of the Internet's media, it's possible to provide a specified QoS for an end-to-end session. But that capability can be severely tested in the more dynamic environment of multicasting, as delivery trees change to accommodate group membership changes. One suggested approach to coupling QoS provisions with multicasting is to use *route pinning*, where the group member's request to join a group also includes requests for specific paths (that would include the appropriate QoS support). Route pinning also includes the option to specify more than one path that meets the QoS specs so that a second path can be maintained and switched to with relative ease should the first one fail.

As this book was being written, some protocols for QoS-based IP routing were proposed and are undergoing debate; these protocols will be designed for both unicast and multicast traffic.

Interoperability

The number of multicast routing protocols currently in use is small. For example, the MBone uses both DVMRP and MOSPF. As new protocols become finalized and deployed on networks, you can expect to see transition periods when a relatively large number of multicast routing protocols are in use. It may be some time (if ever?) before we see only one protocol dominate multicast routing, at least on the Internet. (Intranets, special ISP nets for businesses, and VPNs are a different matter, since more control can be exerted to select a single protocol.) With so many protocols in use, interoperability between the protocols is a major issue.

As its name implies, the PIM (Protocol-Independent Multicast) protocol aims to be interoperable with other multicast routing protocols. But PIM has not yet been accepted as a standard and deployment is limited. Since PIM routers will be forced to support multiple multicast protocols in each interface, increasing PIM's complexity, the deployment of PIM routers is likely to become quite complicated.

Also, as we'll see in Chapter 5, some of the routing protocols, like DVMRP and MOSPF, depend on features of the underlying unicast routing protocols. Effective deployment of these protocols thus depends on interoperability with the unicast protocols.

Tree Maintenance Techniques

One of the fundamental tasks of a multicast routing protocol, whether it's classified as a dense-mode or sparse-mode protocol, is to construct a multicast delivery tree to enable packet-forwarding. Before we discuss the details of each multicast routing protocol in the next chapter, we'll spend some time exploring the techniques routers use to create multicast delivery trees.

It's convenient to classify these techniques according to the way that they create the trees of routers that span between multicast sources and group members. Using this scheme, we'll start out with a discussion of *simple-minded* techniques, such as flooding and spanning trees, then move on to the more complex source-based trees and shared-tree techniques.

Simple-Minded Techniques

Simple-minded multicast routing protocols can be built using either *Flooding* or *Spanning Tree* algorithms. These algorithms are often called simple-minded because they tend to waste bandwidth or require a large amount of computational resources within the multicast routers involved. Protocols built on these algorithms may work for small networks with few senders, groups, and routers, but they do not scale well to larger numbers of senders, groups, or routers. In addition, protocols utilizing these techniques may be limited in their ability to handle arbitrary network topologies, if they can handle them at all.

FLOODING

Flooding is the simplest technique for delivering multicast datagrams to all routers in an internetwork. When a router using a flooding algorithm receives a packet that is addressed to a multicast group, it determines whether it has seen this particular packet before. If it is the first reception of the packet, the packet is forwarded on all interfaces except the one on which it arrived (the flood), guaranteeing that the multicast packet reaches all routers in the internetwork. If the router has seen the packet before, then the packet is discarded.

Flooding algorithms are very simple to implement since a router does not have to maintain a routing table and only needs to keep track of the most recently seen packets. However, flooding does not scale for application to large-scale internetworks since it generates a large number of duplicate packets and uses all available paths across the internetwork instead of just a limited number. Also, even though a flooding algorithm doesn't require the setup and maintenance of a routing table, it does not efficiently use router memory since each router is required to maintain a distinct table entry for each recently received packet.

SPANNING TREE

A more effective solution than flooding would be to select a subset of the internetwork topology which forms a spanning tree. The spanning tree

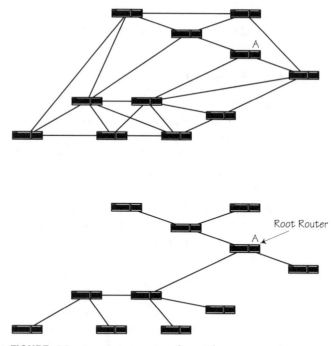

FIGURE 4.9 An internetwork with a spanning tree rooted at router A.

defines a structure in which only one active path connects any two routers of the internetwork (Figure 4.9). A spanning tree has just enough connectivity so that there is only one path between every pair of routers and it is loop-free; messages are replicated only when the tree branches.

The set of selected links forms a tree; it spans to all nodes in the network, thus the name spanning tree. Whenever a router receives a multicast packet, it forwards the packet on all the links which belong to the spanning tree except the one on which the packet has arrived, guaranteeing that the multicast packet reaches all the routers in the internetwork.

Forwarding along the branches of a spanning tree guarantees that the multicast packet will not loop and that it will eventually reach all routers in the internetwork. (Branches at a given level do not connect to each other and are one-way channels for transmitting multicast data, so it's impossible to form loops.)

The spanning tree solution can be quite powerful and it is relatively easy to implement. But a spanning tree algorithm can lead to traffic that's aggregated at a small number of links, leading to strain on some network resources and perhaps formation of bottlenecks and failed transmissions.

In addition, as network topologies become larger and more complex, it is computationally difficult to compute a spanning tree.

Source-Based Tree Techniques

Leaving behind the simple-minded techniques, let's now turn our attention to techniques that generate a source-based delivery tree. These techniques differ in the efficiency of the tree-building process, and the bandwidth and router resources they require to build a source-based tree.

Rather than build a single spanning tree for the entire internetwork, a more efficient solution would be to build a spanning tree for each potential source (i.e., each subnetwork). These spanning trees would result in source-based delivery trees rooted at the subnetworks directly connected to the source stations. Since there may be many potential sources for a group, the system would construct a different delivery tree rooted at each active source.

This class of algorithms has evolved over time, starting with the relatively simple reverse-path broadcasting, then to truncated reverse-path broadcasting and reverse-path multicasting. The latter algorithms were developed to better handle changes in group membership and their affects on trees. These algorithms are often called *reverse-path forwarding* (RPF) algorithms, which refers to the fact that forwarding packets is based on the router's knowledge of the shortest path *back* to the source.

REVERSE-PATH BROADCASTING

The basic algorithm for constructing source-based trees is called Reverse-Path Broadcasting (RPB). It works as follows: As long as a packet from a

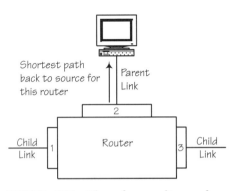

FIGURE 4.10 The forwarding algorithm for Reverse-Path Broadcasting.

source arrives on a link that the local router believes to be on the shortest path back toward the packet's source, then the router forwards the packet on all of its interfaces except the incoming interface (i.e., the interface that the source packet arrived on). If the packet does not arrive on the interface that is on the shortest path back toward the source, then the packet is discarded (Figure 4.10).

> NOTE   The interface over which the router expects to receive multicast packets from a particular source is referred to as the *parent* link. The outbound links over which the router forwards the multicast packet are called *child* links for this source.

The basic algorithm can be enhanced to reduce unnecessary packet duplication. If the local router making the forwarding decision can determine whether a neighboring router on a child link is downstream, then the packet is multicast toward the neighbor. Otherwise, the packet is not forwarded on the potential child link since the local router knows that the neighboring router will just discard the packet (since it will arrive on a nonparent link for the source, relative to that downstream router).

It's relatively easy to derive the information to make this downstream decision from a link-state routing protocol since each router maintains a topological database for the entire routing domain. If a distance-vector routing protocol is employed, a neighbor can either advertise its previous hop for the source as part of its routing update messages or *poison-reverse* the route toward a source if it is not on the distribution tree for that source. Either of these techniques allows an upstream router to determine if a downstream neighboring router is on an active branch of the delivery tree for a certain source.

> NOTE   In the *poison-reverse* process, a router will advertise all distances in its routing table as infinity if the destination is routed on the link. This kills all two-hop loops.

To see how this enhanced algorithm works, take a look at Figure 4.11. In this example, the source station (labeled S in the figure) is attached to a leaf subnetwork directly connected to Router A. Now let's follow what Router B would do using the enhanced RPB algorithm. Router B receives the multicast packet from Router A on link 1. Since Router B considers link 1 to be the parent link for the (source, group) pair, it forwards the packet on links 4 and 5, as well as any of the local leaf subnetworks if they contain group members. Router B does not forward the packet on link 3 because it knows from prior routing protocol exchanges that Router C

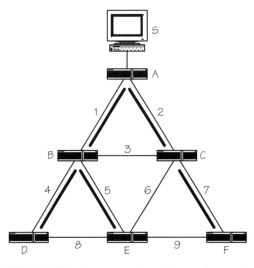

FIGURE 4.11 An example of the enhanced RPB algorithm.

considers link 2 as its parent link for the source. Router B knows that if it were to forward the packet on link 3, it would be discarded by Router C since the packet would not be arriving on Router C's parent link for this source.

The main benefit to reverse-path broadcasting is that it is reasonably efficient and easy to implement. It does not require that the router know about the entire spanning tree, nor does it require a special mechanism to stop the forwarding process (as flooding does). In addition, it guarantees efficient delivery since multicast packets always follow the shortest path from the source station to the destination group. Also, the packets are distributed over multiple links, resulting in better network utilization since a different tree would be computed for each source.

But one of the major limitations of the RPB algorithm is that it does not take into account multicast group membership when building the delivery tree for a source. As a result, datagrams may be unnecessarily forwarded onto subnetworks that have no members in a destination group.

TRUNCATED REVERSE-PATH BROADCASTING (TRPB)

Another source-based tree algorithm, Truncated Reverse-Path Broadcasting (TRPB), was developed to overcome the limitations of Reverse-Path Broadcasting. Using membership information provided by

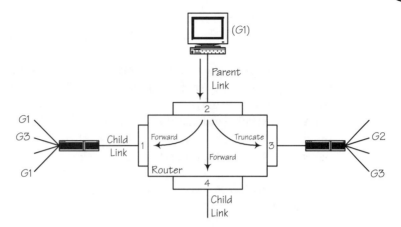

FIGURE 4.12 The TRPB algorithm.

IGMP, multicast routers using TRPB can avoid forwarding datagrams onto a leaf subnetwork if it does not contain at least one member of a given destination group. This way, the delivery tree is *truncated* by the router if a leaf subnetwork has no group members.

The operation of the TRPB algorithm is illustrated in Figure 4.12 (compare this with RPB's operation in Figure 4.10). In this case, the router receives a multicast packet on its parent link for the source for host group G1. The router will forward the datagram on interface 1 since that interface has at least one member of G1. The router does not forward the datagram to interface 3 since this interface has no members in that particular host group; the branch containing the router at interface 3 would be truncated. At the same time, the datagram will be forwarded on interface 4 as long as a downstream router considers this router to be part of its parent link for the source.

Truncated Reverse-Path Broadcasting removes some of the limitations of RPB, but it solves only some of the problems associated with source-based trees. TRPB eliminates unnecessary traffic on leaf subnetworks, but it does not consider group memberships when building the branches of the delivery tree. For that, we must turn to Reverse-Path Multicasting.

REVERSE-PATH MULTICASTING (RPM)

Reverse-Path Multicasting (RPM) creates a delivery tree that spans only subnetworks with group members as well as routers and subnetworks along the shortest path to subnetworks with group members. The source-based, shortest-path tree is pruned by RPM so that datagrams are only forwarded along branches that lead to active members of the destination group.

When a multicast router receives a packet for a (source, group) pair, the first packet is forwarded following the TRPB algorithm across all routers in the internetwork. The TRPB algorithm guarantees that each leaf router will receive at least the first multicast packet. If there is a group member on one of its leaf subnetworks, a leaf router forwards the packet based on its group membership information.

> NOTE   Routers on the edge of the network (which have only leaf subnetworks) are called leaf routers.

If none of the subnetworks connected to the leaf router contain group members, the leaf router may transmit a *Prune* message on its parent link (Figure 4.13), informing the upstream router that it should not forward packets for this particular (source, group) pair on the child interface on which it received the Prune message. Prune messages are sent just one hop back toward the source (TTL=1).

An upstream router receiving a Prune message stores the prune information in memory. If the upstream router has no recipients on local leaf subnetworks and has received Prune messages from each downstream neighbor on each of the child interfaces for this (source, group) pair, then this upstream router does not need to receive additional packets for the

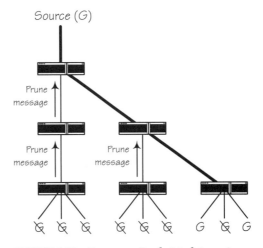

FIGURE 4.13 Reverse-Path Multicasting.

(source, group) pair. Should this be the case, this upstream router will also generate a Prune message of its own, to be sent one hop closer to the source. This cascade of Prune messages results in an active multicast delivery tree, consisting exclusively of branches that lead to active receivers.

Since both the group membership and internetwork topology can change dynamically, the pruned state of the multicast delivery tree must be refreshed periodically. At regular intervals, the prune information expires from the memory of all routers and the next packet for the (source, group) pair is forwarded toward all downstream routers. This allows *stale state* (prune state for groups that are no longer active) to be reclaimed by the multicast routers.

Despite the improvements offered by the RPM algorithm, there are still several scaling issues that need to be addressed when attempting to develop an Internet-wide delivery service. The first limitation is that multicast packets must be periodically flooded across every router in the internetwork, onto every leaf subnetwork. This flooding is wasteful of bandwidth (until the updated prune state is constructed).

This *flood and prune* approach is very powerful, but it wastes bandwidth and does not scale well, especially if there are receivers at the edge of the delivery tree which are connected via low-speed technologies (an ISDN or modem link, for example). Also, every router participating in the RPM algorithm must either have a forwarding table entry for a (source, group) pair, or have prune state information for that (source, group) pair.

It's considered wasteful to place such a burden on routers that are not on every (or perhaps any) active delivery tree, especially as the number of active sources and groups increase. Shared tree techniques are an attempt to address these scaling issues, which become quite acute when most groups' senders and receivers are sparsely distributed across the internetwork.

Shared-Tree Techniques

Rather than build a source-based tree for each source or each (source, group) pair, as the previously discussed shortest-path tree algorithms do, shared-tree algorithms construct a single delivery tree that is shared by all members of a group. Although this approach is similar to that of the spanning tree algorithm, it allows the definition of a different shared tree for each group. Furthermore, users wishing to receive traffic for a multicast group must explicitly join the shared delivery tree. Multicast traffic for each group is sent and received over the same delivery tree, regardless of the source (Figure 4.14).

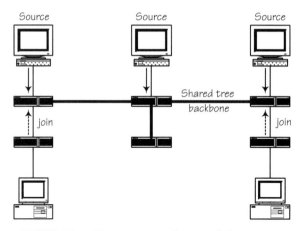

FIGURE 4.14 Sharing a multicast delivery tree.

Just like the other multicast forwarding algorithms we've covered in this chapter, shared-tree algorithms do not require that the source of a multicast packet be a member of a destination group in order to send to a group.

Shared-tree techniques offer several scalability-related advantages over source-based trees. First, shared-tree algorithms make efficient use of router resources since they only require a router to maintain state information for each group, rather than for each source, or for each (source, group) pair. Since the number of sources is no longer a scaling issue, the scalability of applications that have many active senders, such as video-conferencing or groupware applications, improves.

Second, shared-tree algorithms conserve network bandwidth since multicast packets do not have to be periodically flooded across all multicast routers in the internetwork onto every leaf subnet. This can offer significant bandwidth savings, especially across low-bandwidth WAN links, and when receivers sparsely populate the domain of operation.

Finally, since receivers are required to explicitly join the shared delivery tree, data only flows over those links that lead to active receivers.

But even shared-tree algorithms are not perfect. There are still several limitations to protocols that are based on a shared-tree algorithm. Since traffic from all sources traverses the same set of links as it approaches the core, shared trees can result in a concentration of network traffic and formation of bottlenecks near core routers. Also, a single shared delivery tree may create suboptimal routers that lead to increased delays, which may be a critical issue for some multimedia applications.

Summary

No single multicast routing protocol incorporates all of the tree construction algorithms we've discussed. Nor has a single routing protocol yet proved to be suitable for all multicasting topologies. In the next chapter, we'll see the variety of multicast routing protocols that have been proposed for use on the Internet.

5

Multicast Routing Protocols

The previous chapter demonstrated that the requirements for a multicast routing protocol differ greatly from those for a unicast routing protocol. Not only do multicast routers need to respond to changes in network topology, but they also have to respond to changes in group membership. Plus, they need to do this in a timely fashion, not wasting bandwidth by sending unwanted data to resigned members or failing to forward multicast traffic to new members.

Only two multicast routing protocols—DVMRP (Distance-Vector Multicast Routing Protocol) and MOSPF (Multicast Extensions to Open Shortest Path First)—have thus far seen widespread use on the Internet, mainly due to their use on the MBone. Others, like PIM (Protocol-Independent Multicast) and CBT (Core-Based Trees), have been prepared to help deal with scalability problems that are either already self-evident or are likely to occur as multicasting becomes more widespread on the Internet.

Many multicast routing protocols are designed to work well in environments that have plentiful bandwidth and where it is reasonable to assume that receivers are rather densely distributed. In such scenarios, it is very reasonable to use periodic flooding, or other bandwidth-intensive techniques that would not necessarily be very scalable over a wide-area network (WAN).

The designs underlying these protocols assume that the amount of protocol overhead (in terms of the amount of information that must be maintained by each router, the number of router CPU cycles required, and the amount of bandwidth consumed by protocol operation) is appropriate since receivers densely populate the area of operation. The routing protocols that are designed to work on networks with adequate bandwidth and dense group memberships include Distance-Vector Multicast Routing Protocol (DVMRP), Multicast Extensions to Open Shortest Path First (MOSPF), and Protocol-Independent Multicast–Dense Mode (PIM-DM).

The most recent additions to the set of multicast routing protocols are called *sparse mode* protocols. They are designed from a different perspective than the *dense mode* protocols that I've just mentioned. Often, they are not data-driven, in the sense that the forwarding state is set up in advance, and they trade off using bandwidth liberally (which is a valid thing to do in a campus LAN environment) for other techniques that are much more suited to scaling over large WANs, where bandwidth can be scarce and expensive.

While these routing protocols are designed to operate efficiently over a wide area network where bandwidth is scarce and group members may be quite sparsely distributed, this is not to imply that they are only suitable for small groups. Sparse doesn't mean small; rather, it is meant to convey that the groups are widely dispersed. Thus, more attention is paid to preserving bandwidth; for instance, it's wasteful to flood group data periodically across the entire internetwork when the density of groups and group members is sparse. Sparse mode protocols include Protocol-Independent Multicast–Sparse Mode (PIM-SM) and Core-Based Trees (CBT). Let's take a look at the details of each of these protocols in turn.

Distance-Vector Multicast Routing Protocol (DVMRP)

As the name suggests, the Distance-Vector Multicast Routing Protocol (DVMRP) is designed to support the forwarding of multicast datagrams through an internetwork. DVMRP constructs source-based multicast delivery trees using the Reverse-Path Multicasting (RPM) algorithm (see Chapter 4). Originally, the entire MBone ran only DVMRP. Today, over half of the MBone routers still run some version of DVMRP, with MOSPF as the next most popular routing protocol.

DVMRP was first defined in RFC 1075. The original specifications were derived from the Routing Information Protocol (RIP) and employed the Truncated Reverse-Path Broadcasting (TRPB) technique covered in Chapter 4. One major difference between RIP and DVMRP is that RIP calculates the next hop toward a destination, while DVMRP computes the previous hop back toward a source. Since version 3.0 of the mrouted software (the primary routing software for the MBone) was released, DVMRP has employed the Reverse-Path Multicasting (RPM) algorithm.

DVMRP routers can support both direct physical interfaces to an attached subnet and a tunnel interface to another multicast-capable island (as in the MBone). Each interface includes a metric specifying the cost for the given port and a TTL threshold that limits the scope of a multicast transmission, as described in Chapter 3. Each tunnel interface must also be explicitly configured with two additional parameters—the IP address of the local router's tunnel interface and the IP address of the remote router's interface.

Basic Operation

As previously mentioned, DVMRP now implements the Reverse-Path Multicasting (RPM) algorithm (see Chapter 4). According to the RPM algorithm, the first datagram for any (source, group) pair is forwarded across the entire internetwork as long as the packet's TTL and router interface thresholds allow this.

> NOTE   You'll also find me use a shorthand notation for the (source, group) pair, namely (S, G).

Upon receiving this traffic, leaf routers may transmit Prune messages back toward the source if there are no group members on their directly attached leaf subnets. These Prune messages will cause upstream routers to remove all branches that do not lead to group members from the tree, resulting in a source-based, shortest-path tree.

After a set period of time, the prune state for each (source, group) pair expires, allowing for generation of a new multicast tree. A multicast datagram for the (source, group) pair is again flooded across all down-

Administrative Scoping

TTL-based scoping is not always suitable for all applications. Conflicts arise when network managers try to simultaneously enforce limits on topology, geography, and bandwidth. TTL-based scoping cannot handle overlapping regions, which is a necessary characteristic of administrative regions. To help resolve these issues, a new type of scoping called administrative scoping was created in 1994 to provide a way to perform scoping based on the multicast address. Certain addresses would be usable within a given administrative scope (e.g., a corporate internetwork), but would not be forwarded onto the MBone. The range of IP addresses from 239.0.0.0 to 239.255.255.255 has been reserved for administrative scoping.

Administratively scoped IP Multicast can provide clear and simple semantics for scoped IP Multicast. The key properties of administratively scoped IP Multicast are that (1) packets addressed to administratively scoped multicast addresses do not cross configured administrative boundaries, and (2) administratively scoped multicast addresses are locally assigned, and therefore are not required to be unique across administrative boundaries.

stream routers. This flooding will result in a new set of Prune messages, regenerating the source-based shortest-path tree for this (source, group) pair. Since Prune messages are transmitted via UDP and thus their delivery is not guaranteed, the prune lifetime must be kept short to compensate for lost Prune messages.

DVMRP also implements a mechanism to quickly *graft* back a previously pruned branch of a group's delivery tree (see Chapter 3 for an example). If a router that had sent a Prune message for a (source, group) pair discovers new group members on a leaf network (by sending a periodic IGMP-Query on its subnets, for instance), it will send a Graft message to the previous hop router for this source. When the upstream router receives a Graft message, it cancels the previously received prune message. Graft messages reliably cascade hop-by-hop back toward the source until they reach the nearest *live* branch point on the delivery tree. Using this method, previously pruned branches can be quickly restored to a given delivery tree without waiting for the periodic flooding of multicast datagrams to regenerate the tree.

DVMRP Router Functions

It's possible to form redundant links when deploying DVMRP routers, leading to reception of duplicate datagrams. To counter this problem, DVMRP provides for the selection of a dominant router to avoid packet duplication.

Let's see how DVMRP selects a dominant router by investigating the situation shown in Figure 5.1. In this figure, Router C is downstream and can potentially receive datagrams from the source subnetwork through either Router A or Router B. If Router A's metric to the source subnetwork is less than Router B's metric, then Router A is the dominant router for this source. This means that Router A will forward any traffic from the source subnetwork and Router B will discard traffic received from that source.

But if the metrics of the two routers are equal, then the router with the lower IP address on its downstream interface becomes the dominant router for this source. On those occasions when a subnet has multiple routers forwarding to groups with multiple sources, it's possible that a different router may be the dominant router for each source.

If you look at Figure 5.1 again, you'll see that there are both dominant and subordinate routers in this figure. Let's assume in this example that Router B is dominant, Router A is subordinate, and Router C is part of the downstream delivery tree. The dominant router can determine this situation because the subordinate router will *poison-reverse* the route for this source in its routing updates which are sent on the common LAN (i.e., Router A sets the metric for this source to infinity).

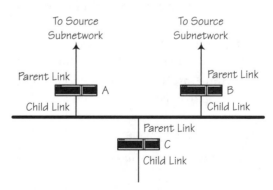

FIGURE 5.1 The DVMRP dominant router in a redundant topology.

NOTE   A subordinate router is one that is not on the shortest-path tree back toward a source.

The dominant router keeps track of subordinate routers for each source; it neither needs nor expects to receive a Prune message from a subordinate router. Only routers that are a part of the downstream distribution tree will ever need to send prunes to the dominant router. If a dominant router on a LAN receives either a poison-reversed route for a source or Prune messages for all groups emanating from that source subnetwork, then it may also send a prune upstream toward the source. If the dominant router uses IGMP to find that there are still local group members on its own leaf subnet, then it will not forward a Prune message upstream, but simply stop forwarding the multicast traffic to the downstream routers that had requested pruning.

In the DVMRP process, each router periodically exchanges routing table updates with its DVMRP neighbors. These updates are independent of those generated by any unicast Interior Gateway Protocol.

Since DVMRP was developed to route multicast and not unicast traffic, a router can often run multiple routing processes in practice—one to support the forwarding of unicast traffic and another to support the forwarding of multicast traffic.

A sample routing table for a DVMRP router is shown in Table 5.1. Unlike the table that would be created by a unicast routing protocol such as the RIP or OSPF, the DVMRP routing table contains Source Prefixes and From-Gateways instead of Destination Prefixes and Next-Hop Gateways.

The items in the DVMRP routing table are:

Source Subnet.   A subnetwork which is a source of multicast datagrams.

Subnet Mask.   The subnet mask associated with the Source Prefix. DVMRP provides the subnet mask for each source subnetwork.

From-Gateway.   The previous hop router leading back toward a particular Source Prefix.

TABLE 5.1   Sample DVMRP Routing Table

Source Subnet	Subnet Mask	From-Gateway	Metric	Status	TTL	InPort	OutPorts
128.1.0.0	255.255.0.0	128.7.5.2	3	Up	200	1	2, 3
128.2.0.0	255.255.0.0	128.7.5.2	5	Up	150	2	1
128.3.0.0	255.255.0.0	128.6.3.1	2	Up	150	2	2, 3
128.4.0.0	255.255.0.0	128.6.3.1	4	Up	200	1	2

Metric.   Cost associated with that port.

Status.   Current availability of port (Up or Down).

TTL.   A time-to-live value is used for table management; it indicates the number of seconds before an entry is removed from the routing table. (Note: This TTL has nothing to do with the TTL used in TTL-based scoping.)

InPort.   Router's interfaces for incoming traffic.

OutPorts.   Router's interfaces for outgoing traffic.

The routing table represents the shortest-path spanning tree to every possible source prefix in the internetwork (i.e., the Reverse-Path Broadcasting tree). Note that the DVMRP routing table does not include information about group membership or received Prune messages.

Since the DVMRP routing table does not include group membership information, the DVMRP router has to build another table, the forwarding table, which is based on a combination of the information contained in the multicast routing table, known groups, and received Prune messages. The forwarding table represents the local router's understanding of the shortest-path source-based delivery tree for each (source, group) pair; in this case, it's the Reverse-Path Multicasting (RPM) tree.

A sample forwarding table for a sample DVMRP router is shown in Table 5.2 with the accompanying message flows in Figure 5.2. (In the figure, a G represents messages for a particular host group of the given address.) The elements in this table include the following items:

Source Prefix.   The subnetwork sending multicast datagrams to the specified groups (one group per row).

Multicast Group.   The Class D IP address to which multicast datagrams are addressed. Note that a given Source Prefix may contain sources for several Multicast Groups.

InPort.   The parent interface for the (source, group) pair. A 'Pr' in this column indicates that a Prune message has been sent to the upstream router.

TABLE 5.2   Sample DVMRP Forwarding Table

Source Subnet	Multicast Group	TTL	InPort	OutPorts
128.1.0.0	224.1.1.1	200	1 Pr	2p 3p
224.1.1.1		100	1	2p 3
224.1.1.1		250	1	2
128.2.0.0	224.1.1.1	150	2	2p 3p

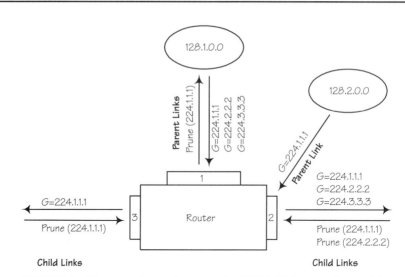

FIGURE 5.2 Message flows for sample DVMRP forwarding table.

OutPorts. The child interfaces over which multicast datagrams for this (source, group) pair are forwarded. A 'p' in this column indicates that the router has received a Prune message from one or more downstream routers on this port.

Since Prune messages are group-specific, messages to a branch can be blocked for one group and passed for another.

Advantages and Disadvantages

DVMRP has the advantage of being relatively simple to deploy because it is based on well-known RIP algorithms. Another advantage is the modest processing demands that DVMRP places on routers. But, even though the processing and state information requirements of DVMRP are less than that needed for other more sophisticated protocols, these requirements can become considerable for large networks using DVMRP.

On the downside, DVMRP's reliance on RIP's distance-vector routing limits convergence performance and the network diameter for large multicast applications (see Chapter 4). DVMRP needs to periodically flood multicast traffic throughout the network to rebuild its trees, which also adversely affects its scalability. Such flooding isn't practical when thousands of multicast groups share the same network infrastructure. Work is progressing on defining hierarchical multicast routing and other approaches for inter-domain routing of multicast traffic to promote better scalability of multicast networks; one such proposed protocol is a hierarchical form of DVMRP called HDVMRP. We'll investigate HDVMRP and some of the other suggested approaches in the last section of this chapter.

Multicast Extensions to Open Shortest Path First (MOSPF)

DVMRP's dependence on the underlying unicast routing protocol makes it impractical to implement DVMRP in a region of the Internet or a corporate intranet which uses a different routing algorithm, such as OSPF. The Multicast Extensions to OSPF (MOSPF) add multicasting support to OSPF by letting routers use their link-state databases to build multicast distribution trees for forwarding multicast traffic. The MOSPF standard, as defined in RFC 1584, allows MOSPF routers to interoperate with nonmulticast OSPF routers for the forwarding unicast IP traffic.

> NOTE   Version 2 of the Open Shortest Path First (OSPF) routing protocol is defined in RFC 1583. OSPF is an *Interior Gateway Protocol* that distributes unicast topology information among routers belonging to a single OSPF Autonomous System. OSPF is based on link-state algorithms which permit rapid route calculation with a minimum of routing protocol traffic.

Basic Operation

Just like all other multicast routing protocols, routers running MOSPF use the Internet Group Management Protocol (IGMP) to monitor multicast group membership on directly attached subnetworks. MOSPF routers maintain a local group database which lists directly attached groups and determines the local router's responsibility for delivering multicast datagrams to these groups.

There are certain noteworthy properties of the MOSPF routing algorithm:

1. For a given multicast datagram, all routers within an OSPF area calculate the same source-based shortest-path delivery tree. Unlike unicast OSPF, MOSPF does not support the concept of equal-cost multipath routing.

2. Synchronized link-state databases containing Group-Membership link-state records allow an MOSPF router to build a source-based shortest-path tree in memory, working forward from the source to the group members. Unlike DVMRP, this means that the first datagram of a new transmission does not have to be flooded to all routers in an area.

3. The *on-demand* construction of the source-based delivery tree has the benefit of spreading calculations over time, resulting in a reduced impact on participating routers. Of course, this may strain the router if many new (source, group) pairs appear at about the same time or if there are a lot of events which force the MOSPF process to flush and rebuild its forwarding cache. But in a stable topology with long-lived multicast sessions, these effects should be minimal.

MOSPF Router Functions

When a subnet or area includes more than one router, one router must be selected as the *MOSPF-designated router* and another selected as a *backup designated router*. The designated router keeps a database of directly attached members for each multicast group and is responsible for communicating group membership information to all other routers in the OSPF area. It accomplishes this by flooding Group-Membership Link State Advertisements (LSAs) within a single area. The backup designated router performs MOSPF duties whenever the primary designated router fails.

Once an MOSPF designated router learns of a new group member on its attached subnets, it sends a special Group-Membership LSA to all other MOSPF routers within the OSPF area. When a MOSPF router receives one of these multicast LSAs, it adds the group membership information to its own link-state database. (This database is the basic OSPF link-state database with the MOSPF multicast extensions.)

On any given subnet, the transmission of IGMP Host Membership Queries is performed solely by the designated router. However, both the designated router and the backup designated router have the responsibility of listening to IGMP Host Membership Reports.

When the initial datagram arrives, the source subnetwork is located in the MOSPF link-state database. The MOSPF link-state database is simply the standard OSPF link-state database with the addition of information obtained from Group-Membership LSA. Using the Router and Network link-state records in the OSPF link-state database, a source-based shortest-

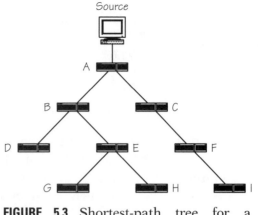

FIGURE 5.3 Shortest-path tree for a (source, group) pair.

path tree is constructed. After the tree is built, Group-Membership LSAs are used to prune the tree so that the only remaining branches lead to subnetworks containing members of this group.

To forward multicast datagrams to downstream members of a group, each router must determine its position in the datagram's shortest-path tree. In Figure 5.3, I've drawn the shortest-path tree for a given (source, group) pair. Router E's upstream node is Router B and there are two downstream interfaces—one leading to G and another leading to H.

Each MOSPF router makes its forwarding decision based on the contents of its forwarding cache. Unlike DVMRP, MOSPF forwarding is not RPF-based. The forwarding cache is built from the source-based shortest-path tree for each (source, group) pair and the router's local group database. After the router discovers its position in the shortest-path tree, a forwarding cache entry is created containing the (source, group) pair, its expected upstream interface, and the necessary downstream interface(s). The forwarding cache entry is now used to quickly forward all subsequent datagrams from this source to this group. If a new source begins sending to a new group, MOSPF must first calculate the distribution tree so that it may create a cache entry that can be used to forward the packet.

Table 5.3 displays the forwarding cache for a sample MOSPF router. The elements in the cache include the following items:

> **Dest. Group.**   A known destination group address to which datagrams are currently being forwarded, or to which traffic was sent

TABLE 5.3   MOSPF Forwarding Cache

Destination	Source	Upstream	Downstream	TTL
224.1.1.1	128.1.0.2	!1	!2 !3	5
224.1.1.1	128.4.1.2	!1	!2 !3	2
224.1.1.1	128.5.2.2	!1	!2 !3	3
224.2.2.2	128.2.0.3	!2	!1	7

recently (i.e., since the last topology or group membership or other event which (re-)initialized MOSPF's forwarding cache).

Source.   The datagram's source host address. Each (Dest. Group, Source) pair uniquely identifies a separate forwarding cache entry.

Upstream.   Datagrams matching this row's Dest. Group and Source must be received on this interface.

Downstream.   If a datagram matching this row's Dest. Group and Source is received on the correct Upstream interface, then it is forwarded across the listed Downstream interfaces.

TTL.   The minimum number of hops a datagram must cross to reach any of the Dest. Group's members. An MOSPF router may discard a datagram if it can see that the datagram has insufficient TTL to reach even the closest group member.

The information in the forwarding cache is not aged or periodically refreshed. Instead, it is maintained as long as there are system resources available or until the next topology change. The contents of the forwarding cache will change either when the topology of the OSPF internetwork changes, forcing all of the shortest-path trees to be recalculated or there is a change in the Group-Membership LSAs indicating that the distribution of individual group members has changed.

Mixing MOSPF and OSPF Routers

Since MOSPF routers can co-exist with OSPF routers in an area, you can plan a gradual deployment of multicasting support by installing MOSPF routers alongside unicast OSPF routers. But each MOSPF router is configured to eliminate all nonmulticast OSPF routers when it builds its source-based shortest-path delivery tree. In addition, the nonmulticast routers do not participate in the flooding of new Group-Membership LSAs (since that is an LSA format they do not recognize). Thus, some care has to be taken when mixing MOSPF routers with nonmulticast OSPF routers or else problems may occur.

One problem can occur when there may be unicast connectivity to a destination, but there is no corresponding multicast connectivity. For example, the only path between two points could require traversal of a nonmulticast-capable OSPF router. Since MOSPF does not support tunneling, multicast data cannot be encapsulated for transfer across a nonmulticast OSPF router.

Second, the designated router for a multi-access network must be an MOSPF router; otherwise, the attached subnet will be able to forward any multicast datagrams. A unicast OSPF router doesn't run IGMP and is incapable of receiving the IGMP Host Membership Reports, so the subnetwork it serves would not be selected to forward multicast datagrams. Also, bear in mind that a unicast designated router cannot generate Group-Membership LSAs for its subnetwork since it doesn't record that type of LSA.

Routing between Areas and Autonomous Systems

OSPF allows sets of networks to be grouped together into what is called an *area* (see Chapter 4). The topology of an OSPF area is hidden from the rest of the system, resulting in a significant reduction in routing traffic. Also, routing within an area is determined only by the area's own net topology, which can help protect the area from bad routing data.

Since OSPF allows for the definition of areas and autonomous systems (ASs) to simplify routing, MOSPF must be able to route multicast traffic between areas and ASs in much the same way as OSPF routes unicast traffic. Inter-area routing is needed when a multicast source and some of the host group members reside in different OSPF areas (see Figure 5.4). Just as for routing within an area, forwarding multicast datagrams is

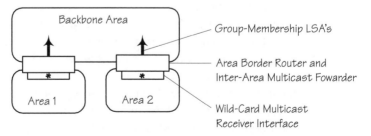

FIGURE 5.4 Inter-area routing.

determined by the contents of the forwarding cache, which is built from the local group database and the source-based trees. But there are differences in the way that group membership information is propagated and the way that the inter-area source-based tree is constructed.

MOSPF introduces the concept of an *inter-area multicast forwarder* that is responsible for forwarding group membership information and multicast datagrams between areas. In most cases, an OSPF Area Border Router (ABR) is configured to also function as an inter-area multicast forwarder.

Inter-area multicast forwarders have to create summaries of their attached area's group membership information for transmission to the backbone. But the transmission of group membership in MOSPF is asymmetric; while group membership information from nonbackbone areas is flooded into the backbone, group membership from the backbone (or from any other nonbackbone areas) is not flooded into any nonbackbone area. Inter-area multicast forwarders transmit their summaries by sending new Group-Membership LSAs into the backbone area.

Another device introduced by MOSPF to handle forwarding of multicast traffic between areas is a *wild-card multicast receiver* that receives all multicast traffic generated in the area in which it's located. In nonbackbone areas, all inter-area multicast forwarders operate as wild-card multicast receivers. This guarantees that all multicast traffic originating in any nonbackbone area is delivered to its inter-area multicast forwarder and then, if necessary, into the backbone area. Since the backbone knows group membership for all areas, the datagram can be forwarded to the appropriate location(s) in the OSPF autonomous system, as long as it is forwarded into the backbone by the source area's inter-area multicast forwarder.

Since the backbone and other areas are not aware of all multicast topology and group membership information, it is usually impossible to build a complete shortest-path delivery tree for situations involving inter-area multicast routing.

Areas introduce another problem when it comes to pruning. If the source of a multicast datagram resides in the same area as the router performing the calculation, the pruning process has to be controlled to ensure that branches leading to other areas are not removed from the tree (Figure 5.5). Only those branches having no group members nor wild-card multicast receivers are pruned. Branches containing wild-card multicast receivers must be retained since the local routers do not know whether there are any group members residing in other areas.

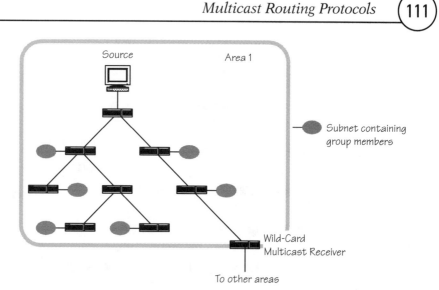

FIGURE 5.5 Shortest-path tree when the source is in the same area as the members.

If the source of a multicast datagram resides in a different area than the router calculating a shortest-path tree, the details of the local topology surrounding the source station are not known. One way around this is to estimate information using information provided by Summary-Links LSAs for the source subnetwork. In such cases, the base of the tree begins with branches directly connecting the source subnetwork to each of the local area's inter-area multicast forwarders (Figure 5.6). Datagrams transmitted from sources outside the local area will enter the area via one of its inter-area multicast forwarders, so they all must be part of the proposed delivery tree.

Since each inter-area multicast forwarder is also an ABR, it must maintain a separate link-state database for each attached area. Thus, each inter-area multicast forwarder is required to calculate a separate forwarding tree for each of its attached areas.

Multicasting between Autonomous Systems follows a procedure that's very similar to the one I just described for inter-area multicasting. The main difference is that, since Autonomous Systems do not use the same routing protocols to communicate between themselves as they do to communicate internally, routers using an Exterior Gateway Protocol have to be selected to help with the multicasting process.

Just as ABRs are used as inter-area multicast forwarders, selected Autonomous System Boundary Routers (ASBRs) are configured as *inter-*

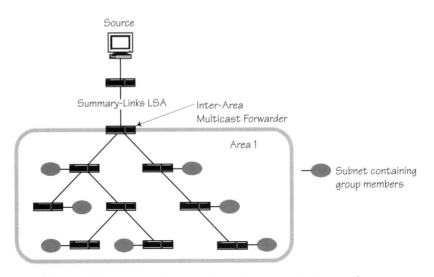

FIGURE 5.6 Shortest-path tree when the source is in another area.

AS multicast forwarders to forward group membership info and multicast traffic between ASs. MOSPF assumes that each inter-AS multicast forwarder uses a multicast routing protocol that forwards multicast datagrams according to the reverse-path forwarding (RPF) algorithm.

In addition, each inter-AS multicast forwarder is a wild-card multicast receiver in each of its attached areas, which guarantees that each inter-AS multicast forwarder is a part of all pruned shortest-path trees and receives all multicast datagrams.

The details of inter-AS forwarding are very similar to inter-area forwarding. On the interior of the OSPF domain, the multicast ASBR must conform to all the requirements of intra-area and inter-area forwarding. Within the OSPF domain, group members are reached by the usual forward path computations. Paths to external sources are approximated by a reverse-path source-based tree, with the multicast ASBR substituting for the actual source. When the source is within the OSPF Autonomous System and there are external group members, the inter-AS multicast forwarders, in their role as wild-card receivers, have to make sure that the data gets out of the OSPF domain and sent off in the correct direction.

Advantages and Disadvantages

Just as link-state routing protocols like OSPF are recognized to possess faster and better convergence properties than distance-vector algorithm, MOSPF's link-state approach allows the system to adapt rapidly to changes in group membership or the availability of network resources. And, since it's a link-state protocol, MOSPF doesn't depend on flooding packets to determine either group membership or network topology.

Since MOSPF can interoperate with OSPF, it can be used to forward normal unicast IP traffic at the same time it handles multicast traffic, making deployment simpler. MOSPF can also use the same flexible-path metrics as OSPF (such as cost, bandwidth, etc.) instead of just a simple hop-count, as DVMRP does, to create source-based trees. This makes MOSPF more amenable to supporting cost-based or QoS-based routing, for example.

For some users, a potential drawback is that networks using MOSPF may need to rely on DVMRP in order to participate on the MBone, since MOSPF does not support tunnels.

On the downside, MOSPF is a computationally intensive routing protocol that requires a router to perform a shortest-path computation for all multicast sources, in fact for each source-group combination. The processing cost of the Dijkstra algorithm to compute the shortest-path tree can also become a limiting factor as networks get larger.

Also, MOSPF isn't well-suited for handling sparse topologies. (See the following section on PIM for more details on sparse topologies.)

Protocol-Independent Multicast (PIM)

The Protocol-Independent Multicast (PIM) protocol is actually two protocols—PIM-Dense Mode (PIM-DM) and PIM-Sparse Mode (PIM-SM). While PIM-DM and PIM-SM do have related control messages, they are actually two completely independent protocols. At the time this book was being prepared, PIM-DM was still being processed as an internet-draft document by the IETF, while PIM-SM had been accepted as an Experimental RFC, RFC 2117.

> NOTE For the sake of convenience, I'll use the term PIM when discussing issues that apply equally well to either of the two protocols and specifically refer to either PIM-DM or PIM-SM when discussing features that are specific to that protocol.

PIM makes a clear distinction between a multicast routing protocol that is designed for dense environments and one that is designed for sparse environments. Dense-mode refers to a protocol that is designed to operate in an environment where group members are relatively densely packed and bandwidth is plentiful. Sparse-mode refers to a protocol that is optimized for environments where group members are distributed across many regions of the Internet and bandwidth is not necessarily widely available. Sparse-mode does not imply that the group has a few members, only that they are widely dispersed across the Internet.

PIM gets its name from the fact that it is independent of any particular unicast routing protocol. PIM-DM and PIM-SM are both designed so that they are not dependent on any specific routing protocol to build and maintain multicast delivery trees. The PIM protocols do not define their own routing update messages in the way that OSPF, RIP, and similar unicast routing protocols do. PIM uses whatever native unicast routing protocol the IP network is running on; therefore, it has to maintain additional state information to compensate for the unicast routing table not being multicast-aware.

Protocol-Independent Multicast—Dense Mode

PIM-DM is similar to DVMRP in the way it floods multicasts out of all interfaces except the source interface. Dense-mode PIM uses Reverse-Path Multicasting (RPM, see Chapter 4) and, like DVMRP, unneeded branches are eliminated with Prune messages. Because it is protocol-independent, however, PIM-DM has to establish its own router-to-router dialogs on top of the unicast routing protocol used for the internetwork.

In DVMRP, information obtained from the poison-reverse process tells a router that other routers on the shared LAN use the LAN as their incoming interface. As a result, even if the designated router for that LAN does not hear any IGMP Reports for a group, the designated router will know that it should continue forwarding multicast datagrams to that group and not send a Prune message to its upstream neighbor. Since dense-mode PIM does not rely on any unicast routing protocol mechanisms, this problem is solved by using Prune messages sent upstream on a LAN. If a downstream router on a LAN determines that it has no more downstream members for a group, then it can multicast a Prune message on the LAN.

There are occasions when PIM-DM can be less efficient than DVMRP because it does not control the interfaces that are flooded during the tree-building process as tightly as does DVMRP. PIM-DM assumes that routers are capable of caching the Prune messages in a context associated with the (source, group) pair. But this won't always be the case—a router lacking sufficient memory can decide to drop the *least recently used* contexts. This will cause a few more packets to be flooded on the network, but isn't considered to be a major problem. Remember that we are talking about networks which are most likely not bandwidth-constrained, which is the case when discussing dense-mode protocols. Should the number of flooded packets become too large, however, the group will be reinserted in the *recently used* list. This compromise also results in PIM-DM requiring a bit less control processing overhead on routers than does DVMRP.

PIM-DM ROUTER FUNCTIONS

A *designated router* (DR) is necessary for each multiaccess LAN so that a single router will send IGMP Host-Query messages to solicit host group membership. The procedure for selecting a designated router is the same for both PIM-DM and PIM-SM: When there is more than one PIM router connected to a multiaccess LAN, the router with the highest IP address is selected as the designated router.

The designated router doesn't have to be responsible for transmitting IGMP Host Membership Query messages, but it does send Join/Prune messages toward the core or rendezvous point (RP), where receivers meet sources (which I'll describe in more detail in the discussion of PIM-SM, in the following section). The designated router also maintains information on the status of the active rendezvous point for local senders to each multicast group.

PIM routers include special procedures for handling multiple paths of equal cost and for handling broadcast networks. The PIM specifications include a very simple solution for the equal-cost multipath problem. When it comes to selecting from two or more neighbors that have equal costs (see Figure 5.1 and the previous discussion of DVMRP dominant routers), a PIM router will accept multicast packets from the neighbor with the largest IP address. (Recall that DVMRP used the interface with the smallest IP address to determine which router was a dominant router in similar situations.)

Broadcast networks pose special problems when several routers are connected to the same cable (see Figure 5.7). When a multicast packet is received by router A, it forwards this packet over the Ethernet cable to two other routers, B and C. Router B will forward the packet on its second interface to the group member. But router C notices that it has no group member attached to its second interface, so it will prune the group, sending a Prune(S,G) message to router A. But if router A acts on the Prune message, no further packets will be forwarded to router B and group mem-

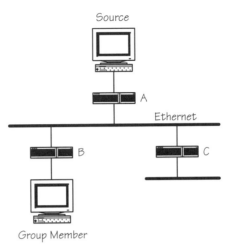

FIGURE 5.7 Handling prune requests on shared media.

ber M, since A has only one interface to the Ethernet cable serving routers B and C.

To deal with this potential problem, PIM requires that Prune messages always be sent to the *all-routers* multicast address, 224.0.0.2. Continuing with our example, this means that router C's Prune message will be received by both routers A and B. As a result of receiving the Prune message from router C, router A does not apply the prune immediately, but schedules the group for deletion. When router B receives the Prune message, it generates a Join message to the same all-routers address, which causes router A to cancel the scheduled prune action.

If there are more than two routers on the Ethernet cable, only one router needs to issue a Join message to keep the branch active since all routers on the cable receive all-routers messages. Other routers on the cable that need to maintain group membership also do not have to send Join messages once they see that a Join message already has been transmitted.

Another problem can arise when several routers are connected to the same broadcast network, such as in Figure 5.8. It's possible that two or more routers may receive the packets from the source through different paths, causing the group member to receive at least two copies of the packets from the source.

But both routers will receive a copy of the packet that the other router sent over Ethernet cable 2. As long as routers C and D keep state

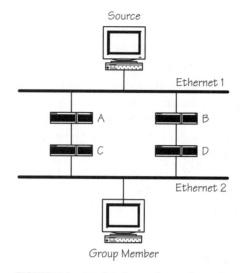

FIGURE 5.8 Multiple paths in broadcast networks.

information for the pair (S,G), they will detect that there is a problem; since the state information mentions that these packets are forwarded on the interface Ethernet2, each router will notice that another router is active on the same link. To resolve the situation, routers C and D will send an Assert(S,G) message which includes the distance between the sender and the source. A router that receives an Assert message will compare the distance with its own; if the distance is shorter, it prunes the interface from the list of selected interfaces for the group and the source.

Protocol-Independent Multicast—Sparse Mode

PIM-Sparse Mode (PIM-SM) was developed as a multicast routing protocol that provides efficient communication between members of sparsely distributed groups. These are the type of groups that are likely to be common in WANs. PIM's designers observed that several hosts wishing to participate in a multicast conference do not justify flooding the entire internetwork periodically with the group's multicast traffic.

To eliminate the potential scaling issues stemming from servicing thousands of small, widely dispersed groups, PIM-SM is designed to limit multicast traffic so that only those routers interested in receiving traffic for a particular group see it.

PIM-SM evolved from the Core-Based Trees (CBT) approach in that it employs the concept of a *core* (or rendezvous point (RP) in PIM-SM terminology) where receivers meet sources. PIM-SM also differs from existing dense-mode protocols by requiring that host group members explicitly join a delivery tree. Rendezvous points are used by senders to announce their existence and by receivers to learn about new senders of a group (see Figure 5.9). An RP may be any PIM-speaking router that is close to one of the members of the group or it may be some other PIM-speaking router in the network.

Routers with adjacent or downstream members are required to explicitly join a sparse-mode delivery tree by transmitting Join messages. If a router does not join the predefined delivery tree, it will not receive multicast traffic addressed to the group. In contrast, dense-mode protocols assume downstream group membership and forward multicast traffic on downstream links until explicit Prune messages are received. Thus, the default forwarding action of dense-mode routing protocols is to forward all traffic, while the default action of a sparse-mode protocol is to block traffic unless it has been explicitly requested.

When joining a group, each receiver uses IGMP to notify its directly attached router, which in turn joins the multicast delivery tree by sending an explicit PIM-Join message which travels hop-by-hop toward the group's rendezvous point. A source uses the rendezvous point to announce its presence, and to act as a conduit to members that have joined the group. This model requires sparse-mode routers to maintain state (the set of RPs for the sparse-mode region) prior to the arrival of data. In contrast,

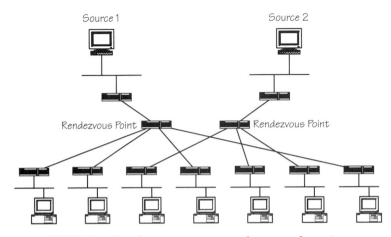

FIGURE 5.9 Rendezvous points and sparse domains.

because dense-mode protocols are data-driven, they do not store any state for a group until the arrival of its first data packet.

There is only one set of RPs per sparse-mode domain, not per group. In addition, the creator of a group is not involved in rendezvous point selection. Also, there is no such concept as a *primary* rendezvous point. Each group has precisely one rendezvous point at any given time. In the event of the failure of an rendezvous point, a new RP-set is distributed which does not include the failed RP.

If there is more than one PIM router connected to a multiaccess LAN, the router with the highest IP address is selected to function as the designated router for the LAN. The designated router does not necessarily have to be responsible for the transmission of IGMP Host Membership Query messages, but it does send Join/Prune messages toward the rendezvous point and maintains the status of the active rendezvous point for local senders to multicast groups.

Whenever the designated router receives an IGMP Report message for a new group, it determines if the group is RP-based by examining the group address.

The designated router creates a multicast forwarding entry for the (*, G) pair and transmits a unicast PIM-Join message toward the primary rendezvous point for this specific group (Figure 5.10). The intermediate routers forward the unicast PIM-Join message, creating a forwarding entry for the (*, G) pair only if such a forwarding entry does not yet exist. Intermediate routers must create a forwarding entry so that they will be able to forward future traffic downstream toward the designated router which originated the PIM-Join message.

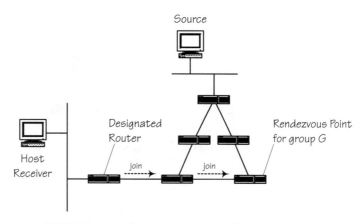

FIGURE 5.10 A host joining a multicast group.

NOTE   The (*, G) notation indicates an (any source, group) pair.

When a source first transmits a multicast packet to a group, its designated router forwards the datagram to the primary rendezvous point for subsequent distribution along the group's delivery tree (Figure 5.11). The designated router encapsulates the initial multicast packets in a PIM-SM-Register packet and sends them toward the primary rendezvous point for the group as unicast traffic. The PIM-SM-Register packet informs the rendezvous point of a new source which causes the active rendezvous point to transmit PIM-Join messages back toward the source's designated router.

The routers between the rendezvous point and the source's designated router use the PIM-Join messages they receive from the rendezvous point to create the forwarding state for the new (source, group) pair. When all routers from the active rendezvous point to the source's designated router have the state information, they are able to forward any future unencapsulated multicast packets from this source subnetwork to the rendezvous point.

But until the (source, group) state has been created in all the routers between the rendezvous point and the source's designated router, the designated router has to continue sending the source's multicast packets to the rendezvous point as packets encapsulated within unicast PIM-Register packets. The designated router may stop forwarding multicast packets using this encapsulation once it has received a PIM-Register-Stop message from the active rendezvous point for this group. The rendezvous point may send PIM-Register-Stop messages if there are no downstream receivers for

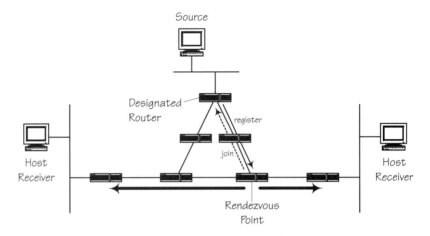

FIGURE 5.11   Source sending to a multicast group.

a group, or if the rendezvous point has successfully joined the (source, group) tree (which originates at the source's designated router).

TREE SELECTION

A tree based on rendezvous points (an RP-tree) provides connectivity for group members, but does not optimize the delivery path through the internetwork. PIM-SM allows routers to either continue to receive multicast traffic over the shared RP-tree, or to create a source-based shortest-path tree on behalf of their attached receivers (see Figure 5.12). Besides reducing the delay between this router and the source, which could be crucial to the attached receivers, the shared tree also reduces the concentration of traffic on the RP-tree.

A PIM-SM router with local receivers has the option of switching to the source's shortest-path tree once it starts receiving data packets from the source. The local receiver's last-hop router may initiate a changeover by sending a Join message toward the active source. After the source-based shortest-path tree is active, a Prune message for the same source would be transmitted to the active rendezvous point, thus removing this router from the shared RP-tree.

Alternatively, the designated router may be configured to continue using the shared RP-tree and never switch over to the source-based shortest-path tree, or a router could perhaps use a different administrative metric to decide if and when to switch to a source-based tree.

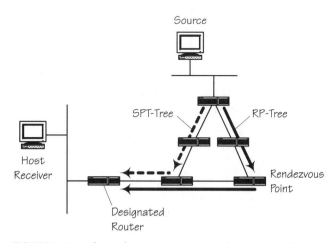

FIGURE 5.12 Shared RP-tree versus shortest-path tree (SPT).

In PIM-SM, switching a group to using a shortest-path tree to a source can also be set via the rendezvous point. In either case, controls such as bandwidth thresholds or administrative weights can be used to program these decisions.

Advantages and Disadvantages

PIM's strengths lie in its sparse-mode implementation. Rather than flooding group membership data over an internetwork (as in DVMRP), PIM-SM's requirement that users actively join groups at rendezvous points reduces the traffic that has to flow over WAN links.

At the same time, PIM-SM's dependence on RPs can lead to bottlenecks at an RP router; the RP also has the potential of being a single point of failure for the host group. PIM-SM's ability to switch a group from the RP to a shortest-path tree once a session is started does alleviate this problem somewhat.

Although it's similar to DVMRP, PIM-DM doesn't offer many of its advantages (such as simple implementation and modest processing demands). That's mainly because it's likely that PIM-DM and PIM-SM will be implemented as a single package in routers and the combination of the two (including the ability to switch between modes) adds to the complexity of the protocol. Also, PIM's complexity is increased by its requirement of interoperability with other protocols, due to its independence of unicast routing protocols.

Core-Based Trees (CBT)

The Core-Based Trees architecture is another multicast system that is based on a shared delivery tree, like PIM-SM. It was designed specifically to address the important issue of scalability when supporting multicast applications across the public Internet. The CBT routing architecture has been recently described in RFC 2201; version 2 of CBT's protocol specifications can be found in RFC 2189.

Similar to PIM-SM, CBT is protocol-independent and employs the information contained in the unicast routing table to build its shared delivery tree. It does not care how the unicast routing table is derived, only that a unicast routing table is present. This feature allows CBT to be deployed without requiring the presence of any specific unicast routing protocol.

Another similarity to PIM-SM is that CBT has adopted the core discovery, or bootstrap, mechanism defined in the PIM-SM specification. For interdomain discovery, efforts are underway to standardize (or at least separately specify) a common RP/Core discovery mechanism. The intent is that any shared tree protocol could implement this common discovery mechanism using its own protocol message types.

But unlike PIM-SM, CBT maintains its scaling characteristics by not offering the option of shifting from a shared tree (e.g., PIM-SM's RP-Tree) to a shortest-path tree to optimize delay. The designers of CBT chose this approach because they believe that the need for routers to maintain large amounts of state information will become the major scaling factor as multicasting becomes widely deployed.

Finally, CBT state is bidirectional, which means that data may flow in either direction along a branch. Again, this is unlike PIM-SM's shared tree state, where data is only allowed to flow in one direction. Thus, data from a source which is directly attached to an existing tree branch does not have to be encapsulated as it does when transmitted over PIM-SM's RP-tree.

Basic Operation

A host that wants to join a multicast group issues an IGMP Host Membership Report. This message informs its local CBT-aware router(s) that it wishes to receive traffic addressed to the multicast group. Upon receipt of an IGMP Host Membership Report for a new group, the local CBT router issues a Join-Request hop-by-hop toward the group's core router (Figure 5.13).

If the Join-Request encounters a router that is already on the group's shared tree before it reaches the core router, then that router issues an acknowledgment hop-by-hop back toward the sending router. If the Join-Request does not encounter a CBT router that's already part of the tree along its path towards the core, then the core router is responsible for responding with an acknowledgment. In either case, each intermediate

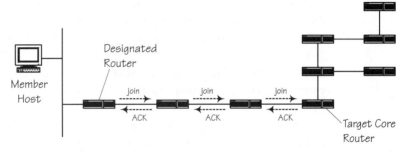

FIGURE 5.13 Process for joining a CBT tree.

router that forwards the Join-Request towards the core is required to create a transient *join state*. This transient *join state* includes the multicast group, and the incoming and outgoing interfaces specified in the Join-Request. This information allows an intermediate router to forward returning acknowledgments along the exact reverse path to the CBT router that initiated the Join-Request.

As the acknowledgment travels towards the CBT router that issued the Join-Request, each intermediate router creates a new *active state* for this group. New branches are established by having the intermediate routers remember which interface is upstream and which interfaces are downstream. Once a new branch is created, each child router monitors the status of its parent router with a keep-alive mechanism, the CBT Echo protocol. A child router periodically unicasts a CBT Echo-Request to its parent router, which is then required to respond with a unicast CBT Echo-Reply message.

If, for any reason, the link between an on-tree router and its parent should fail, or if the parent router is otherwise unreachable, the on-tree router transmits a message on its child interface(s) to initiate the tearing down of all downstream branches for that multicast group. Each downstream router is then responsible for reattaching itself (provided it has a directly attached group member) to the group's shared delivery tree.

The designated router is selected by CBT's Hello protocol and functions as the single upstream router for all groups using that link. The designated router is not necessarily the best next-hop router to every core for every multicast group. The implication is that it is possible for a Join-Request to be redirected by the designated router across a link to the best next-hop router providing access to a given group's core. Note that data traffic is never duplicated across a link, only Join-Requests, and the volume of this Join-Request traffic should be negligible.

When an acknowledgment is received by an intermediate router, it either adds the interface over which the acknowledgment was received to an existing forwarding cache entry or creates a new entry if one does not already exist for the multicast group. When a CBT router receives a data packet addressed to the multicast group, it simply forwards the packet over all outgoing interfaces as specified by the forwarding cache entry for the group. Even though a CBT backbone connects core routers, it's not restricted to only core routers, but can include both core and non-core routers (Figure 5.14).

Similar to other multicast routing protocols, CBT does not require that the source of a multicast packet be a member of the multicast group.

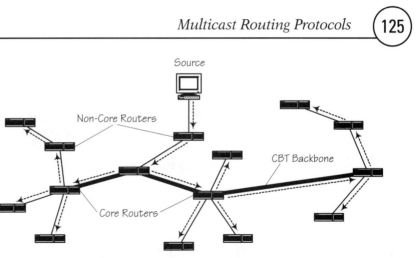

FIGURE 5.14   CBT delivery tree.

However, for a multicast data packet to reach the active core for the group, at least one CBT-capable router must be present on the nonmember source's subnetwork. In such cases, the local CBT-capable router employs IP-in-IP encapsulation and unicasts the data packet to the active core for delivery to the rest of the multicast group.

Advantages and Disadvantages

Since CBT requires that prospective group members specifically issue join messages to a core router to join a host group, the traffic required for maintaining delivery trees is less than that expected for the dense-mode routing protocols. By focusing on shared trees, CBT also provides better scalability, especially for sparsely distributed groups.

CBT also taxes a router's resources less than protocols like DVMRP. Table 5.4, taken from RFC 2201, illustrates estimates that CBT can require as little as 1/50th of the router entries required by DVMRP.

Just as CBT shares some of the same approaches to handling group membership and forwarding multicast traffic as PIM-SM, it has some of

TABLE 5.4   Comparison of DVMRP and CBT Router States

No. of groups	10	10	10	100	100	100	1000	1000	1000
Group size	20	20	20	40	40	40	60	60	60
Sources per group	10%	50%	100%	10%	50%	100%	10%	50%	100%
# DVMRP router entries	20	100	200	400	2000	4000	6000	30000	60000
# CBT router entries	10	10	10	100	100	100	1000	1000	1000

the same shortcomings. For example, the core router can be both a bottle-neck for traffic and a single point of failure.

Additionally, CBT, like PIM-SM, has to deal with the problem of the selection of the initial core router. Either manually configuring the core router or implementing a bootstrap mechanism has been suggested as a possible solution. One concern has been to use the same mechanism for selecting CBT cores and PIM-SM rendezvous points to promote interoperability.

Inter-Domain Routing and Protocol Interoperability

Multicast routing protocols are still in a state of continuing evolution. The different ways for handling group member distribution and for creating multicast trees arose from growing experience with the MBone and other experimental multicast networks. As IP Multicast networks are progressing from the experimental stage to attempts at more widespread adoption, either on the Internet itself or on private corporate intranets, new problems have surfaced, occasionally forcing refinements of routing protocols. Thus, while the MBone uses DVMRP and, to a lesser extent MOSPF, commercial router vendors are moving ahead with support for other multicast routing protocols such as PIM.

The number of multicast routing protocols currently in use is small. As new protocols become finalized and deployed on networks, expect to see transition periods when a relatively large number of multicast routing protocols are in use. It may be some time (if ever?) before we see only one protocol dominate multicast routing, at least on the Internet. (Intranets, special ISP nets for businesses, and VPNs are a different matter, since more control can be exerted to select a single protocol.) With so many protocols in use, interoperability between the protocols can become a major issue. At the same time, a hierarchical scheme for multicast routing protocols, complete with border routers and policy management, has to be invoked to support the growth of IP Multicast beyond that of past MBone implementations to the commercial world.

The MBone was unique in the way it was created as an experimental network, but its design cannot be extrapolated to the current Internet for everyday use by anyone or everyone who is connected to the Net. Even as the MBone grew, it was obvious that the routing protocols designed for multicasting would not scale well. The slate of multicast routing protocols covered thus far in this chapter are not designed for multiple autonomous systems that do not necessarily want to share all their routing information.

In hierarchical routing, the multicast network is divided into a number of individual routing domains. Each routing domain executes its own multicast routing protocol. Another protocol, or another instance of the same protocol, is used for routing between the individual domains. Hierarchical routing reduces the demand for router resources because each router only needs to know the explicit details about routing packets to destinations within its own domain and nothing about the detailed topological structure of any of the other domains. The protocol running between the individual domains maintains information about the interconnection of the domains, but not about the internal topology of each domain.

In general, interoperability between routing protocols will be achieved through the deployment of domain border routers which enable the forwarding of multicast traffic between the domains using different multicast routing protocols. The border (or boundary) router implements the intra-domain and inter-domain routing protocols on different interfaces and is responsible for forwarding data across the domain boundary (Figure 5.15). The border router is also responsible for exporting selected routes out of the domain into the higher-level domain that's responsible for joining other domains at the same level in the hierarchy.

As an example, consider the MBone—it's a collection of autonomously administered multicast regions with each region defined by one or more multicast-capable border routers. Each region independently chooses to run whichever multicast routing protocol best suits its needs and the regions interconnect via the *backbone region*, which currently runs

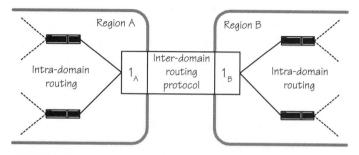

FIGURE 5.15 Schematic of a border (or boundary) router.

DVMRP. Therefore, it follows that a region's border routers must interoperate with DVMRP.

While all the proposals create some type of hierarchy, just like inter-domain unicast routing protocols, some—HDVMRP and HPIM—are built as extensions of current multicast routing protocols. Another approach, M-BGP or Multicast BGP, uses extensions to an existing unicast protocol, BGP4, to support multicasting without consideration for how distribution trees would be constructed. Yet another scheme, GUM or Grand Unified Multicasting, applies the concept of shared trees to inter-domain routing; it too can be written as an extension to BGP4.

Hierarchical Distance-Vector Multicast Routing Protocol (HDVMRP)

The current version of DVMRP treats a multicast network as a single, flat routing domain where each router is required to maintain detailed routing information to every subnetwork on the network. As the number of sub-networks increases, the size of the routing tables and of the periodic update messages will continue to grow, taxing the processing and memory capabilities of DVMRP routers, ultimately leading to routing failures.

In addition to reducing the amount of routing information, a hierarchical version of the DVMRP offers some other benefits. Different multicast routing protocols may be deployed in each region of the network. This permits the testing and deployment of new protocols on a domain-by-domain basis:

- The effects of an individual link or router failures are limited to only those routers operating within a single domain. Likewise, the effects of any change to the topological interconnection of regions is limited to only inter-domain routers. These enhancements are especially important when deploying a distance-vector routing protocol that can result in relatively long convergence times.
- The count-to-infinity problem associated with distance-vector routing protocols places limitations on the maximum diameter of the multicast net topology. Hierarchical routing limits these diameter constraints to a single domain, not to the entire multicasting Internet.

In hierarchical DVMRP, nonintersecting regions are created, each of which is assigned a unique Region ID. The routers internal to a region execute any multicast routing protocols such as DVMRP, MOSPF, PIM, or CBT as what's termed a Level 1 (L1) protocol. Each region is required to

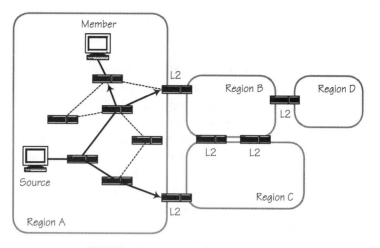

FIGURE 5.16   Hierarchical DVMRP.

have at least one boundary router that is responsible for providing inter-regional connectivity. These boundary routers execute DVMRP as a Level 2 (L2) protocol to forward traffic between regions (Figure 5.16).

The L2 routers exchange routing information in the form of Region IDs instead of the individual subnetwork addresses contained within each region. With DVMRP as the L2 protocol, an inter-regional multicast delivery tree is constructed based on the (region_ID, group) pair rather than the standard (source, group) pair.

When a multicast packet originates within a region, it is forwarded according to the L1 protocol to all subnetworks containing group members. In addition, the datagram is forwarded to each of the boundary routers (L2) configured for the source region. The L2 routers tag the packet with the Region ID and place it in an encapsulation header for delivery to other regions. When the packet arrives at a remote region, the encapsulation header is removed before delivery to group members by the L1 routers.

Although the initial design of HDVMRP only calls for a two-level hierarchy, it's possible to extend the hierarchy to more levels, creating *super regions*. But this would require an additional level of encapsulation, which may not be worth the added overhead.

Hierarchical Protocol-Independent Multicast (HPIM)

Recall that in PIM a rendezvous point (RP) is defined for each sparse-mode group. The designated router (DR) on the same LAN as the receiver's host sends a Join message for the appropriate host group towards the RP for the group, setting up a route from the RP to the receiver along which traffic for that group can flow.

One problem with PIM-SM's construction of an RP-tree is that the DR on a LAN must be able to look up the address of the RP associated with the host group in order to be able to send Register or Join messages to the RP on behalf of the receivers. This RP lookup mechanism must be able to work at gateways between multicast routing protocols.

HPIM differs from PIM in the selection and organization of RP routers. In PIM, a candidate RP router (C-RP) does not know that it is a candidate RP router until it receives a register or Join message from a DR. In HPIM, candidate RP routers not only know they are candidate RP routers, but also are assigned a level in the global hierarchy (similar to HDVMRP's treatment of border routers). Every candidate RP router advertises its availability as a candidate RP router to all other candidate RP routers at the same level in the hierarchy and to all candidate RP routers at the next-lowest level (see Figure 5.17).

It's expected that there will be a small number of levels in the HPIM hierarchy and a small number of candidate RP routers that exist at each level in each scope area.

In HPIM, multicast traffic does not flow from all sources until a join is successfully relayed to the top level RP for that host group. But traffic can start flowing from intermediate sources (i.e., those more local to the

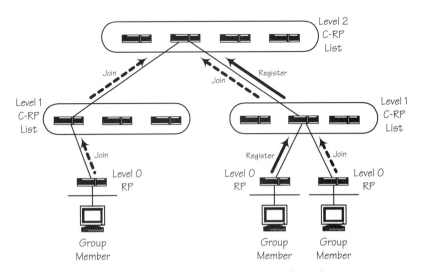

FIGURE 5.17 Formation of an HPIM shared tree.

receiver, as soon as the join message reaches an RP router that they are registered with).

The most important difference between HPIM and PIM is that HPIM does not need to advertise RPs. Each router in the tree makes a local decision about where the next hop RP is, based on the host group address and a candidate RP list which is synchronized across all RPs in the same scope at the same level in the hierarchy.

Multicast Border Gateway Protocol (M-BGP)

As the name implies, Multicast BGP is an extension to BGP, the Border Gateway Protocol. BGP is an exterior routing protocol used to link together autonomous systems allowing administrators to pick their neighboring ASs and enforce inter-AS routing policies. BGP4 is a path-vector protocol where distance vectors are annotated not only with the entire path used to compute each distance, but also with certain policy attributes. These attributes are used by an exterior gateway to compute the routing path. Since BGP includes true costs, it can be used in non-tree topologies. To handle ASs with more than one BGP-speaking border gateway, BGP requires that each gateway in an AS talk to every other gateway in that AS. A unique feature is that BGP routers use TCP to communicate with each other, instead of layering routing messages directly over IP, as every other routing protocol does.

In BGP, unicast traffic flows in the reverse direction of route updates; a network makes itself reachable by advertising itself to all other destinations. At the same time, the set of unicast destinations is the set of all possible multicast sources. Therefore, if an AS can control over which path it sends unicast traffic for advertised destinations, it could control over which path it receives multicast traffic for advertised sources. Given that an AS can potentially receive route updates for a particular network via different AS paths, the multicast path selected by an AS over which to receive multicast traffic from that network need not necessarily be the reverse of the path it selects to route unicast traffic to that same network.

Like BGP, M-BGP's primary function relates to the distribution and selection of AS paths; each AS independently chooses an inter-AS multicast path reflecting its local policy, for each potential multicast source. Any protocol-independent multicast routing protocol can take advantage of M-BGP's framework to build inter-AS multicast distribution trees.

Where unicast and multicast topologies are congruent, an additional policy assumption is applied universally: In order to protect unicast traffic

from multicast, unicast traffic can use multicast paths, but multicast traffic cannot flow over unicast paths unless explicitly permitted.

For each potential source network (unicast destination), a Multicast
Border Router (MBR) may receive multiple multicast paths, or *candidate*
paths. From these it must select one over which to receive multicast traffic
from the specified source(s). An MBR selects such a path that reflects pre-
configured local policy.

Figure 5.18 illustrates AS #1 advertising its networks—A, B, and C—all
of which are potential multicast sources as well as unicast sources. AS #3
has a choice of routes to networks in AS #1. Based on its local policy, AS #3
might decide to accept multicast traffic from networks A, B, and C via AS
#2, but unicast traffic destined to networks A, B, or C should prefer the
direct path. When AS #3 propagates routing information for networks, A, B,
and C to its other neighbors (not shown; arrows to left of AS #3 indicate
these neighbors), it must reflect the divergent unicast and multicast paths
by sending two updates for networks A, B, and C—one with the Multicast
attribute set, which reflects the path multicast traffic takes from sources A,
B, and C, and one without the Multicast attribute set, which reflects the
path taken when routing unicast traffic to networks A, B, and C.

Grand Unified Multicasting (GUM)

Another current approach to inter-domain multicast routing is GUM, or
Grand Unified Multicasting. It's a recent proposal and many of the details
are still being worked out within the IETF's IDMR (Inter-Domain Multicast
Routing) working group.

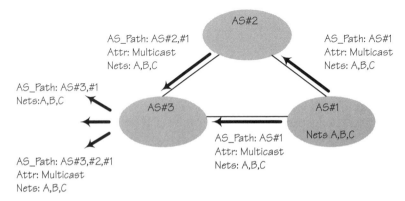

FIGURE 5.18 Propagating route updates from AS #1 using M-BGP.

GUM builds shared trees for active multicast groups and allows receiver domains to build source-specific, inter-domain distribution branches where needed. It requires that each multicast group be associated with a single root. In GUM, the root is an entire domain, rather than a single router, as the normal multicast routing protocols covered in this chapter require. Each of these domains then becomes the root of the shared domain trees for all groups in its range.

GUM depends on associating different ranges of the Class D space with different domains. The mechanism for distributing these address ranges is also still being worked out, with many ideas focusing on a hierarchical scheme.

When a receiver joins a specific group address, the border router towards the root domain generates a group-specific Join message, which is then forwarded Border-Router-by-Border-Router towards the root domain (Figure 5.19). In the example, a Join(B,D) message would be sent via the transit domains (i.e., domains through which multicast traffic might have to pass) towards the root domain when Receiver D wants to join the group hosted by Source B.

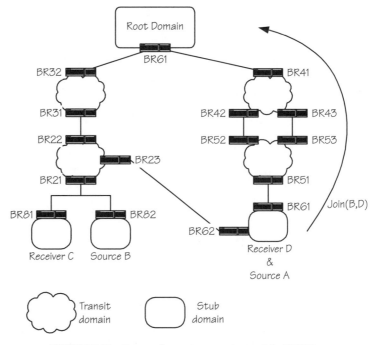

FIGURE 5.19 Inter-domain routing with GUM.

Summary

Routing multicast traffic can be quite complex, as this chapter has demonstrated. Since the early routing protocols such as DVMRP and MOSPF were created to handle dense multicast groupings, the growth of multicasting, both in the MBone and in anticipated new networks, is causing scalability problems that need to be solved in new routing protocols. A major approach is to use shared trees; another solution is to try hierarchical routing in a fashion similar to that of unicast routing. Newer protocols like PIM have yet to see widespread implementation on the Internet, but they're necessary for the effective use of multicasting as its use increases.

6

Transport Protocols

The infrastructures of IP Multicast and interactive applications include much more than just the protocols for group memberships and multicast routing that we've covered so far. End-to-end use of multicasting requires protocols for the transport of data as well as application-level protocols. This chapter focuses on the protocols that have been designed for transporting data, some solely for multicast traffic, but also some that have been designed for either unicast or multicast traffic. These transport protocols are particularly important for multimedia applications and other real-time applications that may require a preset quality of service to either deliver data in a synchronized fashion or because they simply require a higher priority than ordinary traffic.

Some important transport protocols have been developed over the past few years to support real-time multimedia data delivery. The protocols of interest that we'll be covering in this chapter include the Real-Time Transport Protocol (RTP) and its associated protocol, the Real-Time Control Protocol (RTCP), as well as the Real-Time Streaming Protocol (RTSP). These protocols have not been designed with only multicast traffic in mind, although that's likely where they'll see the most application. RTP, RTCP, and RTSP can be used for unicast sessions as well as multicast sessions. It's not until we get to the second half of this chapter, the part focusing on the variety of protocols that have been suggested for reliable multicasting, that we'll delve into protocols designed specifically for multicast sessions (Figure 6.1).

In anticipation of multimedia data becoming more important on packet-based networks like the Internet, the IETF created a framework called the Integrated Services Architecture to guide the development of protocols for multimedia data transfers and related issues on IP networks. RTP and RTCP were developed as part of that original architecture and now the newer protocol for streaming data, RTSP, has become part of the framework. Other parts of the Integrated Services Architecture, such as assigning quality of service and using RSVP for resource reservations, will be discussed in Chapter 7. The protocols proposed for reliable multicasting aren't directly related to the Integrated Services Architecture, but co-exist with it. Since both sets of protocols deal with data transfers, they're covered here in the same chapter.

As I pointed out in previous chapters, TCP serves as one of the principal transport mechanism for IP networks (UDP being the other) and was developed to guarantee the reliable delivery of data in the proper sequence from a sender to a receiver. But the error-control and flow-control mechanisms that are a part of TCP can cause indeterminate delays and bursty data delivery, which doesn't fit the requirements of real-time multimedia data. In order to handle real-time multimedia, other protocols are required. RTP and RTCP form a pair of protocols that were designed to assist in the distribution of multimedia data on IP networks, while RTSP

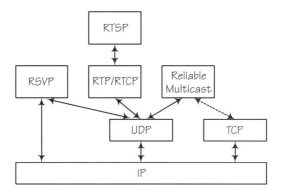

FIGURE 6.1 Protocol relationships.

aims to assist in the delivery of one type of multimedia, streaming multimedia.

Previously, we've talked about the layering of protocols, often using the OSI 7-layer scheme, even though the TCP/IP protocols do not fit neatly into the OSI layers. Over the past few years, it has been proposed that, instead of a strict layering, a more cooperative approach between protocols is needed, especially when dealing with real-time applications.

This approach, *application layer framing,* provides a simple framework that applications can use directly instead of relying on a complex transport protocol like TCP. (It was first formally proposed by D. D. Clark and D. L. Tennenhouse of MIT in 1990.) For example, much of TCP's complexity isn't needed by real-time applications. Rather than deal with delays introduced by retransmissions, a real-time audio application can simply forget about missing data. RTP and RTCP were designed with application layer framing (ALF) as a guiding principle. We'll see later in the chapter that some of the frameworks for reliable multicasting also make use of ALF in their design. These specifications define a framework for a protocol, defining only the basic roles, operations, and message formats, allowing specific applications to add to them to form the complete protocol.

Real-Time Transport Protocol (RTP)

RTP was designed to assist the delivery of multimedia data by providing sequence numbering and time stamping along with an extensible architecture for identifying payloads. A second protocol, RTCP, is defined as part of the RTP specifications—its purpose is to provide control and monitoring of RTP data transfers. The latest version of RTP, version 2, includes descriptions of both of the protocols and has been approved for RFC publication as a proposed standard (RFC 1889).

Despite the name of the protocol, the use of the term "real-time" here does not mean that users receive data streams as soon as they have been sent. Network latency prevents that. In this case, real-time stands for an attribute of stream-based transmissions (i.e., the original framing and timing of data chunks can be reproduced after transmission by any and all of the receivers). Thus, at least in principle, the user should be unable to distinguish between a data stream that has its source on his or her local machine and one that is transmitted over the network.

RTP provides end-to-end delivery services, but it does not provide all of the functionality that is typically provided by a transport protocol. For instance, RTP typically runs on top of UDP to utilize that protocol's multiplexing and checksum services. But it can also run over IPX or ATM. RTP has no notion of a connection and may operate over either connection-oriented or connectionless lower-layer protocols (Figure 6.2).

RTP also does not provide any mechanisms to ensure timely delivery or provide quality-of-service guarantees. It does not guarantee delivery or prevent out-of-order delivery, nor does it assume that the underlying network is reliable. Some applications that can adapt to changes in data delivery do not require such guarantees, but for those that do, RTP has to be accompanied by other mechanisms, such as RSVP, to support resource reservation and to provide reliable service.

Although RTP can be used for unicast sessions, it has primarily been designed with multicast sessions in mind. Not only is the data multicast from the sender, but recipients multicast their reports back to all members of the group. As we'll see when we discuss RTCP in the next section, this multicast feedback lets all the participants see the bandwidth required for their session and the load they may have on the sender (which may cause them to throttle back and use less bandwidth).

In addition to the usual roles of sender and receiver, RTP defines two other roles, *translator* and *mixer*. Translators and mixers lie on the network between senders and receivers and process RTP packets as they pass through. Translators simply translate from one payload format to another; for example, this might be required when a video file has to be encoded

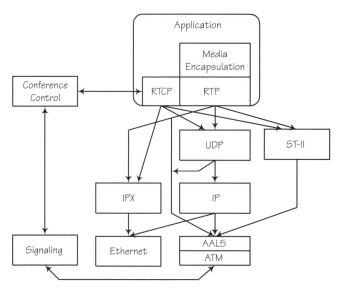

FIGURE 6.2 RTP and other protocols.

with a different codec in order to meet reduced bandwidth availability on a network leg. Mixers are similar to translators but, instead of translating individual streams to a different format, they combine multiple streams into a single stream, preserving the original format. Not all applications can support mixers; this approach works well for audio conferences, for example, but multiple video sources usually cannot be combined into one stream.

Packet Format

RTP uses the same format for all of its messages. Because it supports application layer framing, this message format lends itself to various interpretations and for additions that particular applications may need.

The RTP header (Figure 6.3) provides the timing information needed to synchronize and display audio and video data, and to determine whether packets have been lost or arrived out of order. The header also includes the payload type, allowing for multiple data and compression types.

RTP packets consist of a 12-byte header followed by the payload (e.g., a video frame or a sequence of audio samples). The payload may also be wrapped into an encoding-specific layer. The header contains the following information:

Payload type. A 1-byte payload type identifies the kind of payload contained in the packet (JPEG video or GSM audio, for example).

Timestamp. A 32-bit timestamp describes the generation instant of the data contained in the packet. The timestamp frequency depends on the payload type.

Sequence number. A 16-bit packet sequence number allows loss detection and sequencing within a series of packets with the same timestamp.

Marker bit. The interpretation of a market bit depends on the payload type. For example, for a video payload, it marks the end of a frame, while for audio, it marks the beginning of a *talkspurt*.

Synchronization source identifier. A randomly generated 32-bit number that uniquely identifies the source within a session.

A *payload* format defines the manner in which a particular payload, such as an audio or video encoding, is to be carried in RTP. Table 6.1

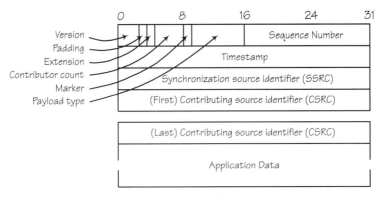

FIGURE 6.3   RTP packet header.

includes the currently defined payload types for RTP. A *profile* assigns payload type numbers for the set of payload formats that may be used in an application. A profile may also define application-specific extensions or modifications to RTP. An initial profile for carrying audio and video data over RTP was defined in RFC 1890.

TABLE 6.1   RTP-defined Static Payload Types

Payload Type	Encoding Name	Audio/Video (A/V)	Clock Rate (Hz)	Channels (audio)
0	PCMU	A	8000	1
1	1016	A	8000	1
2	G.721	A	8000	1
3	GSM	A	8000	1
5	DV14	A	8000	1
6	DV14	A	16000	1
7	LPC	A	8000	1
8	PCMA	A	8000	1
9	G.722	A	8000	1
10	L16	A	44100	2
11	L16	A	44100	1
14	MPA	A	90000	
15	G.728	A	8000	1
25	CelB	V	90000	
26	JPEG	V	90000	
28	nv	V	90000	
31	H261	V	90000	
32	MPV	V	90000	
33	MP2T	AV	90000	
72–76	reserved	N/A	N/A	N/A
96–127	dynamic	?		

Other payload types have been proposed for H.263 video streams, redundant audio data, bundled MPEG, MPEG1/MPEG2 video, QuickTime media streams, and DTMF digits.

Basic Operation

To set up an RTP session, the application using RTP defines a pair of destination addresses (i.e., one network address and two ports, one for RTP, the other for RTCP). The address can be either a unicast network address or a multicast address. In a multimedia session, each medium is carried in a separate RTP session, with its own RTCP packets reporting the reception quality for each session (see the next section for a description of RTCP). In other words, audio and video would travel in separate RTP sessions.

If RTP packets are carried in UDP datagrams, data and control packets use two consecutive ports, with the data port always as the lower, even-numbered one. If other protocols serve underneath RTP (e.g., RTP directly over ATM AAL5; AAL5 = ATM Adaptation Layer type 5), it is possible to carry both the data part and control part in a single lower-layer protocol data unit, with control followed by data.

The RTP header provides the timing information necessary to synchronize and display audio and video data, and to determine whether packets have been lost or have arrived out of order. In addition, the header specifies the payload type, thus allowing multiple data and compression types. RTP is tailored to a specific application via auxiliary profile and payload format specifications.

To allow a higher level of synchronization or to synchronize nonperiodically transmitted data streams, RTP uses a monotonic clock. This clock is usually incremented in time units that are smaller than the smallest block size of the data stream. The initial clock value is random. An application does not use the RTP timestamp directly; rather it extracts the NTP (Network Time Protocol) timestamp and RTP timestamp from the transmitted RTCP packets for every stream that it wants to synchronize.

Let's use the audio-conferencing scenario originally presented in RFC 1889 to illustrate the use of RTP. Suppose each participant sends audio data in segments of 20-millisecond duration. Each segment of audio data is preceded by an RTP header, then the resulting RTP message is placed in a UDP packet. The RTP header indicates the type of audio encoding that is used, for example PCM (Pulse Code Modulation). Users can opt to change the encoding during a conference in reaction to network congestion or, for example, to accommodate low-bandwidth requirements of a new conference participant. Timing information and a sequence number in the RTP header are used by the receivers to reconstruct the timing produced by the source, so that in this example, audio segments are contiguously played out at the receiver every 20 milliseconds.

Real-Time Control Protocol (RTCP)

RTP's sister protocol, RTCP, is used for controlling RTP data transfers. An RTCP message consists of a number of packets that can be embedded within each other, each with its own type code and length indication. Their format is fairly similar to that of RTP data packets.

In a multicast session, RTCP packets are multicast periodically to the same host group as RTP data packets. Thus, they also serve as an indicator of live connections and session members, even in the absence of actual data transmissions.

RTCP performs the following four functions:

Provide information to application.   The primary function is to provide information to an application regarding the quality of data distribution. Each RTCP packet contains sender and/or receiver reports that report statistics useful to the application. These statistics include number of packets sent, number of packets lost, inter-arrival jitter, and so forth.

Identify RTP source.   RTCP carries a transport-level identifier for an RTP source, called the canonical name (CNAME). This CNAME is used to keep track of the participants in an RTP session. Receivers use the CNAME to associate multiple data streams from a given participant in a set of related RTP sessions (e.g., to synchronize audio and video).

Control RTCP transmission interval.   To prevent control traffic from overwhelming network resources and to allow RTP to scale up to a large number of session participants, control traffic is limited to at most five percent of the overall session traffic. This limit is enforced by adjusting the rate at which RTCP packets are transmitted as a function of the number of participants. Since each participant sends control packets to everyone else, each can keep track of the total number of participants and use this number to calculate the rate at which to send RTCP packets.

Convey minimal session control information. As an optional function, RTCP can be used as a convenient method for conveying a small amount of information to all session participants. For example, RTCP might carry a personal name to identify a participant on the user's display. This function is useful in loosely controlled sessions where participants informally enter and leave the session.

As a result of its functionality, RTCP can be used to support at least four session-related tasks: quality-of-service monitoring and congestion control, synchronizing between media, source identification, and session size estimation.

In RTCP, applications that have recently sent audio or video data generate a sender report that is multicast to all session members. Since the report contains information cumulative counters of the packets and bytes sent, the receivers can estimate the actual data rate.

Session members issue receiver reports for all video or audio sources they have heard from recently. The reports contain information on the highest sequence number received, the number of packets lost, a measure of inter-arrival jitter, and timestamps needed to compute an estimate of the round-trip delay.

As I previously mentioned, RTP and RTCP generate different sessions for different media streams. The RTCP sender report contains an indication of real time and a corresponding RTP timestamp which can be used to synchronize multiple media streams at the receiver.

RTP data packets identify their origin only through a randomly generated 32-bit identifier while RTCP messages contain a *source description (SDES) packet* which in turn contains a number of pieces of information, usually textual. One such piece of information is the so-called canonical name, a globally unique identifier of the session participant. Other possible SDES items include the user's name, e-mail address, telephone number, and application information.

Since RTCP is purposely scaled so that it makes up five percent of the nominal data rate of a session, monitoring the control traffic can serve as an indicator of the number of members participating in the session. (Recall that each session periodically transmits RTCP packets.)

RTCP provides feedback on current network conditions and reception quality, allowing applications to automatically adapt to those conditions. For example, a slowdown experienced by many recipients would most likely be due to a network problem (a failed T1 link backed up by slower

56-Kbps line) and not to an individual computer. In this case, the source application might choose to make an on-the-fly change to its encoding scheme, temporarily eliminate the video portion of a transmission, or switch from color to monochrome to improve the transfer of information.

In other cases, network managers can use information in the RTCP packets to evaluate the performance of their networks for multicast distribution. Since RTCP sends feedback not only to the sender, but also to all other recipients of a multicast stream, it lets an individual user determine whether a problem is specific to the local end node or attributable to systemwide problems.

The basis for flow and congestion control is provided by RTCP sender and receiver reports. By analyzing the inter-arrival jitter field of the sender report, we can measure the jitter over a certain interval and indicate congestion before it becomes consistent, resulting in packet loss.

Packet Formats

RTCP defines five different message types: the Sender Report (SR), Receiver Report (RR), Source Description (SDES), Bye, and App messages. The *Sender Report* is used for transmission and reception statistics from session participants that are active senders. The *Receiver Report* handles reception statistics from participants that are not active senders. The *Source Description* message is used to transmit more information about packets, including such items as synchronization information and source identifiers. The *Bye* message indicates the end of participation on the part of one of the participants while the *App* message is used for application-specific functions.

Each RTCP packet begins with a fixed part similar to that of RTP data packets, followed by structured elements that may be of variable length according to the packet type; the variable length fields always end on a 32-bit boundary.

SENDER AND RECEIVER REPORTS

Senders in a conference periodically transmit sender report packets to let the other participants know what they should have received. The Sender Report packet (Figure 6.4) consists of three sections, possibly followed by a fourth profile-specific extension section if defined.

The only difference between the Sender Report (SR) and Receiver Report (RR) forms, besides the packet type code, is that the Sender Report includes a 20-byte sender information section for use by active senders. I'll

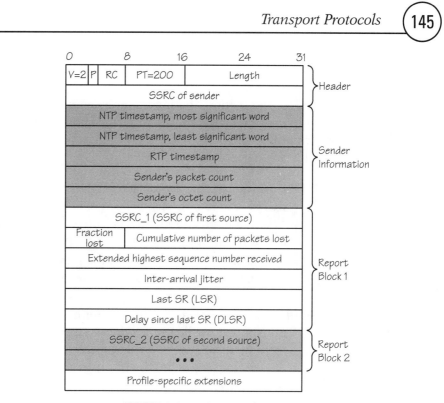

FIGURE 6.4 RTCP sender report.

use Figure 6.4 to describe both packet formats, indicating where the two reports differ in the following text.

The first section, the header, is 8 octets long. The fields have the following meaning:

Version (V).   Identifies the version of RTP, which is the same in RTCP packets as in RTP data packets. Currently this is 2.

Padding (P).   If the padding bit is set, this RTCP packet contains some additional padding octets at the end which are not part of the control information.

Reception report count (RC).   The number of reception report blocks contained in this packet. A value of zero is valid.

Packet type (PT).   Contains the constant 200 to identify this as an RTCP SR packet. A packet type of 201 makes this an RTCP RR packet.

Length.   The length of this RTCP packet in 32-bit words minus one, including the header and any padding.

SSRC. The synchronization source identifier for the originator of this SR (or RR) packet.

The second section, the sender information, is 20 octets long and is present in every Sender Report packet. It summarizes the data transmissions from this sender. This section is omitted in receiver report packets. The fields have the following meaning:

NTP timestamp. Indicates the wall-clock time when this report was sent so that it may be used in combination with timestamps returned in reception reports from other receivers to measure round-trip propagation to those receivers.

RTP timestamp. Corresponds to the same time as the NTP timestamp, but in the same units and with the same random offset as the RTP timestamps in data packets.

Sender's packet count. The total number of RTP data packets transmitted by the sender since starting transmission up until the time this SR packet was generated. The count is reset if the sender changes its SSRC identifier.

Sender's octet count. The total number of payload octets (i.e., not including header or padding) transmitted in RTP data packets by the sender since starting transmission up until the time this SR packet was generated. The count is reset if the sender changes its SSRC identifier.

The third section contains zero or more reception report blocks depending on the number of other sources heard by this sender since the last report. Each reception report block conveys statistics on the reception of RTP packets from a single synchronization source.

Receivers do not carry over statistics when a source changes its SSRC identifier due to a collision. These statistics are:

SSRC_n (source identifier). The SSRC identifier of the source to which the information in this reception report block pertains.

Fraction lost. The fraction of RTP data packets from source SSRC_n lost since the previous SR or RR packet was sent. This fraction is defined as the number of packets lost divided by the number of packets expected.

Cumulative number of packets lost. The total number of RTP data packets from source SSRC_n that have been lost since the beginning of reception.

Extended highest sequence number received. The low 16 bits contain the highest sequence number received in an RTP data packet from source SSRC_n, and the most significant 16 bits extend that sequence number with the corresponding count of sequence number cycles. Different receivers within the same session will generate different extensions to the sequence number if their start times differ significantly.

Inter-arrival jitter. An estimate of the statistical variance of the RTP data packet inter-arrival time, measured in timestamp units and expressed as an unsigned integer.

Last SR timestamp. The middle 32 bits out of 64 in the NTP timestamp received as part of the most recent RTCP sender report (SR) packet from source SSRC_n. If no SR has been received yet, the field is set to zero.

Delay since last SR. The delay, expressed in units of 1/65536 seconds, between receiving the last SR packet from source SSRC_n and sending this reception report block. If no SR packet has been received yet from SSRC_n, the DLSR field is set to zero.

SOURCE DESCRIPTIONS

The third type of RTCP packet, the source description or SDES packet (Figure 6.5), is a three-level structure composed of a header and zero or more *chunks,* each of which is composed of items describing the source identified in that chunk:

Version (V), padding (P), length. As described for the Sender Report packet (see earlier section).

Packet type (PT). Contains the constant 202 to identify this as an RTCP SDES packet.

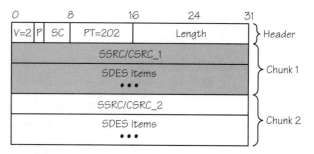

FIGURE 6.5 RTCP source description packet.

TABLE 6.2   SDES Items

CNAME	Canonical end-point identifier (mandatory)
NAME	User name
EMAIL	Electronic mail address
PHONE	Phone number
LOC	Geographic user location
TOOL	Application or tool name
NOTE	Notice/status
PRIV	Private extensions

Source count (SC).   The number of SSRC/CSRC chunks contained in this SDES packet. A value of zero is valid, but meaningless.

Each chunk consists of an SSRC/CSRC identifier followed by a list of zero or more items, which carry information about the SSRC/CSRC, and starts on a 32-bit boundary. Each item consists of an 8-bit type field, an 8-bit octet count describing the length of the text (thus, not including this two-octet header), and the text itself. Table 6.2 includes the currently defined items used in SDES.

BYE PACKET

A source uses a Bye packet (Figure 6.6) to announce that it is leaving a conference. Although other participants would eventually detect the source's absence without this packet, it does make things faster, which can lead to more efficient usage of available bandwidth:

Version (V), padding (P), length.   As described for the Source Report packet (see earlier section).

Packet type (PT).   Contains the constant 203 to identify this as an RTCP Bye packet.

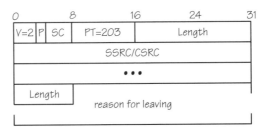

FIGURE 6.6   RTCP Bye packet.

Source count (SC).   The number of SSRC/CSRC identifiers included in this Bye packet.

APP PACKET

The App packet (see Figure 6.7) is intended for experimental use as new applications and new features are developed, without requiring packet type value registration. Should a particular application-specific packet prove to be useful, it would most likely be converted to a full RTCP packet with its own official packet type:

Version (V), padding (P), length.   As described for the Sender Report packet (see earlier section).

Subtype.   May be used as a subtype to allow a set of App packets to be defined under one unique name or for any application-dependent data.

Packet type (PT).   Contains the constant 204 to identify this as an RTCP App packet.

Name.   A name chosen by the person defining the set of App packets to be unique with respect to other App packets this application might receive.

Application-dependent data.   Application-dependent data may or may not appear in an App packet. It is interpreted by the application and not RTP itself. It must be a multiple of 32 bits long.

Basic Operation

To set up an RTP session, the application using RTP defines a pair of destination addresses (i.e., one network address and two ports, one for RTP, the

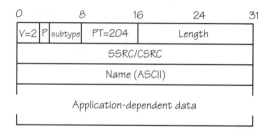

FIGURE 6.7 RTCP App packet.

other for RTCP). The address can be either a unicast network address or a multicast address. In a multimedia session, each medium is carried in a separate RTP session, with its own RTCP packets reporting the reception quality for each session. If network resources need to be allocated to the session, RSVP (which we'll cover in Chapter 7) would most likely be used to reserve the resources (see Figure 6.8).

To keep track of just who is participating in a session, each site will periodically multicast its user name and a reception report over the RTCP port. While this report reveals reception quality, it can also be used to control adaptive encodings, allowing the application to change compression techniques on-the-fly.

Since multiple related streams, such as audio and video, are not coupled together during transmission, receivers have the option of choosing just one of the streams if they desire. One user might want to receive just the audio portion because he's using a low-bandwidth link that would otherwise be overloaded by the video stream. But, if both streams are delivered, they can be synchronized at the receiver by using the timing information that's carried in the RTP and RTCP packets for both streams.

Although RTP and RTCP are responsible for controlling the flow of one data stream, they do not automatically synchronize multiple data streams (such as audio and video). This has to be accomplished at the application level by either using a playback buffer that's large enough to compensate for most of the jitter in all streams or by using an additional RTCP-like management stream containing feedback about relative arrival times between the associated streams.

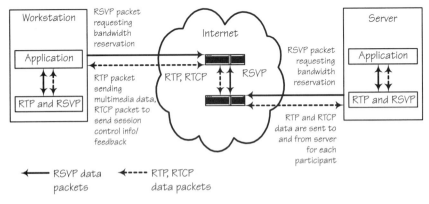

FIGURE 6.8 RTP/RTCP operation.

Real-Time Streaming Protocol (RTSP)

One of the interesting types of data currently common to Internet-based multimedia is streaming multimedia. *Streaming* breaks data into many packets sized appropriately for the bandwidth available between the client and server. When the client has received enough packets, the user software can be playing one packet, decompressing another, and receiving a third. The user can begin listening almost immediately without having to download the entire media file. Sources of data for streaming can include both live data feeds and stored clips.

The Real-Time Streaming Protocol, RTSP, is an application-level protocol that aims to provide a robust protocol for streaming multimedia in multipoint applications over either unicast or multicast. RTSP is currently an IETF draft specification in the early stages of development, but products using RTSP are already available.

In many ways, RTSP is more of a framework than it is a protocol. It is intended to control multiple data delivery sessions, and provide a means for choosing delivery channels such as UDP, TCP, IP Multicast, and delivery mechanisms based on RTP. RTSP can be used with RSVP to set up and manage reserved-bandwidth streaming sessions. We'll be discussing RSVP and resource reservation in detail in Chapter 7.

RTSP acts as a *network remote control* for multimedia servers. It establishes and controls either a single or several time-synchronized streams of continuous media such as audio and video, but does not typically deliver the continuous streams itself—that's left to protocols like RTP.

The set of streams to be controlled is defined by a presentation description (which has not yet been defined in the RTSP internet-draft). The client can request a presentation description via HTTP or some other method. If the presentation is being multicast, the presentation description contains the multicast addresses and ports to be used for the continuous media. Each media stream can reside on a different server; the client automatically establishes several concurrent control sessions with the different media servers and synchronization of the media is performed at the transport level.

RTSP has been designed to work on top of RTP to both control and deliver real-time content. This enables RTSP to take advantage of any future RTP improvements. Since RTSP can be used with unicast traffic, its use can help smooth the transition for environments moving from unicast to IP multicasting with RTP.

RTSP also has some overlap in functionality with HTTP (HyperText Transfer Protocol). It is similar in syntax and operation to HTTP 1.1 so that extensions to HTTP can, in most cases, also be added to RTSP. For example, RTSP can use PICS (Platform for Internet Content Selection) for associating labels with content. One significant difference between RTSP and HTTP is that RTSP maintains state by default in almost all cases (HTTP is a stateless protocol). Also, both RTSP servers and clients can issue requests.

RTSP may also interact with HTTP since the initial contact with streaming content is often made through a Web page. The current protocol specification for RTSP allows different hand-off points between a Web server and the media server implementing RTSP.

Basic Operation

RTSP can be used to retrieve media from a media server, invite a media server to a conference (in a distributed teaching environment, for example), or add media to an existing presentation.

A standard sequence of events (see Figure 6.9) would be for the client to obtain a session presentation description from a Web server using HTTP, then control is passed to the client's media layer and the multimedia server, which communicate via RTSP. The actual multimedia stream is transferred via RTP. The setup and teardown of the session is controlled by RTSP.

Each presentation and media stream may be identified by an RTSP URL (Uniform Resource Locator), such as in the following example (showing two different streams from two different servers):

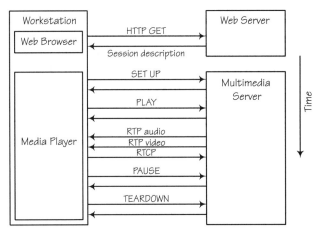

FIGURE 6.9 RTSP operation.

```
<session>
    <group>
        <track src="rtsp://audio.mtv.com/movie">
        <track src="rtsp://video.mtv.com/movie">
    </group>
</session>
```

A presentation can contain more than one media stream. The presentation description file contains encodings, language, and other parameters than enable the client to choose the most appropriate combination of media. Each media stream that is individually controllable by RTSP is identified by an RTSP URL, which points to the media server handling that particular media stream and names the stream stored on that server. Table 6.3 lists the named methods that RTSP can use; of these, only five—SETUP, PLAY, RECORD, PAUSE, and TEARDOWN—play a central role in defining the allocation and usage of stream resources on the server.

There is no notion of an RTSP connection; instead a server maintains a session labeled by an identifier. During an RTSP session, an RTSP client may open and close many reliable transport connections to the server to issue RTSP requests.

Since RTSP delivery of a stream can be sent via a separate protocol independent of the control channel, data delivery continues even if no RTSP requests are received by the media server. Therefore, the server needs to maintain a *session state* to be able to correlate RTSP requests with a stream.

Reliable Multicasting Protocols

Most of our discussion of IP multicasting so far has focused on a bare-bones approach, using generic protocols for transporting data. In such

TABLE 6.3 RTSP Methods

OPTIONS	Get available methods
SETUP	Establish transport
ANNOUNCE	Change description of media object
DESCRIBE	Get (low-level) description of media object
PLAY	Start playback, reposition
RECORD	Start recording
REDIRECT	Redirect client to new server
PAUSE	Halt delivery, but keep state
SET PARAMETER	Device or encoding control
TEARDOWN	Remove state

cases, delivery is accomplished via IP and UDP, leading to unreliable delivery. This is unsuitable for many applications that can use multicasting. Therefore, other protocols have to be designed to add reliable delivery to multicasting.

But reliable multicasting brings with it a series of unique problems: (1) the possibility that feedback from the receivers might overwhelm a source (a *feedback implosion*); (2) how lost packets are recovered; and (3) the different requirements that different multicasting applications can impose. It shouldn't be surprising that so many protocols for reliable multicasting have been proposed, but it's likely that no single protocol will be a solution for all situations.

In unicast transmissions, feedback for error and flow control is conveniently handled by TCP and other protocols, but multicasting protocols need other procedures to handle feedback. Since multiple sources of feedback can be expected in a multicast session, unicast-style methods would easily lead to feedback implosions at the source (see Figure 6.10).

Dealing with feedback control in multicast situations usually takes one of two approaches. In the first approach, the system attempts to suppress feedback implosions by introducing random delays among the receivers and multicasting the acknowledgment to others in the group. Another approach is for the protocol to aggregate the feedback by intermediate receivers, often using a hierarchy of intermediaries. In either case, the feedback used must not be specific to the receiver which sends the feedback.

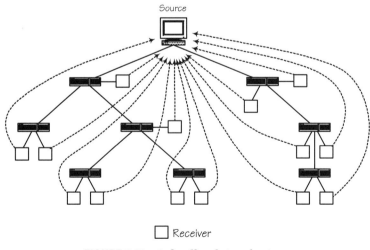

FIGURE 6.10 A feedback implosion.

Loss recovery can be accomplished in a number of ways. The sender can simply retransmit the lost packets by multicast to the group. The disadvantage is that all receivers, whether they lost the packets or not, receive the retransmitted packets again. One possible solution is to set up another group specifically for retransmission and expect receivers to join that group when they detect packet losses.

Another approach is *local repair,* where receivers may also carry out retransmissions. This takes advantage of scoping in IP Multicast, since it aims to restrict requests for retransmissions to a given area of the internet. When a receiver detects packet losses, it first would send a retransmission request by multicast with a small scope (a small TTL); if a local receiver has the lost packets, it can retransmit them to the requestor. If this first try is unsuccessful, then a retransmission request is repeated with a large scope.

An alternative is to use Forward Error Correction (FEC) as a preventive rather than corrective step; it can be particularly effective for multicast error recovery. For this to work, resource reservations have to be made in advance so that receivers and intermediate nodes are always able to support the sender's data rate. In this context, FEC is actually the simple part to implement, but resource reservation can be more problematic. (We'll talk about some of the problems with resource reservation when we discuss RSVP in Chapter 7.)

Lastly, reliability guarantees and group size requirements are different for each application and network. For example, different protocols would most likely be used for each of these situations: a small group of servers replicating files on a LAN, satellite-based file distribution, a video-conference, and a group of users collaborating via a shared whiteboard.

Classifying and Comparing Protocols

One of the major issues in reliable multicast protocols is how retransmission of lost packets is controlled. First, there's which end of a session maintains the state of the connection and controls the retransmission of lost packets—the senders or the receivers. Secondly, considering the situations when receivers control the retransmissions, there's the question of how the receivers are organized—as clouds, trees, or rings, for instance.

If we choose to classify these protocols according to which end of a session maintains control of packet retransmissions, we have two classes: sender-based and receiver-based (Figure 6.11). In *sender-based* approaches, the source maintains the state of all receivers to whom it has sent informa-

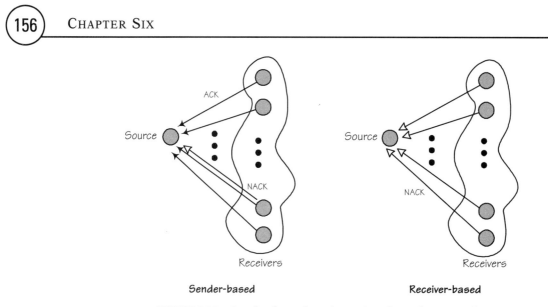

FIGURE 6.11 Sender-based and receiver-based protocols.

tion and from whom it has to receive acknowledgments (ACKs). In the *receiver-based* approach, each receiver informs the source of the information that is in error or missing; the source multicasts all packets, giving priority to retransmissions and the receiver sends a negative acknowledgment (NACK) when it detects an error or lost packet.

In a receiver-based system, the retransmission task is distributed to all receivers and the sender keeps no state about each receiver but simply replies to requests for data (the NACKs in Figure 6.11). In a receiver-based system, the sender may need to poll the receivers when it is about to remove the data from its buffer.

In general, receiver-based protocols are more scalable than sender-based protocols. That's because the maximum throughput of sender-based protocols depends on the number of receivers which can strain both network resources (e.g., the bandwidth necessary to handle incoming ACKs) and the sender's computing resources (RAM for tracking the state of each receiver and for buffering previously sent packets until their recipient has been acknowledged by every receiver).

Turning now to the receiver-based class of protocols, these systems differ in how they organize the receivers and make use of that structure to transmit packets. The way the receivers are organized can have a significant impact on the scalability of a protocol.

Cloud-based protocols do not attempt to impose any structure on the receivers (hence the use of the word "cloud"). These protocols are usually connectionless, delivering data on a best-effort basis and they do not maintain membership information, which helps give them good scalability. But the applications are responsible for handling exception and fault conditions, which can lead to poor performance.

Tree-based protocols are characterized by dividing the set of receivers into groups and distributing the retransmission responsibility over a tree structure built from the set of groups, with the source as the root of the tree (Figure 6.12). The tree structure prevents receivers from directly contacting the source in order to maintain scalability over a large set of receivers.

Tree-based protocols eliminate the feedback implosion problem, free the source from having to know the receiver set, and operate solely on messages exchanged in local groups. If aggregate ACKs are used, a tree-based protocol can work correctly in the presence of receiver failures and network partitions.

Ring-based protocols organize all nodes into a ring and each node in the ring maintains global membership information (Figure 6.13). A token is based among all nodes to synchronize data transmissions and acknowledgments, and to provide the basis for ordering the receiving hosts.

Ring-based topologies have the advantages of high performance and high reliability. But the complexity of the algorithm and the large number of protocol states make them difficult to implement. And, since each member must maintain a membership list, the scalability of ring-based protocols is usually rather limited.

For some applications, the definition of reliability has to include one more aspect—ordering of the data. In other words, does the protocol

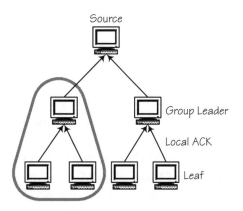

FIGURE 6.12 Schematic of a tree-based protocol.

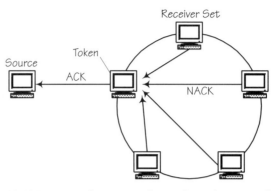

FIGURE 6.13 Schematic of ring-based protocol operation.

deliver a set of packets to the receiver in the same order in which they were transmitted? There are three categories of ordering. A protocol with *unordered* delivery does not make any guarantees on the order in which packets are delivered to the receiver. The delivery is termed *source-ordered* if the protocol maintains the order of the transmission for each sender. Source-ordered protocols do not make guarantees on the order in which packets from different senders are received by a receiver. Lastly, a *totally-ordered* protocol ensures that all packets are received by all receivers in the same order; this order may follow some global rule.

As we cover the protocols that have been developed for reliable multicasting, we'll emphasize certain characteristics for comparison of the protocols. These characteristics include:

Reliability Mechanism. How the protocol recovers from data loss.

Repair Request. How the protocol requests retransmission of lost data.

Feedback Control. How the protocol controls the amount of control information receivers generate.

Retransmission. How retransmitted data is propagated.

Flow Control. The mechanism used to prevent the source from overflowing the receivers and from causing network congestion.

Locus of Control. Whether the protocol uses a central site to perform certain control functions.

Ordering. What ordering guarantees the protocol offers.

Late Join/Leave. Whether the protocol allows receivers to join or leave a multicast session after it starts.

Scalability.   What size group can the protocol support.

Target Applications.   Which applications can best make use of the protocol.

The following paragraphs contain some of the details of these various protocols. At the end of this section, there's a summary table (Table 6.4) to show how the different methods compare.

Adaptive File Distribution Protocol (AFDP)

As the name suggests, AFDP provides a reliable multicast framework for distributing files. It's built to run on top of UDP and can be run in any of three modes—unicast, broadcast, or multicast—although multicast is AFDP's preferred mode of transmission.

AFDP groups are organized according to three entities: publishers, subscribers, and a secretary. AFDP senders, or *publishers,* send data to AFDP *subscribers.* The special group member, the *secretary,* is responsible for managing group membership, authorizing publishers, and determining the appropriate transmission mode to be used (see Figure 6.14). Although the group secretary controls group membership, subscribers can join or leave a host group at any time.

AFDP's reliability stems from its subscribers' use of NACKs to request retransmission of lost packets. NACKs are generated by the subscribers at fixed intervals, with a statistically varying delay to reduce the possibility of a NACK implosion at the publisher. Publishers retransmit lost packets to the entire group.

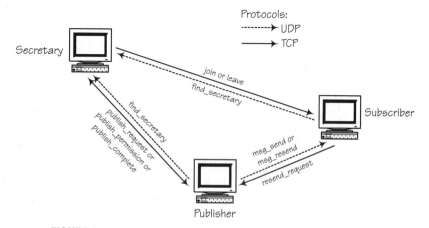

FIGURE 6.14   Communications between AFDP members.

The rate-based flow-control mechanism used by AFDP slows down publishers every time they receive a NACK, but they can increase their transmission rate after successful transmissions.

Descriptions of AFDP have not specified a probable limit to the size of a host group, but estimates put it between 10 and 1,000 subscribers, varying with network bandwidth and workstation capabilities.

Log-Based Receiver-Reliable Multicast (LBRM)

LBRM was designed to help solve the problem of providing fast updates of terrain and related data to a multicast group in distributed simulations.

A unique feature in LBRM is its use of a logging server to log all of the packets that are transmitted by the source. A primary logging sever resides near the source, but it is not part of the multicast group. The server provides a reliable unicast log of all multicast transmissions to the primary logging server. This logging server is then used to retransmit any lost packets upon request as either unicast or multicast packets. Receivers send unicast NACKs to the logging server to request lost packets. Logging servers decide whether they should multicast or unicast a lost packet based on the number of NACKs that they receive.

Even though the logging server takes care of retransmitting lost packets, the original source is expected to store all data that has been sent until it gets an ACK from the logging server.

With LBRM, it's possible to organize multiple logging servers into a hierarchy to help perform local recovery. Secondary logging servers are members of the multicast group and, like primary logging servers, log all received packets. LBRM allows receivers to determine the nearest secondary server using a series of scoped multicast (increasing TTL) or by a static configuration similar to that used for a name server (DNS, for example).

Local Group Multicast Protocol (LGMP)

The Local Group Multicast Protocol is based on the Local Group Concept; the idea is to enable the receivers to dynamically organize themselves into subgroups (called Local Groups) and use a *group controller* within each Local Group to coordinate local retransmissions of lost packets and to handle status reports (see Figure 6.15).

LGMP does not include the protocol specifications for selecting group controllers; instead, they're defined in a separate protocol called DCP or Dynamic Configuration Protocol.

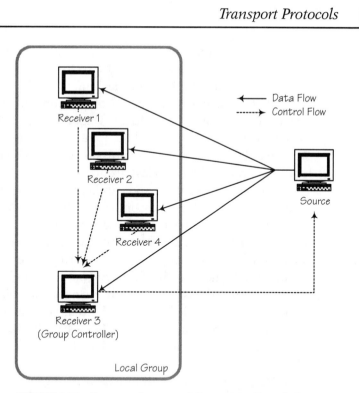

Data Flow
Control Flow

Receiver 1

Receiver 2

Receiver 4

Source

Receiver 3
(Group Controller)

Local Group

FIGURE 6.15 Data and control flows in a Local Group.

Packet losses are monitored by receivers and requests for retransmissions are transmitted as unicast packets. Packet retransmissions are first handled inside local groups and missing packets are only requested from the sender or a higher-level group controller if no member of the local group has a copy of the requested packets.

Simulations have indicated that LGMP can support host groups containing as many as 2000 members.

Multicast File Transfer Protocol (MFTP)

MFTP was designed with one type of application in mind—multicasting large files to many receivers. MFTP builds on the concepts of *blocks,* which consist of hundreds or thousands of frames and *multiple passes,* where the first pass consists of transmission of the entire file and subsequent passes contain only the missing frames.

Receivers transmit an acknowledgment after receipt of each block and use a NACK to indicate those frames within a block which are missing or in error. After completion of a pass, the sender accumulates the list of missing frames and starts another pass (see Figure 6.16), consisting of only those frames that were NACKed. Other passes are initiated if needed until all receivers obtain all of the data.

MFTP consists of two protocol components: the Multicast Control Protocol (MCP) and the Multicast Data Protocol (MDP). MCP allows the server to dynamically control the joining and leaving of receivers while MDP handles the reliable transmission of data products to the receivers that have joined the multicast group.

The sender has the responsibility for managing the host group, initiating any file transfers and controlling the transfer operation. Data transmissions are announced to receivers by the sender. The Announce message identifies the data that will be transmitted, its size, and other parameters, such as the private group address (described later). Two different multicast groups are defined by MFTP: the *public group* and the *private group*. The public group address is where any receiver may join and listen for announcements made by any sender that is transmitting to the public address. However, only receivers that are authorized by the application to receive a particular transmission actually join the address for the private group.

MFTP supports two different types of group management—Closed Groups and Open Groups. In Closed Groups, the sender restricts the membership of the group at two levels: (1) the members of the group are restricted either by prior configuration or by use of MCP, and (2) the product announcement itself includes a list of receivers that are authorized to

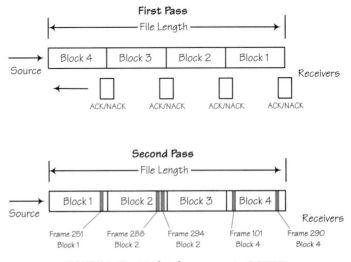

FIGURE 6.16 Multiple passes in MFTP.

participate. This method allows the sender to keep detailed statistics on each receiver.

In the Open Groups model, the receivers are not known to the sender. This means that the sender is not able to configure the multicast groups via MCP. A receiver must be able to obtain the public group address of senders that it is interested in, either by using the MCP Group Query message or by using an external session description protocol (see Chapter 8).

Experiments with MTFP have succeeded in supporting as many as 10,000 receivers using the Open Groups model.

Multicast Transport Protocol—Version 2 (MTP-2)

We've already covered many of the details of the Multicast Transport Protocol in Chapter 3, so I'll just briefly recap the pertinent details here.

A revised version of MTP, the Multicast Transport Protocol, MTP-2 has been used for a number of applications for some time since the original standardization of MTP in RFC 1301. MTP-2 was designed to avoid some of the practical problems experienced in using MTP and introduces a number of additional facilities that increase its utility. In particular, MTP-2 no longer has a single point of failure.

Using the MTP nomenclature, the master is responsible for the ordering of messages for all web members and for rate control for any data transmissions. Members that cannot maintain a minimum flow are requested to leave the group.

Consumers can request a retransmission of data packets when there is a gap in the packet sequence numbers of a message or no further packets are received for more than a given time period while the message is still incomplete. In order to handle retransmissions, a producer keeps a copy of every data packet it sends. To limit the number of packets it stores, a producer will delete these copies after a special period of time set by the MTP system.

Another, newer version of MTP is Self-Organizing Multicast or MTP/SO. MTP/SO uses MTP-2 as a basis and adds spontaneous self-organization of the members of the group into a hierarchy of local regions. Scalability is increased by providing passive group joining and local retransmission of lost packets.

Reliable Adaptive Multicast Protocol (RAMP)

The Reliable Adaptive Multicast Protocol is designed to be layered atop a network-layer multicast protocol like IP Multicast.

Group membership is maintained by the RAMP sender. This does not scale as well as receiver-based membership approaches (see Chapter 3). Receivers are allowed to join or leave the host group at any time.

A RAMP sender starts a session by sending a Connect message to an IP Multicast address. The sender can then start transmitting multicast data once it receives at least one Accept message. Data messages contain increasing sequence numbers; when a receiver detects a gap in the message sequence, it will request a retransmission by sending a NACK back to the sender as a unicast message. The sender's application has the responsibility of determining whether to retransmit messages as multicast to the group or as unicast to the requester.

RAMP senders can operate either in burst mode or idle mode. In burst mode, the sender marks the start of a burst by setting the ACK flag in the Connect message and sets the end of a burst by sending an Idle message. If the sender does not hear from a known reliable receiver, it will retry the transmission and eventually eject the receiver from the membership list if it does receive a reply. In idle mode, the sender multicasts an Idle message immediately after it receives the first Accept message and whenever it has no data to send. If a receiver does not receive either a data message or an Idle message, it will assume that data has been lost and will request retransmission.

Flow control is a simple rate-based mechanism in which the sender adjusts its transmission rate based on feedback received from the slowest receiver in the group. The packet rate is measured as a linear function of returned NACKs.

Reliable Broadcast Protocol (RBP)

RBP is one of the original protocols designed for reliable multipoint communications, focussing on broadcast networks, but its algorithm has served as the basis for a number of the multicast protocols discussed in this section. The Reliable Broadcast combines negative and positive acknowledgments to achieve reliability and ordering.

All group members are ordered in a logical ring, with one initially designated as the master token site. Messages are multicast to the group through a token site; the token site multicasts an ACK for each message that it receives. To limit the resources each site needs to maintain the state of a session, the role of the token site rotates among all members of the group. A member accepts the role of becoming the next token site only if it has received all the messages with a timestamp earlier than that of the token-passing message.

The ACKs sent by a token site include a global timestamp, enabling receivers to use them to globally order the messages and detect if any messages have been lost. When a receiver detects a lost message, it sends a NACK to the current token site, which replies with the missing message.

Because the token site is responsible for all acknowledgments and retransmissions, it becomes the bottleneck whenever any losses occur. The scheme also requires re-formation of the ring whenever a member joins or leaves the group. Both of these factors keep the system from scaling well with the size of the group.

Reliable Multicast Protocol (RMP)

The Reliable Multicast Protocol (RMP) seeks to provide ordered, reliable multicast delivery on top of the traditional unreliable multicast service. To ensure guaranteed delivery, RMP uses a ring-based algorithm for passing a token to group members.

Messages are multicast to the host group through a primary receiver called the *token site;* the token site multicasts an ACK for each message that it receives, informing the sender that the token site has received a message. The ACKs include the sending host's number and message sequence identifier, as well as a global timestamp, enabling receivers to use them to order the messages and to detect lost messages.

The token site is passed among all sites in the RMP token ring. The token is passed at least once for each ACK that's sent, where each ACK contains the name of the new token site. When the new token site receives the ACK, it checks to see if it has received all of the messages and ACKs with timestamps smaller than that of the current ACK. If not, it requests the messages from the group by multicasting a NACK for each missing message. Any group member on the ring can transmit the missing message to the site issuing the NACK. Once it has received all the messages, it declares itself to be the new token site.

The protocol creates an explicit list of intended destinations so the sender always knows who is in the group and what each member has received. But group members can join and leave at any time.

One unique advantage offered by RMP is its support for non-multicast members. A host that occasionally needs to send data to an RMP group can do so via a proxy member.

For flow control, RMP uses a rate-based control that allows the administrator to specify the maximum amount of traffic that any sender can send in a given time period. RMP is best suited for environments where a group consists of less than 100 members.

Reliable Multicast Transport Protocol (RMTP)

RMTP is a tree-based reliable multicast protocol which helps reduce the likelihood of an ACK implosion by aggregating acknowledgments at midpoints in the network.

In this protocol, each branch of the delivery tree has a designated receiver which receives acknowledgments from its *children* on the branch and aggregates them before sending them upstream to the sender (see Figure 6.17).

Designated receivers cache the received multicast data and respond to retransmission requests from other receivers on their branch. This approach also reduces the end-to-end latency for retransmissions; repeat transmissions are selective, based on each packet, which can result in higher throughput.

RMTP allows receivers to join an ongoing session at any time and still receive the entire data stream reliably. In order to provide this feature, the senders and the designated receivers have to buffer the entire file during the session. This allows receivers to request the retransmission of any transmitted data from the corresponding designated receiver. Although the designated receivers are chosen statically for a host group, a receiver can dynamically choose a designated receiver as its ACK processor.

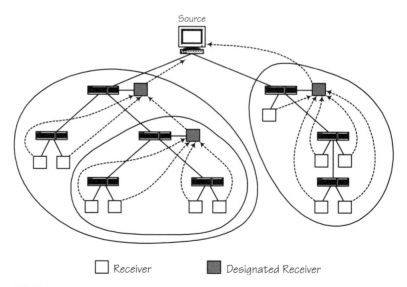

FIGURE 6.17 Aggregating ACKs via a hierarchy of designated receivers.

RMTP is unique in that it describes an effective technique called *subtree multicasting* for limiting the scope of retransmissions using multicast. Subtree multicasting allows a designated receiver to multicast a retransmitted packet such that it is carried strictly away from the original source of the packet down the subtree that the original packet would have followed. Although this scheme effectively controls delivery of a retransmitted packet, it is not supported by the current slate of multicast routing protocols.

Reliable Multicast Transport Protocol (RMTP)

Another protocol called RMTP has been developed by groups working at NTT Information & Communication Systems Laboratories and IBM Research in Japan. This protocol does not utilize a hierarchy of intermediates for aggregating ACKs or NACKs, but instead depends on direct end-to-end communications between receivers and the source when packets are lost.

> NOTE To prevent confusion between the two protocols with the same name, I'll refer to it as RMTP-J in the following summary table.

When a receiver detects a lost packet (by noting a missing number in the sequence of packet IDs, for instance), it sends a unicast NACK to the sender. RMTP also requires the receiver to send an ACK for confirmation of receipt of the complete data set. Despite the concern about feedback implosions, the protocol's designers found that their system was able to handle as many as 10,000 senders by using a backoff time algorithm to control receiver's NACKs and ACKs.

Lost packets are retransmitted to the group as multicast packets. The sender will continue retransmissions of the data until no packet loss is reported by the receivers. Receivers are instructed to ignore duplicate packets.

Two different procedures are used for flow control (i.e., separate transmission and monitor-based rate control). In separate transmission, when the performance decline (due to a failed connection, for instance) of a receiver is detected by the sender, the sender will halt the retransmission control to that receiver until retransmission to other receivers is completed. This effectively isolates temporarily unavailable receivers while normal state receivers receive a higher priority. The monitor-based rate control is used to offset global performance declines, such as those due to network congestion.

RMTP uses an explicit connection establishment procedure in order to pass to the receivers the information they need for retransmission control. After obtaining a list of likely receivers from another source (such as IGMP), the sender transmits connection establishment request packets to all receivers via multicast. Each receiver is expected to respond with an acknowledgment sent to the sender via unicast. If the sender does not receive the expected acknowledgments after a set period of time, it can transmit another round of connection requests to specific receivers as unicast packets.

Group membership is static during the session. Connections to receivers can be removed at the end of a transmission by responding to a Release packet that's sent from the sender after each transmission.

Single Connector Emulation (SCE)

SCE has been designed as an architecture that sits between the Transport layer interface and the Network layer interface so that it can aggregate the multicast capabilities of the Network layer, adapting them to the expected single connection features of the Transport layer. The SCE receives acknowledgments and other control packets from the multicast group members and aggregates them for forwarding to the overlaying Transport layer.

The transport service created by SCE is connection-oriented. Prior to any data transmission, a connection has to be established from the source of the multicast data to the set of targeted destinations. In order to reconcile the expectations for a successful single connection and setting up similar criteria for multiple connections, SCE uses a set of minimal success criteria that depend on the number of responding receivers.

As with many other systems, when a connection is established and data is transferred, the source will keep track of the status of the destinations through control packets it receives from them. In SCE, this requires keeping track of the individual destinations even though the success of a transmission is aggregated to a single status variable for the entire group. SCE maintains a database of member-specific information to keep track of each group member.

SCE places additional restrictions on group membership. The initial membership of a group is set at the establishment of the connection. All receivers that respond are made part of the group and a list is maintained at the source. Receivers are allowed to leave an existing group, but no new receivers may join after the connection is established. A group member may be dropped if it consistently does not acknowledge received packets for prolonged periods. But a former group member may also be readmitted into the group if it starts responding correctly after some set interval of time.

Scalable Reliable Multicast (SRM)

Scalable Reliable Multicast provides a best-effort multicast delivery. SRM uses a cloud-based algorithm which requires the receivers to be responsible for recovering lost packets by noticing gaps in sequence numbers. SRM does not maintain an explicit membership list.

Cloud-based protocols like SRM are usually connectionless. Since they do not maintain membership information but deliver data on a best-effort basis, they are more scalable than ring-based protocols.

SRM was originally designed to support Wb, the distributed whiteboard tool. Participants transmit multicast NACKs to request retransmission of lost data; any member that has the information can answer the NACK and retransmit the data. To avoid generating multiple copies of retransmitted data, the retransmissions are multicast to the group. Sites also wait a random period of time before sending a NACK or retransmitting data to reduce the problem of multiple copies; if another member of the group either requests or retransmits the packet in question, the other site will suppress its own transmission.

New sites can join an ongoing whiteboard conference by transmitting a Join message at any time. Periodic Session messages are generated by current members to update the new site's view of the group if no other data are transmitted for a certain period of time.

Tree-Based Multicast Transport Protocol (TMTP)

TMTP is a combination of both sender-based and receiver-based techniques. Group members are organized into domains, with each domain containing a domain manager that's responsible for error recovery and local retransmissions within the domain.

Domain managers are also responsible for sending unicast ACKs, time-outs, and retransmission requests to the sender when necessary. ACKs are returned to the sender upon receipt of each multicast packet from the sender.

Flow control is accomplished by a combination of rate-based and windowing techniques. A maximum transmission rate solves problems that can arise from bursty traffic or packet loss at receivers that are rate-dependent. The windowing technique delays retransmissions as long as possible to increase the likelihood of an ACK reception and to allow domain managers to resolve problems within their domains.

Although demonstrations of TMTP have been performed with up to 30 members, analyses of the protocol indicate that it should be scalable to much larger groups.

Express Transport Protocol (XTP)

XTP is another protocol that we discussed earlier in this book (Chapter 3). It's a rather all-inclusive approach to multicasting, since it defines its own network and transport level protocols. But, recall that the use of XTP does not preclude the use of the regular IP protocols on the same network devices; rather, it's designed to coexist with them.

XTP relies on NACKs to support reliable communications. In XTP's multicast mode (it can also run as a unicast protocol), retransmissions are multicast to the group, but NACKs are unicast back to the sender. The status of receivers can also be checked by a synchronized handshake process. In this case, receivers each wait a random delay before sending their control packet to reduce the possibility of a feedback implosion.

Both window- and rate-based flow control are supported by XTP. The rate-based flow control allows a receiver to dynamically pace a sender using rate and burst control parameters.

In order to make it easier to compare the protocols for reliable multicasting, Tables 6.4a and 6.4b present a summary of the salient features of each of the protocols that I've covered in this section.

In addition to all of these protocols, two frameworks have been proposed to ease the building of reliable multicasting applications. These are RMF, the Reliable Multicast Framework, and RMFP, the Reliable Multicast Framing Protocol.

Reliable Multicast Framework (RMF)

RMF is one of the two schemes discussed here that is not a reliable multicast protocol, but a framework for applications to employ such protocols. (The other framework is RMFP, which will be discussed next.)

RMF has three key features. First, it includes the concept of self-identifying packets. These permit fine-grained reliability semantics on a per-packet basis that allow a sender to induce a desired behavior at the

TABLE 6.4a Summary of Reliable Multicasting Protocols

	AFDP	LBRM	LGMP	MFTP	MTP-2	RAMP	RBP
Reliability mechanism	NACK	ACK, NACK		NACK, ACK	NACK	NACK	ACK, NACK
Repair request	unicast	unicast	unicast, multicast	unicast	unicast	unicast	unicast
Feedback control		structure-based	structure-based				
Retransmission	multicast, unicast,	multicast	unicast	multicast	multicast, unicast	multicast	unicast
Flow control	rate-control		rate		rate	rate	
Locus of control	centralized	centralized	distributed per source	centralized	centralized	distributed per source	centralized
Ordering		supported	supported		total	supported	total
Late join/leave group	supported				supported		
Scalability	10–1000	>50	2000	10,000	no estimate	small groups	
Target applications	file distribution	interactive multimedia	distr. simulation	file distribution	many types	interactive multimedia	many types

TABLE 6.4b Summary of Reliable Multicasting Protocols *(continued)*

	RMP	RMTP	RMTP-J	SCE	SRM	TMTP	XTP
Reliability mechanism	ACK, NACK	ACK	NACK, ACK	ACK	NACK	ACK	NACK
Repair request / Feedback control	multicast	multicast structure-based	unicast backoff timing	unicast	multicast timer-based	multicast structure-based	unicast
Retransmission	unicast	multicast, unicast	multicast	multicast	multicast	unicast	multicast
Flow control	window	rate & window	rate	rate		rate & window	rate & window
Locus of control	centralized	distributed	centralized	centralized	distributed	distributed	centralized
Ordering	total	supported	packet reordering	per source		ordered delivery	supported
Late join/leave group	supported		no-static	leave only	supported	supported	supported
Scalability	<100	18 nets (demo)	10,000	<20	>1,000	>30	limited
Target applications	file transfer	file transfer	file transfer	file transfer	interactive media		many types

receiver when the packet is received. For example, an RMF packet could indicate whether an ACK should be transmitted upon receipt of the packet. Second, a *universal multicast receiver* is defined; this is an RMF-based receiver that can interoperate with any sender through the use of self-identifying packets (as opposed to having a specific receiver for each reliable multicast protocol). Lastly, RMF provides clear separation of functionality at the data level and the session level. By using session-level control protocols, the system can define the default behavior of the protocol, including such items as the address to which ACKs or NACKs should be delivered (see Figure 6.18), or the receiver timer algorithm to be used.

RMF assumes a sender-based model, with a single sender and multiple receivers. Some of the configurable features within RMF are shown in Table 6.5.

Reliable Multicast Framing Protocol (RMFP)

Rather than design a protocol for specific application or type of multicast data, RMFP attempts to define a framework for building reliable multicast applications, moving developers one level away from the details of the reliable multicast protocols.

RMFP follows the principles of application-level framing and integrated layer processing. It is designed for integration into an application rather than implementation as a separate layer. RMFP includes extension mechanisms to allow modifications and additions required by individual applications. A complete specification of RMTP for a particular application will require a profile document which specifies extensions and modifications for the application.

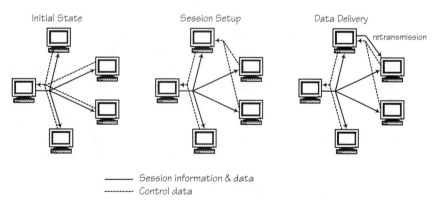

FIGURE 6.18 Flow of initial and repair data during RMF session.

TABLE 6.5   RMF's Configurable Features.

Reliable Multicast Service	RMF Configurable Alternatives
■ Error Control	
Detection	Unreliable, sender (ACK), receiver (NACK) (P)
Who retransmits missing packets?	Source, repair server, unspecified (S)
How are retransmits performed?	Multicast, unicast (P)
■ Performance Monitoring	
Frequency	Polling, uniform intervals, event-driven (S)
■ Algorithm Options	
Control packet aggregation	Individual, sequential block, bit vector (S)
Ordering	Unordered, source ordering (S)
Miscellaneous	Streaming/burst; fragmentation/ reassembly (P)

Note: P = configurable on per-packet basis; S = configurable for session.

RMFP runs over UDP and does not provide any reliability (or functionality in a larger extent) on its own. Reliability and other protocol functionalities would be defined in specific profiles and implemented as part of the reliable multicast applications. Like RTP, RMFP defines a data packet format and a control packet format.

Summary

Many of the protocols we've just described use application layer framing to achieve the best importance, which is crucial for the transmission of real-time multimedia data. Neither RTP nor RTCP comprise a single, usable protocol. RTP and RTCP combined with a specific payload format do define a complete protocol, however.

RTSP has been specifically designed to control the presentation of one or more multimedia streams, especially in conjunction with HTTP. It relies on RTP to handle the actual transmission of the streams and expects other protocols to be developed for delivering the presentation information.

More than a dozen protocols have been designed to provide reliable multicasting. This relatively large number of protocols is due to the varying requirements of different multicast applications along with the different methods available for suppressing feedback in a multicast group. How these schemes control or aggregate feedback from multiple receivers has a large impact on their scalability.

C H A P T E R

7

Integrated Network Services and Quality of Service

In previous chapters we've already seen how complicated systems can get in order to deliver data reliably over a multicast delivery tree. And although we've touched on the different demands that traffic from interactive real-time applications place on networks, we haven't yet discussed how packet-switched networks using IP can provide such services. It's time to turn our attention to the methods that have been proposed for providing guaranteed service and QoS to interactive applications on IP networks.

Recall that packet-switched networks like the Internet traditionally offer best-effort delivery of network traffic. But that's unsuitable for real-time applications such as interactive multimedia that often cannot tolerate retransmitted packets or indeterminate delays. If packet-switched networks are to support real-time applications, a system other than best-effort delivery is required. Convinced that the packet-switched Internet could, in fact, offer such services in addition to best-effort delivery, the IETF set out in 1990 to define the Integrated Services Architecture to do just that. This chapter focuses on the different service requirements of real-time applications and the way that the Integrated Services Architecture aims to provide these services. As part of our discussion we'll go into the details of RSVP, the Resource ReSerVation Protocol that's been designed to work with the Integrated Services Architecture.

Requirements of Real-Time Applications

A wide variety of applications can run on networks. In addition to the bulk transfer applications like FTP, netnews, and e-mail, there are interactive applications ranging from a terminal emulator that requires entering commands to control responses from a remote host or using a Web browser to view pages on another site to interactive simulations between players in a multiplayer network and the even faster interactions required for transaction processing of online orders.

Some of the simpler multimedia data, such as text combined with graphics, or animation files, do not pose special transmission problems on networks. These files may be larger than the norm, but they don't require synchronization of different parts of the data. But more complex multimedia data, such as that used in interactive applications—videoconferencing and streaming video, for example—impose special restrictions on networks beyond demands for more bandwidth.

While bandwidth is the crucial factor when precise amounts of data must be delivered within a certain time period, latency affects the response time between clients and servers. *Latency* is the minimum time that elapses between requesting and receiving data, and can be affected by many different factors, including bandwidth, an internetwork's infrastructure, routing techniques, and transfer protocols.

A network can contribute to latency in a number of ways:

Propagation delay. The length of time it takes information to travel the distance of the line. This type of delay is mostly determined by the speed of light and isn't affected by the networking technology in use.

Transmission delay. The length of time it takes to send the packet across a given medium. Transmission delay is determined by the speed of light and the size of the packet.

Processing delay. The time required by a router for looking up routes, changing the header, and other switching tasks.

Another factor, that of jitter, also affects real-time network traffic. *Jitter* is the variation in the latency. Irregular packet delays due to jitter can introduce distortion, making the multimedia signal unacceptable.

If we take a look at the best-effort delivery offered by IP, we see that IP networks treat every message independently—a source may transmit a packet to a destination without any prior negotiation or communication. Furthermore, the network has no information that a particular packet belongs to a suite of packets, such as a file transfer or a video stream. The network will do its best to deliver each of these packets independently. This approach often introduces considerable latency and jitter in end-to-end paths (see Figure 7.1), that aren't compatible with much of the data generated by the newer applications seen on networks, which depend on known delays and little, if any, data loss.

The many multimedia applications already running on networks can best be classified by first taking into account the format of the information they process and, second, by describing the time dependencies of the data (Figure 7.2). Multimedia data can either be a collection of text and graphics formats which are usually called *discrete* or time-independent media, or audio and video that are often called *continuous* or time-dependent media.

We can subdivide applications dealing with continuous media into two classes according to their requirements of network performance. In *intolerant* or *rigid* applications, they require either absolute or statistical performance guarantees of the network. In return for network-provided guarantees, these applications produce constant quality output. The other class, *tolerant* or *adaptive* applications, expects a consistent quality of service (QoS) at any point in time, but can adjust their operation to adapt to changes in the actual QoS that's provided. These applications are able to gracefully adapt their output quality depending on the QoS provided by the network.

Due to the bandwidth of continuous-media streams and the strict delay and jitter bounds of interactive applications, retransmissions are not viable for most of these applications. Fortunately, many continuous-media

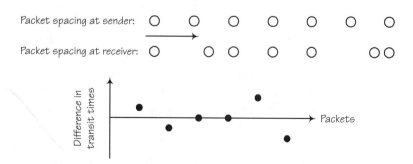

FIGURE 7.1 Variations in packet arrivals at a receiver.

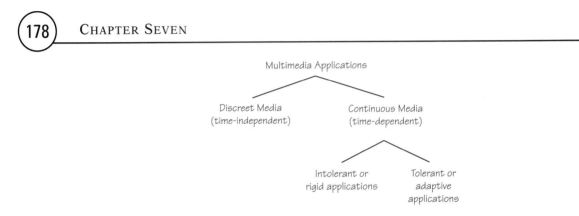

FIGURE 7.2 Multimedia application categories.

applications can tolerate moderate error rates without significant quality degradation, with the degree of tolerance depending both on the nature of the application and the methods used for encoding and compressing the media. While rigid applications may only be able to recover from sporadic problems that are masked by the nature of the media, adaptive applications may also dynamically adapt to long-term QoS modifications.

With the move to interactive multimedia, applications now require control over the quality of service they receive from the networks. To support the different latency and bandwidth requirements of multimedia and other real-time applications, networks can use QoS parameters to accept an application's network traffic and prioritize it relative to other QoS requests from other applications. QoS provides network services that are differentiated by their bandwidth, latency, jitter, and error rates.

As you might expect, there's more than one approach to providing network quality of service for real-time applications (see Figure 7.3). First, one could simply attempt to avoid congestion altogether by over-provisioning your network (i.e., providing more bandwidth than would ever be needed). This might work for a while, but it's highly likely that eventually the increase in the number of users and the applications they use, as well as the type of data they transmit, will use all the available bandwidth. This can also be a very expensive solution.

Another approach to avoiding congestion is to charge users on the basis of the volume of their network traffic. As we've seen repeatedly on the Internet and corporate networks, when the services are free, they're often utilized beyond the breaking point. Charging for their use tends to reduce the use of resources. But metered service is not particularly popular on the Internet and it will most likely be some time before it's widely accepted.

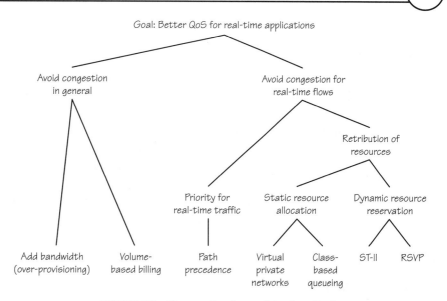

FIGURE 7.3   Strategies for achieving QoS.

But rather than avoid congestion in general, you can try to avoid congestion only for the real-time traffic. This can be accomplished either by supporting higher priorities for real-time traffic or by redistributing the resources between real-time and nonreal-time traffic.

Routers can differentiate between service classes according to the precedence field in the header of each packet (IPv4's Type of Service, or TOS, field). Also called the Class of Service or CoS approach, this method offers a small fixed number of service classes and only guarantees that packets with higher precedence get better service than packets with lower precedence. Since there is no admission control, there is no mechanism to prevent classes from becoming overloaded. Despite a lack of predictable quality and flexibility, precedence-based CoS may well prove to be the only current strategy that's feasible for providing QoS on a large scale.

Should you choose to allocate network resources between real-time and nonreal-time applications, then you have two choices. Either you can statically allocate the resources or you can allow resources to be reserved dynamically. Static resource allocation combines the advantages of resource sharing with the advantages of a dedicated line, but with the loss of flexibility; if you don't use the entire bandwidth of the reserved line, you cannot use it for other traffic. Class-based queueing can be more useful than a virtual private network, since it allows you to statically reserve a portion of a single link, rather than the entire link.

Last, but not least, we come to dynamic resource reservation, which is best suited for the dynamics of multicasting. We've already discussed ST-II as a multicasting protocol that supports end-to-end reservations (Chapter 3). But ST-II does not support heterogeneous reservations and the scalability is limited since admission is controlled by the sender.

The approach that has received most of the attention and efforts of Internet engineers is Integrated Services and RSVP, which is the focus of the remainder of this chapter. For more details on QoS and the many ways to provide it on IP, ATM, and frame relay networks, take a look at Paul Ferguson and Geoff Huston, *Quality of Service: Delivering QoS on the Internet and in Corporate Networks*, John Wiley & Sons, Inc., 1998.

The Integrated Services Architecture

Anticipating the variety of real-time applications and services that could be used on IP networks, the IETF formed the Integrated Services (INTSERV) Working Group, which set out to design a set of extensions to the best-effort delivery model that's currently used on the Internet.

> NOTE This effort has been expanded to include two other working groups—the Integrated Services over Specific Link Layers (ISSLL) Working Group and the RSVP Working Group.

This framework, the Integrated Services Architecture, provides special handling for certain types of traffic flows and includes a mechanism for applications to choose between multiple levels of delivery services for their traffic. A fundamental precept of the Integrated Services Architecture is that network resources must be controlled in order to deliver QoS which requires the inclusion of admission controls. Along with this, there must be a way to reserve resources (an important aspect in providing differentiated services).

> NOTE For those of you familiar with ATM, you'll probably see parallels between the Integrated Services Architecture and ATM—the Integrated Services Architecture provides signaling for quality-of-service parameters at Layer 3 of the OSI model, while ATM provides similar signaling for QoS parameters at Layer 2.

Note that the Integrated Services Architecture isn't designed to provide better quality of service for short-lived, nonreal-time applications like

Flows

In general, IP networks deal with traffic on a packet-by-packet basis. But, especially when dealing with real-time data, it's important to preserve relations between the packets generated by a source. This brings us to the concept of data flows.

The concept of a flow in networking is a very general one. A flow might consist of "all web traffic from the marketing server," "all file-server traffic to and from teller machines," or "all traffic from the CEO's laptop, wherever it's located." On the other hand, a flow can also consist of a particular sequence of packets from an application running on a particular host that's transmitted to another, specific host at a particular time each day.

Flows are typically identified on IP networks by the tuple (source address, destination address, source port, destination port, protocol). In the multicast case, the destination address would be the host group address. When flows are identified at network nodes, they are usually categorized into classes. These classes can contain more than one flow and usually have a service model associated with them. Flow specifications are cast in terms of the class of service, combined with the quantitative parameters as needed. For example, a mean rate combined with a measure of burstiness suffice to characterize many applications. IPv6 incorporates tags known as *Flow identifiers* to make the classification of packets by newer routers a more efficient task. The Flow identifier has been designed with networks such as ATM in mind. Thus, its size is 24 bits, just like the VCI/VPI field which in ATM is used for roughly the same function.

FTP, TELNET, WWW, or e-mail. Although interactive nonreal-time applications can also suffer from congested networks, their short lifetime does not justify the overhead of setting up and tearing down a reservation.

The Integrated Services Architecture consists of five major components—QoS requirements, resource-sharing requirements, allowances for dropping packets, provisions for feedback on usage, and a model for resource reservation. We'll concentrate on the first four components for the moment and leave the resource reservation component, RSVP, for the last half of the chapter.

Quality-of-Service Parameters

Since the Integrated Services Architecture is predominantly concerned with real-time application traffic, control of QoS has to include provisions for setting maximum acceptable latencies and jitter for the data. To characterize the QoS capabilities of a node in the path of a packet flow, the Integrated Services Architecture defines the following control parameters:

NON_IS_HOP.   Provides information about the presence of nodes which do not implement QoS control services along the path.

NUMBER_OF_IS_HOPS.   Used to inform the flow endpoints of the cumulative number of IS-aware nodes (IS = Integrated Services) which lie in the data path.

AVAILABLE_PATH_BANDWIDTH.   A local parameter providing an estimate of the bandwidth (in bps) that's available for traffic following this path.

MINIMUM_PATH_LATENCY.   A local parameter representing the latency of the forwarding process associated with this node.

PATH_MTU.   Maximum transmission unit (in bytes) for packets traversing the data path.

TOKEN_BUCKET_TSPEC.   Token bucket specification plus a peak rate (in bps), the minimum policed unit, and the maximum packet size (in bytes); the token bucket specification includes an average token rate and a bucket depth.

NOTE   The token bucket is a system to reshape traffic by allowing a flow to transmit traffic whenever tokens are present in a predefined container (the bucket). Tokens are specified to represent a given unit of bytes. A flow can transmit traffic up to its peak burst rate if there are adequate tokens in the bucket.

These parameters should be used by any network element (hosts and routers, for example) that supports the Integrated Services Architecture. Network elements can support more than one service class (i.e., they can offer different combinations of the QoS parameters). In such cases, each service-specific parameter is associated with a service number, where a service number of 1 indicates the default service.

Service Classes

As part of the architecture, the Integrated Services Working Group has defined several service classes that, if supported by routers, can provide a data flow with certain QoS commitments. This contrasts with best-effort traffic, which receives no such service commitment from a router and has to make do with whatever resources are available. The level of QoS provided by these enhanced QoS classes is programmable on a per-flow basis according to requests from the end applications. These requests can be passed to the routers by network management procedures or, more commonly, using a reservation protocol such as RSVP. The requests dictate the level of resources (e.g., bandwidth, buffer space) that must be reserved along with the transmission scheduling behavior that must be installed in the routers to provide the desired end-to-end QoS commitment for the data flow.

Five service classes have been defined so far. They are:

Best Effort. The traditional service model of the Internet, typically implemented through FIFO (First In, First Out) queueing in routers.

Fair. An enhancement of the traditional model, where there are no extra requests from the users, but the routers attempt to partition network resources in some fair-share sense. This is typically implemented using a random drop approach to handling overloads, possibly combined with some simple round-robin serving of different sources.

Controlled load. An attempt to provide a guarantee that a network appears to the user as if there were little other traffic. It makes no other guarantees and is essentially a way of limiting the traffic admitted to the network so that the performance is perceived as if the network were over-engineered for those that are admitted.

Predictive or controlled delay. The delay distribution that a particular flow perceives is controlled. It requires the source to make some prestatement to the routers that a particular throughput is required.

Guaranteed. Where the delay perceived by a particular source or to a group is bounded within some absolute limit. This may entail both an admission test as with controlled-load, and a more extensive queueing system for forwarding packets.

These classes of traffic roughly correspond with those developed in the Broadband ISDN (Integrated Services Digital Networks) standards communities for ATM networks (i.e., the International Telecommunications Union and the ATM Forum).

The first of these classes, best-effort delivery, is of course the default delivery mode for Internet traffic and doesn't receive any special consideration within the Integrated Services Architecture. Of the remaining classes only two, guaranteed service and controlled-load service, have been formally specified within the framework of the Integrated Services Architecture for use with RSVP.

CONTROLLED-LOAD SERVICE

Controlled-load service provides approximately the same quality of service under heavy loads as under light loads. The important difference from the traditional Internet best-effort service is that the controlled-load flow does not noticeably deteriorate as the network load increases. This will be true regardless of the level of load increase. By contrast, a best-effort flow would experience progressively worse service (greater delay and packet loss) as the network load increased.

The controlled-load service is intended for those classes of applications that can tolerate a certain amount of loss and delay, provided it is kept to a reasonable level. Examples of applications in this category include adaptive real-time applications.

One possible example of controlled-load service is using it for multicast applications over an intranet where traffic conditions and global policies can be managed. This should ensure that a statistical throughput guarantee is enough and propagation delays will be low enough for most users so that they can use interactive multimedia conferencing tools with adequate performance.

A description of the traffic characteristics (called the TSpec) for the flow desiring controlled-load service must be submitted to the router, although it is not necessary to include the peak rate parameter. If the flow is accepted for controlled-load service, then the router makes a commitment to offer the flow a service equivalent to that seen by a best-effort flow on a lightly loaded network.

Controlled-load service can be implemented fairly simply in the queueing systems in routers and functions adequately for the existing multicasting applications, which can adapt to the small-scale end-to-end delay, and variations and jitter that it may introduce, through the use of adaptive buffering. It is not suited to applications that require very low latency such as distributed virtual reality systems.

GUARANTEED SERVICE

Guaranteed service means that packets will arrive within a guaranteed delivery time and will not be discarded due to queue overflows, as long as the flow's traffic stays within the bounds of its specified traffic parameters.

The guaranteed service does not control the minimal or average delay of traffic, nor does it control or minimize the jitter; it controls only the maximum queueing delay. It is intended for applications with stringent real-time delivery requirements such as certain audio and video applications that have fixed playout buffers and are intolerant of any datagram arriving after their playback time. Guaranteed service is designed to address the support of legacy applications that expect a delivery model similar to traditional telecommunications circuits.

> NOTE   A playout buffer is one way of accommodating different arrival times of data that was sent at a regular interval. As long as a mean rate of delivery is maintained, an application can buffer the data and play it back with the proper interval, even if the arrival times are irregularly spaced, but not out-of-order.

Every node in the data path must implement the guaranteed service in order for this service class to function, due to the end-to-end and hop-by-hop calculation of two error terms. As with the controlled-load service, links on which the guaranteed service is run are not allowed to fragment packets.

There are two types of traffic policing associated with the guaranteed service—simple policing and reshaping. Policing is done at the edges of the network and reshaping is done at intermediate nodes within the network. Simple policing can be described as the act of comparing traffic in a flow against the TSpec for conformance. Reshaping consists of an attempt to restore the flow's traffic characteristics to conform to the TSpec.

Other Requirements

Under the Integrated Services Architecture, the allocation of network resources is performed on a flow-by-flow basis. Even though each flow is subject to the appropriate admission criteria, many flows share the available resources in the network. The aggregate bandwidth of the network can thus be shared by different types of traffic.

The Integrated Services Architecture also outlines scenarios where it may be necessary to control traffic by dropping packets. For example, the network may be in danger of reneging on established service commitments and the only course of action may be to preempt some flows. Traffic reshaping may make it necessary to drop packets as well.

Finally, although the Integrated Services Architecture recognizes the need to provide usage feedback and accounting data, this topic has not yet been covered in any detail by the working group.

Now that we've taken a brief tour of the components of the Integrated Services Architecture, let's briefly review how it works.

Traffic Control

The Integrated Services Architecture defines four mechanisms that make up the traffic control functions at OSI layers 3 and above. Figure 7.4 shows the architectural components as they're defined for implementation on a router. A brief discussion of some possible implementations follows. In general, the details of these schemes is best left to books on routing algorithms; selection of an appropriate algorithm is best left to router vendors.

The first, the packet scheduler, assumes the function of traffic policing—it must determine whether a particular flow can be admitted entry to the network. The basic function of packet scheduling is to reorder the output queue. The simplest approach is to use a priority scheme, giving some packets absolute preference over others. An alternative scheme is to use a round-robin system or a similar variant, which gives different classes of packets access to a share of the link.

The second, the packet classifier, maps each incoming packet into a specific class for traffic differentiation. One approach is to use a *virtual circuit* model in which a circuit is set up with specific service attributes and

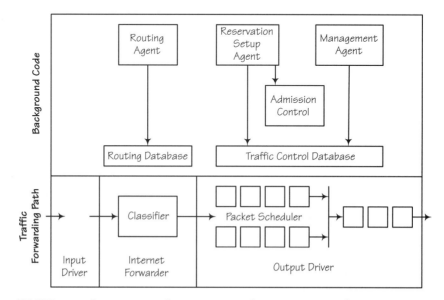

FIGURE 7.4 The Integrated Services Implementation Reference Model.

the packet carries a circuit identifier. This is the approach used by ATM as well as ST-II. Another approach is to provide a Flow-ID field in the IP packet header which can be used for shortcut classifications of the packet as part of a flow.

Admission control is simply responsible for determining whether a flow can be granted the requested QoS without affecting other established flows. This usually implies that there's a way to monitor the current (and occasionally the past) load on the router's resources to determine if a new request can be fulfilled.

Lastly, resource reservation is needed to set up the flow state in the requesting hosts as well as the routers along the end-to-end transit path. This currently is largely the purview of RSVP, although other protocols may be suggested; the Integrated Services Architecture does not restrict resource reservation to RSVP, although that's the protocol that's received the most attention.

Resource ReSerVation Protocol (RSVP)

In the Integrated Services Architecture, there's a logical separation between the QoS control and the protocol designed for resource reservation, RSVP. That's because RSVP can be used with a variety of QoS services, and the QoS services that were designed as part of the Integrated Services Architecture can be used with a variety of setup schemes. If we think of RSVP as the signaling system, then the QoS control information is the signal content. With that in mind, let's look at the details of RSVP. (Even more details on RSVP and its relation to the Integrated Services Architecture can be found in RFCs 2205-2216.)

In the previous chapter on Transport Protocols, we covered the inter-relationship between RTP and RTCP, and also pointed out a scenario where RSVP could be used to reserve resources for use by an RTP stream (see Figure 6.8 on page 150). (Applications can also use protocols other than RTP and RTCP in conjunction with RSVP to reserve network resources.) Although RTCP can provide feedback on reception quality (see Chapter 6), other protocols are needed to request timely delivery and guarantee a specific QoS for a session between a sender and its receivers. RSVP provides access to an internetwork's integrated services, as described in this chapter, and there is a guaranteed quality of service end-to-end.

Even though other protocols, such as ST-II (see Chapter 3), have been proposed for requesting and controlling QoS on IP networks, RSVP has a few unique features that are better suited to today's Internet. For example,

RSVP supports heterogeneous QoS, which means that different receivers of the same multicast group can each request a different QoS. For example, different QoS might involve different costs, or users might have different network resources available. RSVP also supports dynamic QoS—the resources which are requested by a receiver may be changed at any time for any reason. Also, RSVP is receiver-based, which is better suited for dynamic situations like those associated with multicast groups. For multicast, the reservation request need only travel to a point where it merges with another reservation for the same source stream. This receiver-oriented design is intended to accommodate large multicast groups and dynamic group membership.

RSVP operates on top of IP, occupying the place of a transport protocol in the protocol stack, but provides session layer services (that is, it does not transport any data). RSVP is an Internet control protocol like IGMP or ICMP and is not a routing protocol. It uses underlying routing protocols to determine to where it should carry reservation requests. As routing paths change, RSVP adapts its reservation to new paths if reservations are in place. The RSVP protocol is used by routers to deliver QoS control requests to all nodes along the paths of the flows and to establish and maintain state to provide the requested service. After a reservation has been made, routers supporting RSVP determine the route and the QoS class for each incoming packet, and the scheduler makes forwarding decisions for every outgoing packet.

> NOTE RSVP messages are sent as raw IP datagrams, identified as protocol #46. They can also be encapsulated in UDP packets for systems which cannot accommodate raw network I/O services.

Basic Operation

To start the process of reserving network resources, an RSVP sender sends a Path message downstream towards an RSVP receiver destination.

Each intermediate RSVP-capable router along the delivery tree intercepts Path messages and checks them for validity. If an error is detected, the router will drop the Path message and send a PathErr message upstream informing the sender, so he can then take appropriate actions.

For a valid Path message, the router will update the path state entry for the sender and set a cleanup timer and restart timer. These timers are used to help schedule the refresh of RSVP's *soft state*. The router is also responsible for generating Path messages based on the stored path state

RSVP's Soft State

Since the membership of a large multicast group and the resulting multicast tree topology are likely to change with time, the RSVP design assumes that state for RSVP and traffic control state will be built and destroyed incrementally in routers and hosts. For this purpose, RSVP establishes what is called a *soft* state; that is, RSVP sends periodic refresh messages to maintain the state along the reserved path(s). In the absence of refresh messages, the state automatically times out and is deleted.

and forwarding them down the routing tree until the Path message reaches its destination receiver.

Upon receipt of the Path message, the RSVP receiver then sends Resv messages back upstream to the sender along the same hop-by-hop traffic path which the Path messages traversed when traveling towards the receiver (see Figure 7.5). (For IP Multicast, a host sends IGMP messages to join a host group and then sends RSVP messages to reserve resources along the delivery path(s) of that group.)

A host receiver uses RSVP to request a specific QoS from the network for a particular data stream from a data source. An elementary RSVP reservation request consists of a specification for an end-to-end desired QoS (e.g., peak/average bandwidth and delay bounds—see Figure 7.6) and a definition of the set of data packets to receive the QoS.

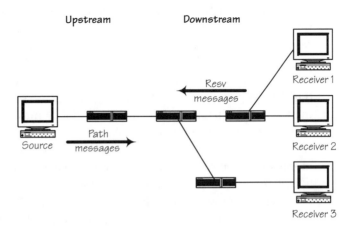

FIGURE 7.5   Directions of RSVP messages.

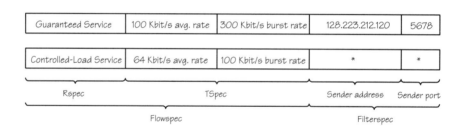

FIGURE 7.6   Examples of reservation requests.

During reservation setup, an RSVP QoS request is passed to two local decision modules, *admission control* and *policy control*. Admission control determines whether the node has sufficient available resources to supply the requested QoS. Policy control determines whether the user has administrative permission to make the reservation.

The request is granted or rejected according to these admission and policy controls which utilize information from underlying integrated services mechanisms that are not part of RSVP. If the reservation is rejected, RSVP returns an Error message to the appropriate receiver. If the reservation can be accommodated, the node configures a packet classifier to select the appropriate incoming data packets and a packet scheduler to achieve the desired QoS on the outgoing interface. One RSVP session might have priority over others.

The reservation request is propagated to nodes upstream towards the appropriate sender. Upon successful receipt of the Resv message, the sender begins sending its data.

The basic RSVP reservation model is *one pass*—a receiver sends a reservation request upstream, and each node in the path either accepts or rejects the request. This scheme does not provide an easy way for a receiver to find out the resulting end-to-end service. RSVP therefore supports an enhancement to one-pass service known as *One Pass With Advertising* (OPWA). With OPWA, RSVP control packets are sent downstream, following the data paths, to gather information that may be used to predict the end-to-end QoS. The results (*advertisements*) are delivered by RSVP to the receiver hosts and to the receiver applications if necessary. The advertisements may then be used by the receiver to construct, or to dynamically adjust, an appropriate reservation request.

When a flow has a multicast destination, different destinations systems may require different reserved resources. Just as merging group membership requests is important for IP multicasting, so too is the merging of RSVP reservations. At each replication point in a multicast delivery tree, RSVP must merge reservation requests; it does this by selecting the largest Flowspec from all those received (see Figure 7.7).

Merging of Flowspecs occurs whenever Resv messages that originated from different receivers and traversed different traffic paths converge at a *merge point*. The guidelines for merging reservations for both the controlled-load and guaranteed service classes are given in RFCs 2211 and 2212, respectively.

Message Formats

RSVP defines six types of messages: Path, Resv, PathErr, ResvErr, PathTear, and ResvTear. Each RSVP message begins with a common header (Figure 7.8); that header contains eight defined fields and two reserved fields.

Version. Current version is 1.

Flags. Reserved 4-bit field for future extensions.

RSVP type. Identifier for message type.

Checksum. Standard ones complement checksum of message.

send_TTL. The IP TTL value with which the message was sent.

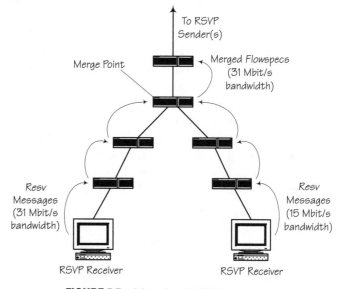

FIGURE 7.7 Merging RSVP requests.

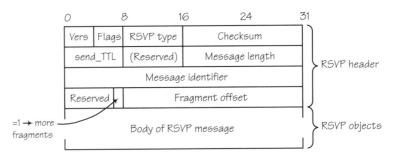

FIGURE 7.8   RSVP message format.

Message length.   Length of entire message.

Message identifier.   Used when message is fragmented.

Reserved.   Unspecified.

Fragment offset.   Relation between current fragment and rest of message.

More fragments.   Flag to indicate if more fragments should be expected; =1 for all but the last fragment.

After the common information, RSVP messages consist of a series of objects. These objects make up the contents of the message's body; each has the same basic format—an object length, class number, class type, and the object contents. RSVP currently defines 15 different objects types (Table 7.1).

Some objects deserve particular note. The SENDER_TSPEC carries the traffic specification generated by each data source within an RSVP session. The FLOWSPEC object carries reservation request information (RSpec and TSpec) generated by data receivers. The ADSPEC object carries information which is generated at either data sources or intermediate network elements to help determine the characteristics of the end-to-end communications path (the *advertisements* I referred to earlier). This information includes the minimum path latency, path bandwidth, number of IS-aware devices, and the path MTU (Maximum Transmission Unit); other parameters can be included for either guaranteed load or controlled load services.

A typical path message might look like the one shown in Figure 7.9. Following the header, this message contains four different objects which identify the destination (SESSION), the message's previous hop (RSVP_HOP), the frequency at which it will be refreshed (TIME_VALUES), and the flow itself (SENDER_TEMPLATE).

TABLE 7.1 RSVP Defined Objects

Number	Object Type	Value	Description
0	NULL		Ignored by recipient
1	SESSION	1	IPv4 session
		2	IPv6 session
3	RSVP_HOP	1	IPv4 previous or next-hop address
		2	IPv6 previous or next-hop address
4	INTEGRITY		Keyed MD5 authentication data
5	TIME_VALUES	1	Frequency of path or reservation refreshes
6	ERROR_SPEC	1	Error information from an IPv4 system
		2	Error information from an IPv6 system
7	SCOPE	1	List of IPv4 hosts to which WF reservation refresh applies
		2	List of IPv6 hosts to which WF reservation refresh applies
8	STYLE	1	Reservation style
9	FLOWSPEC	1	Controlled delay
		2	Predictive QoS
		3	Guaranteed QoS
		254	Several unmerged flows
10	FILTER_SPEC	1	IPv4-based filter to apply to flow
		2	IPv6-based filter using source port values
		3	IPv6-based filter using flow label values
11	SENDER_TEMPLATE	1	IPv4-based flow description from sender
		2	IPv6-based flow description from sender
12	SENDER_TSPEC	1	Upper bound on traffic that sender will generate
13	ADSPEC		Sender's advertised information for flow
14	POLICY_DATA	1	Policy information for flow
		254	Several unmerged policy data objects
20	TAG	1	Collection of objects to be associated with a given name

Like path messages, reservation requests have a prescribed set of objects and an order for those objects. A sample request is shown in Figure 7.10.

The SESSION object describes the destination object; the RSVP_HOP object describes the previous system that handled the reservation request, while the TIME_VALUES object tells the sender how often the sender will refresh its reservation. The STYLE object indicates the reservation style (FF, SE, or WE—see next section); the option vector part permits a more flexible specification of the style if it's needed. The FLOWSPEC object

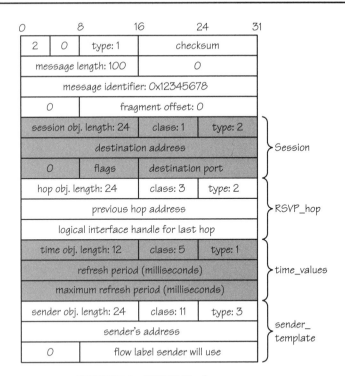

FIGURE 7.9 RSVP Path message.

identifies the resources that the flow needs, while the **FILTER_SPEC** specifies a sending address and IP flow label.

    RSVP includes two error messages, one for errors in Path messages (PathErr), another for Reservation Errors (ResvErr). In both cases, the error message follows the reverse path of the original message. In addition, RSVP defines two teardown messages that can be used to terminate a connection before the timers would normally shut down the connection. A Reservation Teardown message, ResvTear, sent by recipients of a flow, would tell the network that the reserved resources are no longer needed. A sender can generate a Path Teardown message, PathTear, telling systems to disregard any information they have been maintaining for the flow.

Reservation Styles

A reservation request includes a set of options that are collectively called the *reservation style*. These styles are described by RSVP FILTER_SPECs.

    As part of its design, RSVP separates the description of a reserved resource from whom the resource is reserved for. The first function is han-

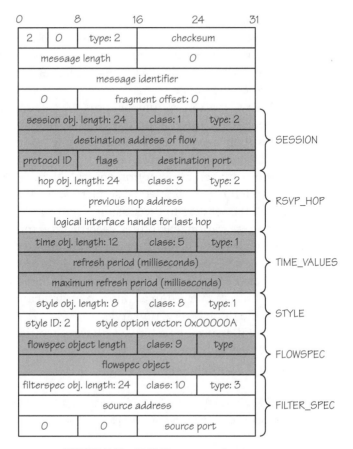

FIGURE 7.10 RSVP reservation request.

dled by the filter specification (FILTER_SPEC), while the second function is the purview of the flow specification (FLOWSPEC). This separation is important, as the filter specification can be reused in a number of ways.

The simplest way that the filter specification is reusable is by having the specification refer to a flow received by an application, rather than to one that is sent. This means that senders can transmit video at a rate convenient to them, but that receivers can select the sub-band rates that are most convenient to each of them. This receiver-based reservation is quite different from the telephony model of how to do things, and fits well with the IP Multicast model.

The second way that the filter generalizes the idea of a reservation is that it can include a wild card, so that it can refer to groups of sources. For example, in an audio conference, there is no necessity to set aside resources for all the audio feeds at once, since humans are typically capable of organizing themselves in a conversation so that there is usually only one person speaking at any one time. Thus, sources will ask for reservations that are only marginally more than a unicast audio reservation for a multiway multicast audio conference.

One reservation option concerns the treatment of reservations for different senders within the same session. Establish a distinct reservation for each upstream sender or else make a single reservation that is shared among all packets of selected senders.

Another reservation option controls the selection of senders; it may be an explicit list of all selected senders or a wild card that implicitly selects all the senders to the session (Figure 7.11). In an explicit sender-selection reservation, each filter specification must match exactly one sender, while in a wild card sender-selection, no filter spec is needed.

Three reservation styles have been defined for use in RSVP so far: fixed filter (FF), wild card filter (WF), and shared explicit (SE). When reservations are merged in a router, merging can only occur between messages of the same reservation style.

The Filterspec of each fixed-filter reservation consists of only a single sender. The effective Flowspec of the reservation is the maximum of all FF reservation requests received on that interface for that particular sender.

NOTE   When the router's interface connects to a shared-medium LAN, it's possible to receive Resv messages from multiple next hops.

The Filterspec of each wild card-filter reservation at an interface matches any upstream sender. The effective Flowspec is the maximum from all WF reservation requests received at that particular interface.

The Filterspec of each shared-explicit reservation at an interface contains a specific set of senders from upstream and is obtained by taking the

Sender Selection	Reservations	
	Distinct	Shared
Explicit	Fixed-Filter (FF) Style	Shared-Explicit (SE) Style
Wild card	(No Style Defined)	Wild Card-Filter (WF) Style

FIGURE 7.11 Relation between sender selection and reservation style.

union of the individual Filterspecs from each SE reservation request received on that interface. The effective Flowspec installed is the maximum from all SE reservation requests received on that particular interface.

The SE and WF styles are useful for conferencing applications where only one sender is likely to be active at one time. In such cases, reservation requests for twice the sender bandwidth could be reserved to allow some amount of overspeaking. The difference between the two styles is how tightly the application must specify the flows that share the resource. With a shared explicit reservation, the application must explicitly identify every participating sender. The wild card-filter style lets an application share a resource without identifying every sender. Any flow that matches the reservations specification may use the resource, regardless of its sender. Wild card filters thus offer convenience in exchange for control and security.

Resource ReSerVation Protocol and Multicasting

Although RSVP can be used for unicast sessions, its main area of applicability is for multicast sessions such as video and audio conferencing, and other interactive multimedia group applications. Thus RSVP message transmission and maintenance of its soft state is interwoven with the processes of maintaining host group memberships. The general procedure is for a host to send IGMP messages to join a multicast group and then send RSVP messages to reserve resources along the delivery paths of the group (see Figure 7.12).

The basic procedure is described in Figure 7.12. In step A, a source is multicasting data to two group members. When a new receiver wishes to join the host group, it sends an IGMP group membership request to its local router (step B), which is forwarded up the delivery tree. Data from that multicast session is then forwarded to the new member, but no special network resources are yet associated with the new member. Since the source periodically sends RSVP Path messages down the delivery tree to maintain the soft state of the system, the new member will eventually receive a Path message that it can act on, sending an appropriate Resv message upstream to reserve whatever resources it feels necessary (step C). As this new Resv message is merged with other Resv messages from the other receivers, it may be necessary to have some receivers change their requests or reallocate network resources, changing the multicast delivery tree.

Even as this simple example shows, the changes in host group membership and in reservation requests can lead to frequent changes in the multicast delivery tree. In many cases, a more stable delivery tree is desired.

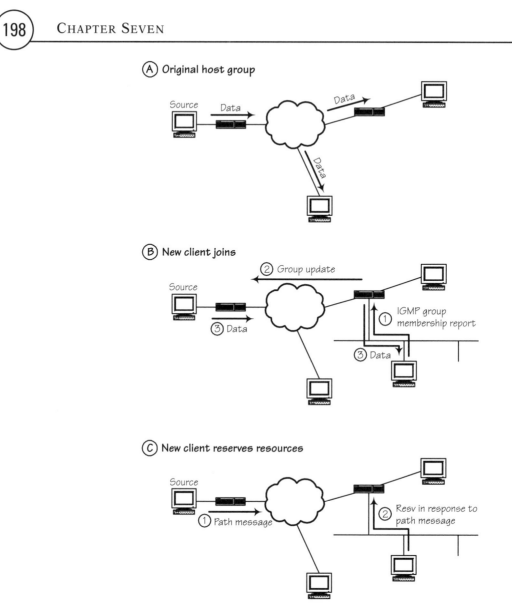

FIGURE 7.12 Adding RSVP support for a new multicast receiver.

Unicast routing in most internetworks is dynamic in order to guide packets around hosts and links that are down and to adapt to variations in network load. Even though this is sufficient for best-effort service, it creates problems when routes are carefully planned to support QoS guarantees for multicast sessions.

One way that has been proposed to help deal with this problem is to make the multicast routing algorithm ignore unnecessary routing changes (i.e., changes that reduce route costs, but are not due to failed links or switches). The rationale is that load variations should not significantly affect streams for which resource reservations have already been made, but should instead be dealt with by rerouting best-effort traffic. This approach, called *route pinning,* preserves the quality guarantees as long as a path remains physically connected. As part of the approach, it has been suggested that alternate paths also be defined as part of the setup of a delivery tree, thus allowing for a smoother transition in the case of a primary path's failure.

Issues

RSVP has yet to see wide-scale deployment; many of the protocols were only admitted to the IETF standards track in the last half of 1997. Although some commercial routers have already shipped with RSVP support, there are still concerns about RSVP's scalability.

There are at least three scaling issues involved in large-scale deployment of RSVP: scaling of control traffic within a multicast group, scaling of reservations state for many reservations, and scaling of reservation enforcement for many reservations.

In multicast sessions, Path messages are also sent as multicast messages, thus minimizing traffic. Reservation requests are merged at each branch point of the multicast distribution tree, so there is only one Resv message on each branch of the tree. Each additional reservation request in a large multicast group travels only a short distance before it merges with another reservation request. Shared and wild card filters allow aggregation of reservations for flows with the same destination.

The second issue in scaling is managing the reservation state for a large number of sessions. The number of RSVP control messages processed by each router is proportional to the number of QoS flows going through the router. Managing state and processing control messages scales linearly with the number of flows. (Aggregation of multicasting routing state across groups is impossible with the current addressing scheme.) The amount of unicast and multicast routing state in a router depends only on the network topology and is insensitive to the size of the router's links. In contrast, the state required for RSVP (reservation state and path state) grows with the bandwidth of the links. The larger the links, the more flows can be served, but the more state information needs to be managed.

The third scaling problem is enforcement of reservations. All incoming packets go through a packet filter. The packet classifier has to check the list of reservations for each packet to determine which service the flow should get. Thus, the cost of classifying is proportional to the number of packets going through the router, not to the number of reservations or the number of flows.

Various issues surrounding RSVP need to be resolved to make it a more useful QoS protocol. First, regarding admission control, either a centralized or distributed algorithm needs to be developed to determine if the network can admit more traffic from new sources without disrupting existing traffic. Second, RSVP needs a mechanism for QoS-based routing; some work has already been started on this, and a preliminary specification for QoS extensions to OSPF has been published. Third, RSVP needs a mechanism to pin down the route used to deliver packets, including a self-healing mechanism so that a new router is computed if the original one fails; this can be especially important for dynamically changing multicast host groups. Fourth, the network needs a mechanism to aggregating flows as having the same qualities in order to simplify their processing at intermediate nodes.

Some other concerns need to be addressed if usage feedback and billing are ever to be implemented as part of the Integrated Services Architecture and RSP. First, accounting and billing needs to be integrated into the architecture in a scalable way. Second, RSVP requires a method for authenticating users to ensure that the appropriate parties are billed for the proper resources. Lastly, some scheme to permit settlements will need to be evolved to allow deployment of RSVP and Integrated Services across paths that entail more than a single intranet or commercial Internet Service Provider.

Considering all of the concerns about RSVP deployment, it's most likely that initially RSVP will be used mainly on corporate networks and in experimental networks of limited range.

Summary

Real-time applications often place special, stricter requirements on the delivery of network traffic. The Integrated Services Architecture designed by the IETF aims to satisfy these requirements on the packet-switched IP networks by defining standard methods for describing traffic requirements and for reserving the network resources needed to meet those requirements.

RSVP, the Resource ReSerVation Protocol, has also been designed by the IETF as part of the Integrated Services Architecture to provide one method for reserving network resources for either unicast or multicast traffic. Although paths are defined by the senders, RSVP is primarily a receiver-based protocol; it's the receivers who take on the responsibility of requesting specific resources to meet their bandwidth and latency requirements for a given session.

Session Management and Security

While the dynamic nature of IP multicasting may make it easy for users to join and leave multicast sessions at their leisure, this dynamism also makes it difficult both to control session participation and to learn what sessions are available.

Take the MBone for example. An MBone session can be scheduled by selecting an appropriate Class D address; then the creator of the session announces it to the MBone community, perhaps by direct e-mail, a mailing list, or posting the information to a special Web site. Anyone who can access the MBone can join the session and listen in.

While this rather casual approach may have worked in the initial stages of an experimental net like the MBone, more formal, standardized methods are needed to promote regular commercial use of multicasting. This includes creating protocols for scheduling events and selecting appropriate group addresses, notifying users of scheduled sessions, and restricting participation in sessions.

Session Management

Session management revolves around a number of issues. First, there needs to be a way to distribute the Class D multicasting addresses to minimize the chance of selecting an address that's already been chosen for a different multicast session. Second, different methods must be in place for notifying potential participants of available sessions; these methods should support both posted announcements (on *bulletin boards* and Web pages, for instance) as well as select invitations sent by e-mail or via a session directory server. Third, session management can also involve restricting multicasts and session participants (the latter via passwords or encryption keys, for instance); in a related issue, there's the question of securing session information and multicast data for private sessions. Lastly, session participants may need a routine way to negotiate the media required for a session if anticipated participants are unable to use the media originally defined for a session.

Much of the current work on session management, especially regarding session announcement and invitation, has grown out of the MBone's primary uses, namely as a medium for either audio and video conferencing or for shared whiteboards and similar collaborative applications. In many of these situations, a session organizer may want to invite particular users to be conference participants; he may also choose to keep the session private, perhaps by encrypting the data. Other applications on the Internet, such as IP telephony, are also creating a need to ring up speakers and join in either one-to-one or multiparty conversations.

A series of protocols are currently being designed and evaluated for session announcement and management or the *session directory service* by the MMUSIC (Multiparty Multimedia Session Control) Working Group of the IETF. These protocols include the Session Description Protocol (SDP), the Session Announcement Protocol (SAP), and Session Initiation Protocol (SIP). Another protocol, the Session Conference Control Protocol (SCCP) has recently been added to the group (Figure 8.1). These protocols have yet to be completely formalized and approved by the IETF, so some features may change even as this book goes to print.

The Session Description Protocol outlines the parameters for describing the proposed session, including information such as the scheduled time, the originator, the host group address, and the media required. The Session Announcement Protocol was designed to provide a standardized way of periodically distributing descriptions of planned multicast sessions. The Session Initiation Protocol (previously called the Session Invitation Protocol) offers the means to invite specific users to participate in a con-

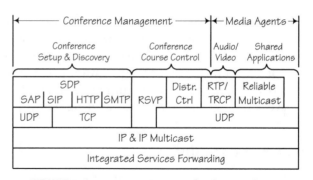

FIGURE 8.1 Session Protocol relationships.

ference other than by e-mail. Lastly, the Session Conference Control Protocol is designed to organize speakers in a conference, helping to decide who speaks next and impose some order on what would otherwise become a chaotic situation. Another protocol, the Conference Control Channel Protocol (CCCP), also works for more loosely organized conferences such as are common on the MBone. We won't cover these protocols in great detail in the chapter, mainly because they were still in the early stages of definition as this book was being written.

There are two different classes of session management. First, there's managing the setup of multicast sessions on an internetwork and disseminating information about the session to prospective participants. This is the type of session management that will be covered in the greatest detail in this chapter. But there's another kind of session management, more properly called conference control, that also needs to be discussed here. Conference control is concerned with the procedures surrounding running an established session, such as allocating time to participants, controlling polling and so on. We'll cover conference control towards the end of this chapter.

Before we delve into the details of the protocols that make up the session directory service, we need to cover some basic concepts of security, and particularly cryptography, since these items haven't yet been covered in the book, but are an integral part of some of the protocols that we'll be covering in this chapter.

Security

These days, security on networks covers a wide variety of problems and solutions. Issues such as protecting intranets from unauthorized access, encrypting data on desktop PCs and for transmission on a network, as well as identifying legitimate users and business partners have all given rise to a number of books on the subject. A good starting point is *Internet Security for Business,* by Terry Bernstein et al. (John Wiley and Sons, Inc., 1996). For the moment, though, I just want to cover a few basics regarding security and cryptography to familiarize you with terms that will come up every so often as we discuss securing multicast sessions.

A Primer on Cryptography

Cryptographic techniques offer four essential services: identification, authentication, non-repudiation, and privacy. Identification is pretty obvious—it's verifying that the sender of a message is really who he or she says. Authentication goes a step further—not only do you verify the sender's identity, but you also verify that the message he or she sent has not been altered. Non-repudiation is a requirement that's of more importance to commercial transactions than to multicast sessions (at least so far); this concept prevents anyone from denying that he or she sent or received a certain file or data, and is similar to sending a letter Certified, Return Receipt Requested through the U.S. Postal Service. Finally, privacy is the ability to shield communications from unauthorized viewing.

Secure communications start with authentication and encryption. Encryption, or encoding data into an unreadable form to ensure privacy, is probably the first use for cryptography that we'd think of. But new uses for authentication of individuals or computers has increased the utility of cryptography (see Table 8.1). Digital signatures, which can be generated quickly and bind a document or message to the owner of a particular key, are also proving useful for identifying users and authenticating messages.

Encryption is based on two components—an algorithm and a key. A cryptographic algorithm, or cipher, is a mathematical function that takes

TABLE 8.1 Uses of Cryptographic Technology

Use	Technology
Authentication of users without sending name and password in the clear	Digital certificates
Message privacy	Encryption/decryption
Message integrity	Authentication codes using message digests, digital signatures
Protection of confidential documents from unauthorized access	Digital certificates, digital signatures

intelligible information (often called *plain-text* even if it's a different type of data) as input and changes it into unintelligible *cipher text.* In order to encrypt the original information, most algorithms use a key as input in conjunction with an encryption formula. Both the key and the function used are crucial to the encryption. The same key used in two different encryption functions will produce two different results, and two keys used with the same function also produce two different results. The number of possible keys each algorithm can support depends on the number of bits in the key.

The difficulty of cracking an encrypted message is a function of the key length. For example, an 8-bit key allows for only 256 possible keys (2^8). Even using a brute-force method (i.e., having a computer sequentially guess each possible key and decrypting the message to see if it makes sense) would lead to finding the correct key quickly. Now try the same thing with a computer guessing 1 million keys every second for a 100-bit key (which equates to searching 2^{100} keys)—it would take many centuries to discover the right key.

There are two types of cryptography, based on the nature of the key that's used to encrypt and decrypt data. One is symmetric cryptography, which uses the same key to encrypt and decrypt data. The other is asymmetric cryptography, which uses two keys, one to encrypt the data and the second to decrypt the data.

The oldest form of key-based cryptography is called secret-key or symmetric encryption (see Figure 8.2). In this scheme, both the sender and recipient possess the same key, which means that both parties can encrypt and decrypt data with the key. This presents some drawbacks. A shared secret key must be agreed upon by both parties. If you have *n* correspondents, then you have to keep track of *n* secret keys, one for each of your correspondents. (If you don't mind letting all multicast recipients see each other's messages, then one key distributed to all users would suffice; the situation is much more complex if each conference member needs to keep his or her responses private from the other participants.) If you use the same key for more than one recipient, then each recipient will be able to read the other's messages.

> NOTE   The oldest known cipher is called the caesar cipher after Julius Caesar, who was noted for using it to communicate with his field commanders. This simple cipher shifts all characters in a message by an arbitrary number of characters, say 13. As long as the Caesar's field commander knew that's what was done to Caesar's message, he could subtract 13 characters from the message he received and read the orders in the message.

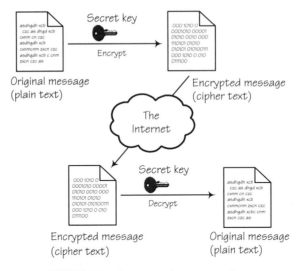

FIGURE 8.2   Symmetric encryption.

Symmetric encryption schemes also have the problem that the authenticity of a message's originator or recipient cannot be proved. Since both possess the same key, either of them can create and encrypt a message and claim that the other person sent it. This built-in ambiguity about who authored a message makes it impossible for one person to prove that he did or did not send a message (non-repudiation). By using what is called public-key cryptography, which makes use of asymmetric encryption algorithms (see Figure 8.3), the non-repudiation issues can be resolved.

Public-key cryptography is based on the concept of a key pair. Each half of the pair (one key) can encrypt information so that only the other half (the other key) can decrypt it. One part of the key pair, the private key, is known only by the designated owner; the other part, the public key, is published widely but is still associated with the owner. Key pairs have a unique feature: Data encrypted with one key can be decrypted with the other key in the pair. In other words, it makes no difference if you use the private key or public key to encrypt a message, the recipient can use the other key to decrypt it.

These keys can be used in different ways to provide message confidentiality and to prove the authenticity of a message's originator. In the first case, you would use the recipient's public key to encrypt a message; in the other, you would use your private key to encrypt a message. For example, in order to create a confidential message, Tim would first acquire

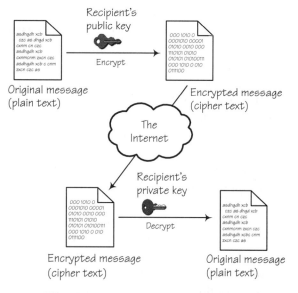

FIGURE 8.3 Asymmetric encryption.

Ann's public key. Then he uses her public key to encrypt the message and sends her the encrypted message. Since the message was encrypted with Ann's public key, only someone with Ann's private key (and we presume only Ann has that) can decrypt the message.

Although encrypting a message with a part of a public key pair isn't very different from using secret-key encryption, public-key systems offer some advantages. For instance, the public key of your key pair can be readily distributed (on a server or via e-mail) without fear that this compromises your use of your private key. (Of course, this means that anyone who gets the public key of your key pair can read any intercepted messages that you encrypted with your private key. If you want to ensure privacy in a message, use the recipient's public key to encrypt the data.) You don't have to send a copy of your public key to all your respondents; they can get it from a key server maintained by your company or from what are called certificate authorities.

> **NOTE** No official hierarchy of certificate authorities yet exists on either a national or international scale. Companies like Verisign, GTE Cybertrust, and Nortel sell digital certificates to individuals and corporations and the U.S. Postal Service is also experimenting with offering certificates to properly identified individuals.

Another advantage of public-key cryptography is that it allows you to authenticate a message's originator. The basic idea is this: You are the only person who can encrypt something with your private key since you're the only one who has it; if someone can use your public key to decrypt the message, then the message must have come from you. Thus, the use of your private key on an electronic document is similar to your signing a paper document.

But using public-key cryptographic algorithms to encrypt messages is computationally slow, so cryptographers have come up with a way to quickly generate a short, unique representation of your message called a *message digest* that can be encrypted and then used as your digital signature.

Some popular fast cryptographic algorithms for generating message digests are known as one-way hash functions. A one-way hash function doesn't use a key; it's simply a formula to convert a message of any length into a single string of digits called a *message digest* or *hash*. (One of the most common one-way hash functions is called MD5, which we'll run into as we discuss securing multicast data.) For example, if I were using a 16-byte hash function, any text I process with that hash function would produce 16 bytes of output, say CBBV235ndsAG3D67. The important thing to remember is that each message should produce a random message digest. Now encrypt that message digest with your private key and you've got a digital signature.

As an example, let's have the sender, Tim, calculate a message digest for his message, encrypt it with his private key, and send that digital signature along with the plain-text message to Ann.

After Ann uses Tim's public key to decrypt the digital signature, she has a copy of the message digest that Tim calculated. Since she was able to decrypt the digital signature with Tim's public key, she knows that Tim created it, authenticating the originator (see Figure 8.4). Ann then uses the same hash function (which was agreed upon beforehand) to calculate her own message digest of Tim's plain-text message. If her calculated value and the one Tim sent her are the same, then she can be assured that the digital signature is authentic.

The one problem with this approach is that a copy of the plain text is sent as part of the message and therefore Tim's message is not protected from snooping. Although it further complicates matters, a standard approach is to use a symmetric algorithm with a secret key to encrypt the plain text of the message. The computational intensity of public-key encryption makes it unsuitable for encrypting the entire message.

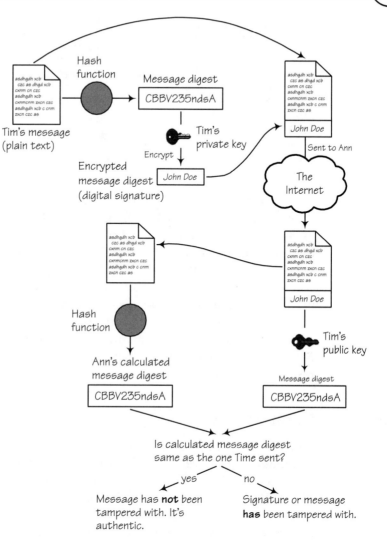

FIGURE 8.4 Verifying a digital signature.

KEYS AND SECURITY

One of the best discussions of key lengths and the efforts required to break a key is found in Chapter 7 of *Applied Cryptography* by Bruce Schneier (2d ed. John Wiley and Sons, Inc., 1996). Table 8.2 is a condensation of his table estimating the cost of building a computer in 1995 to crack symmetric keys and the time required to crack certain length keys.

TABLE 8.2 Time Required to Break Different Length Keys

	Length of key in bits				
Cost	*40*	*56*	*64*	*80*	*128*
$100 K	2 secs	35 hrs	1 yr	70,000 yrs	10^19 yrs
$1 M	.2 secs	3.5 hrs	37 days	7000 yrs	10^18 yrs
$100 M	2 msecs	2 mins	9 hrs	70 yrs	10^16 yrs
$1 G	.2 msecs	13 secs	1 hr	7 yrs	10^15 yrs
$100 G	2 microsecs	.1 sec	32 secs	24 days	10^13 yrs

Remember that this is not a static situation either. Computing power is always going up and costs falling (Moore's law), so it'll get easier to break larger keys in the future. These estimates are for brute-force attacks (i.e., guessing every possible key). There are other methods for cracking keys, depending on the ciphers used (that's what keeps cryptanalysts employed), but estimates for brute-force attacks are commonly cited as a measure of the strength of an encryption method.

Secret- and public-key ciphers use different key lengths, so the previous table cannot be used for setting all of your security requirements. Schneier has a table (Table 8.3) comparing the two systems for similar resistance to brute-force attacks.

Security and Multicasting

It's tempting to believe that multicast is inherently less private than unicast communication since the traffic visits so many more places in the network. But this isn't really the case except with multicast routing protocols like DVMRP which depend on a broadcast-and-prune process to maintain delivery trees. On the other hand, IP Multicast does make it easy for a host to anonymously join a multicast group and receive traffic destined for that group without the knowledge of other senders and receivers. If you require

TABLE 8.3 Secret- and Public-key Key Lengths for Equivalent Levels of Security

Secret-key Key Length	*Public-key Key Length*
56 bits	384 bits
64 bits	512 bits
80 bits	768 bits
112 bits	1792 bits
128 bits	2304 bits

that communication occurs among a restricted set of users, then strict privacy can only be enforced through adequate end-to-end encryption.

Some protocols already provide the means for encrypting data. For example, RTP specifies a standard way to encrypt RTP and RTCP packets using secret-key encryption schemes such as DES (Data Encryption Standard). It also specifies a standard mechanism to manipulate plain text keys using MD5 so that the resulting bit string can be used as a DES key. This allows simple out-of-band mechanisms such as privacy-enhanced mail to be used for encryption key exchange.

Another approach is to encrypt all packets that are transmitted over IP, regardless of the application that generated them. The IETF has been working on defining the protocols for a secure Internet, mainly in their IP Security (IPSec) Working Group. A series of Internet standards for authenticating and encrypting IP datagrams have been published as RFCs 1825 to 1829. These protocols were originally designed for use in IPv6, but can be used as extensions to IPv4. Efficient deployment of this kind of security system depends greatly on selecting a system for distributing the keys required for authentication and encryption, and that has yet to be finalized.

In the IPSec architecture, two different datagram headers have been designed for two different tasks. The IP Authentication Header, or AH, is supposed to take care of authentication and data integrity, (i.e., assuring the receiver that a received datagram was, in fact, transmitted by the party identified as the source, and that the datagram wasn't altered since transmission.) The Encapsulating Security Payload (ESP) header has a different role, that of maintaining the privacy of the IP datagrams.

The IP ESP header can be used to encrypt either a transport-layer segment or the entire IP datagram. In the first case, this is called transport-mode ESP; the second case is tunnel-mode ESP. Using transport-mode ESP still allows for potential security risks; for added security, tunnel-mode ESP can be invoked, where the entire IP datagram is encrypted and a new IP header is generated for routing the secure datagram from sender to receiver. The information in the unencrypted IP headers is then used to route the secure datagram from origin to destination.

Both of these protocols depend on what is called the *Security Association*. A Security Association between a sender and a receiver contains mutually agreed upon information needed for authentication and encryption; information such as the authentication or encryption algorithm, the lifetime of the cryptographic key, and other details for the use of the algorithm. When datagrams are received, they can only be verified or decrypted if the receiver can link them to the sender by means of a

Security Association. In the IPSec architecture, the information comprising a Security Association is exchanged as part of the key management session, which precedes any exchange of sensitive data. Although the primary focus of IPSec thus far has been unicast traffic, it's possible to extend IPSec's architecture to multicasting; for the moment, more work along these lines needs to be done.

Key distribution is closely tied to authentication. Conference or session directory keys can be securely distributed using public-key cryptography on a one-to-one basis (by e-mail, a directory service, or by an explicit conference setup mechanism), but this is only as good as the certification mechanism that's used to certify that a key given by a user is the correct public key for that user. Certification mechanisms such as X.509 are not specific to multicast conferencing, and no standard mechanisms are currently in use for conferencing purposes other than sending the information via secure e-mail (PEM (Privacy Enhanced Mail) or S/MIME (Secure MIME), for instance).

Key management for multicast sessions requires quite a lot more traffic compared to the key management for unicast sessions. First, the common group key has to be distributed to each group member and all the senders. If the traffic also has to be authenticated, then each sender has to distribute their authentication key to all group members. This can be accomplished by using a centralized trusted party, such as a group owner. In this case, members would send their join and leave requests to the group owner, who generates and distributes the necessary keys. Recall that some of the protocols for reliable multicasting that we've described in Chapter 6 depend on either control by the sender or a series of intermediate group servers and could be used to handle key distribution if necessary. Some, like ST-II and MTP, already include provisions for secure transmissions. And RFC 1949 outlines a procedure for using the core routers in CBT as points for controlling access and distributing cryptographic keys for secure multicasting sessions.

The many types of data that can be multicast and the modular nature of IP multicasting applications further complicate the issue of securing a session. Take a videoconference, for example—participants are likely to receive two different media streams, one for the audio portion, the other for the video portion. If one application is used to play the audio stream and another to play the video stream, then both have to be capable of decrypting the data. They both may require separate keys, adding to the complexity of key management and distribution.

Now let's turn our attention to the details of session directories and session management.

Session Directories

There are two basic ways to locate and participate in a multicasting session—either by advertising (i.e., potential participants see a posted notice for a session and join the host group) or by invitation (i.e., users are specifically invited by others to participate in a session). Sessions on the MBone were originally advertised on mailing lists and in news groups; eventually, some Web sites were created as central distribution points for information about MBone sessions.

But none of these methods are proving adequate as the MBone gets larger and other multicast networks are created. The growth of the MBone has pointed out some of the navigation difficulties associated with multicast sessions, in particular how session addresses are chosen and information on sessions is distributed. This has led to the creation of a *session directory service*, which serves as the framework for SDP, SAP, and SIP. This service has several functions (see Figure 8.5):

1. A user creating a conference needs to choose a multicast address that is not in use. The session directory system has two ways of doing this. First, it allocates addresses using a pseudo-random strategy based on how widespread the conference is going to be according to the originator and where the originator is. Second, it multicasts the session information; if it detects a conflict with an existing session announcement, it changes its allocation.

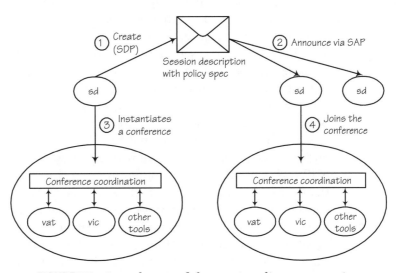

FIGURE 8.5   Sample use of the session directory service.

2. Users need to know what conferences are on a multicast internetwork (the MBone, for instance), what multicast addresses they are using, and what media each session is using. They can use the session directory messages to discover all of this. Also, since administrative scoping can be used to restrict multicasts to specific regions of interest, both announcements and session traffic can be controlled to avoid affecting other areas of the internetwork.

3. The session directory tools currently implemented can also launch the appropriate multicast applications for the user, simplifying the actions he needs to perform to join a session.

Van Jacobson's *sd* session directory tool has been the major tool for advertising MBone conferences for some time (see Chapter 10 for more details on sd); it distributes the conference addresses and conference-specific information (such as the applications required) for participation. Since then, the approach has been refined to separate the directory information into two classes: the actual description of a session (handled by SDP) and the dissemination of the description (handled by SAP).

As session directories have evolved, the content of a session description has grown and security issues are being addressed. First, there's the information a potential participant in a conference or multicast session needs to know before he or she joins the conference. The basic information should include the session's subject, the time and date of the session, the host group address, and what media are required. Added information might include such items as the length of the session, the session originator and some verification that the originator of the information is legitimate (a digital signature, for instance), and other participants.

In addition to disseminating information about session names and purposes, the session directory can be used to provide information relating to the privacy or security of session announcements and session content. For instance, shared secrets, such as public keys for encrypting data, can be disseminated via the session directory.

Although the primary focus of the MMUSIC Working Group has been on the development of the session directory service using protocols like SDP, SAP, and SIP, there are other proposals for session directories. In particular, LDAP (Lightweight Directory Access Protocol) has received a great deal of interest as a means of providing many different directory-related services on the Internet, including authentication information and access privileges as well as contact information. Since LDAP is designed to be extensible, it's been proposed that LDAP directories could be used to store information about multicast sessions as well as the media capabilities of each participant.

> NOTE LDAP was originally designed as a protocol for accessing directory-based data that's stored in X.500 directories. It's now evolved into a glue that's used for exchange of data between a variety of directories. The extensibility of LDAP, particularly starting with version 3, also makes it useful for storing additional objects like digital certificates as well as user profiles.

Having outlined what's expected of a session directory service, let's take a look at some of the capabilities that have been designed into the supporting protocols, SDP, SAP, and SIP.

The Session Description Protocol (SDP)

Simply put, SDP is designed to convey information about conference sessions and relevant setup information to recipients. Thus, SDP is purely a format for session descriptions and relies on other protocols, such as SAP, SIP, RTSP, SMTP or IMAP e-mail using MIME, and HTTP for distribution of the session descriptions.

When announcements of multicast sessions are made only via e-mail or the World Wide Web, they can reach a greater audience than when dispatched via SAP. This may raise control issues. When SAP is used to disseminate a session description, only legitimate participants will receive the announcement, since SAP messages are subject to the same TTL control or administrative scoping control that the original SDP message defines. But Web servers and e-mail don't have the same restrictions.

SDP includes the session name and purpose, times the session is active, the media comprising the session and information (addresses, ports, etc.) to receive the media. Other optional information can include such items as the bandwidth to be used by the conference and contact information for the person responsible for the session.

The session description is a simple ASCII text message that can be transmitted as part of a UDP packet or as a part of a MIME message. For both e-mail and WWW distribution, the use of the MIME content type "application/sdp" should be used. There are three classes of parameters in SDP: session description parameters (Table 8.4), time description parameters (Table 8.5), and media description parameters (Table 8.6). Of these parameters, only the protocol version, owner, session name, session time,

TABLE 8.4   Session Description Parameters

Symbol	Description	Format
v	Protocol version	
	Owner/creator and session identifier	\<username>\<session id>\<version>\<network type>\<address type>\<address>
s	Session name	
i	Session information	
u	URI (Uniform Resource Identifier) of description	
e	E-mail address	
p	Phone number	
c	Connection data	\<network type>\<address type>\<connection address>
b	Bandwidth information	\<modifier>:\<bandwidth-value> (e.g., modifier = CT (Conference total), AS (Application-specific maximum))
z	Time zone adjustments	\<adjustment time>\<offset>...
k	Encryption key	\<method>:\<encryption key> (e.g., base64:\<encoded encryption key>;uri:\<URI to obtain key>; prompt)
a	Session attribute lines (may be zero)	

and media name/transport address are required in a session description; all others are optional.

The connection address that's included in the session connection data can take on one of three forms. It can be a simple unicast IP address or a multicast IP address, in which case it must include a TTL (appended to the IP address using a slash as the separator). It can also be a contiguous range of addresses. This last case is included to support hierarchical encoding schemes for media streams where applications may require multiple multicast groups. For example, a connection description of

```
c=IN IP4 224.2.1.1/127/3
```

is identical to multiple "c" lines in a media description:

TABLE 8.5   Time Description Parameters

Symbol	Description	Format
t	Time the session is active	\<start time>\<stop time>
r	Zero or more repeat times	\<repeat interval>\<active duration> \<list of offsets from start-time>

TABLE 8.6   Media Description Parameters

Symbol	Description	Format
m	Media name and transport address	<media><port><transport><format list>
i	Media title	
c	Connection information	
b	Bandwidth information	
k	Encryption key	
a	Attribute lines (may be zero)	

```
c=IN IP4 224.2.1.1/127
c=IN IP4 224.2.1.2/127
c=IN IP4 224.2.1.3/127
```

Encryption keys can be obtained in a number of ways. The AV profile created for RTP in RFC 1890 includes provisions for encrypting the data stream with a key; this key can be distributed either in the clear or as a base64-encoded string. Alternatively, a URI can be provided that points the recipient to a Web server storing the key. Additional authentication may be required before the user can obtain the key from the server. Lastly, if the prompt option is selected, no key is included in the session description, but the user will be prompted to enter the key when he attempts to join the session.

A session announcement may contain a number of media announcements, starting with an "m" field; the media announcement is terminated either by another media announcement (another "m" field) or the end of the session announcement.

Only three transport protocols have thus far been defined. They are RTP/AVP, or RTP using the audio/video profile carried over UDP, VAT (the Video Audio Tool packet format) carried over UDP, and UDP alone.

Possible items that can be included in the attribute lines of session descriptions and media descriptions include: category, keywords, tool, packet time (length of time, in milliseconds, of media in packet), conference type (broadcast, meeting, moderated, test, H.332, etc.), character set, frame rate, and format specific parameters.

An example SDP description from the IETF Internet-Draft is:

```
v=0
o=mhandley 2890844526 2890842807 IN IP4 126.16.64.4
s=SDP Seminar
i=A Seminar on the session description protocol
u=http://www.cs.ucl.ac.uk/staff/M.Handley/sdp.03.ps
e=mjh@isi.edu (Mark Handley)
c=IN IP4 224.2.17.12/127
```

```
t=2873397496 2873404696
a=recvonly
m=audio 3456 RTP/AVP 0
m=video 2232 RTP/AVP 31
m=application 32416 udp wb
a=orient:portrait
```

In this example, AVP is the audio/video profile that's been defined for RTP sessions in RFC 1890. In the application item, wb is the whiteboard tool developed by Van Jacobson (see Chapter 10 for more details).

The Session Announcement Protocol (SAP)

Now that we've created a standard session description, we need a way to disseminate that description to prospective participants. As I mentioned in the previous section, this can be accomplished via the Web or e-mail. However, the designers of the session directory service have another possible method in mind, that of multicasting the session description to session directory applications that are listening to a particular multicast address. This approach makes dissemination of session information much easier than maintaining mailing lists or submitting the material to a webmaster. The distribution can be pretty much automatic, just as distribution of other multicast data is automatic (once a host group address is selected).

A SAP client that announces a conference session periodically multicasts an announcement packet to a well-known multicast address and port (224.2.127.254, UDP port 9875). The time period between repetitive announcements is dependent on the scope of the session and the number of other sessions currently being announced by other session directory instances.

Administrative Scoping of Announcements

For each administrative scope zone in force at a particular site, a session directory running at that site needs to know the following: the multicast address to be used for the announcement (normally the highest multicast address in the relevant scope zone), the UDP port to which announcements should be sent, the TTL announcements should be made with, the address range to be used for sessions in this scope zone, and the total bandwidth to be used by the session directory for session announcements in the administrative scope zone (the recommended default is 500 bps).

The announcement is multicast with the same scope as the session it is announcing; the scope is determined by the group address range or the TTL. This helps keep session announcements restricted to the locale in which the session is likely to take place. For instance, a departmental conference doesn't have to be announced to the entire corporation.

If different media in the announcement are given different TTLs, then multiple announcements are needed to ensure that anyone joining the conference can receive data for each media. Some may choose to receive only the audio data, for instance, and not the video. A TTL for video would likely be smaller than the TTL for an audio conference, so the smaller TTL wouldn't be used to announce the audio part of the conference.

The key properties of administratively scoped IP multicasts are that packets addressed to administratively scoped multicast addresses do not cross configured administrative boundaries and administratively scoped multicast addresses are locally assigned; they do not have to be unique across administrative boundaries. Administratively scoped multicast addresses are defined as the range 239.0.0.0 to 239.255.255.255. The address range 239.255.0.0/16 (in this shorthand notation,/16 is the TTL) is called the IPv4 Local Scope and can grow downward (i.e., from 239.255.0.0/16 into the reserved ranges 239.254.0.0/16 and 239.253.0.0/16). The range 239.192.0.0/14 is defined as the IPv4 Organization Local Scope and is the space from which an organization should allocate subranges when defining scopes for private use. Some of the other global scopes are given in Table 8.7.

In IPv6, the scope field determines the extent of the address, affecting the distribution of multicast messages through the internetwork's hierarchy. Although the group ID is independent of the scope field, the scope field still controls the distribution of the packet on the network. Using the previous examples, the IPv4 prefix of 239.254.0.0/16 corresponds to an IPv6 scope of 3, while 239.192.0.0/14 has an IPv6 scope of 8 and 224.0.1.0 to 238.255.255.255 has an IPv6 scope of 14.

TABLE 8.7 Some IPv4 Scopes

Address Range	Class
224.1.0.0 - 224.1.255.255	ST multicast groups
224.2.0.0 - 224.2.127.253	Multimedia conference calls
224.2.127.254	SAPv1 announcements
224.2.127.255	SAPv2 announcements
224.2.128.0 - 224.2.255.255	SAP dynamic assignments

Packet Contents

A session announcement contains a session description and an optional authentication header (Figure 8.6). The session description may be encrypted.

If the originator chooses to encrypt the session announcement, then the SAP packet includes a few additional fields, as shown in Figure 8.7. If the data packet is encrypted, the padding and random fields are encrypted as well as the text payload.

The following briefly describes the contents of each packet's field:

V. Version number=1

Message type. 0=announcement packet, 1=description deletion packet

E. Encryption bit; if set, means text payload is encrypted

C. Compressed bit; if set, payload is compressed using gzip

auth len. Authentication length (no. of 32-bit words)

auth hdr. Authentication header; digital signature of text payload

msg id hash. Message identifier hash; globally unique ID for this announcement

Originating source. IP address of original source of message

Key ID. 32-bit hint to identify which encryption key was used to encrypt packet

Timeout. Additional timestamp, used when payload is encrypted

P. Encryption padding

Random. Initialization vector for encryption algorithms like CBC DES

SAP can also be used to modify or delete session descriptions. A previously announced session can be modified simply by announcing the

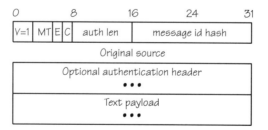

FIGURE 8.6   Unencrypted SAP data packet.

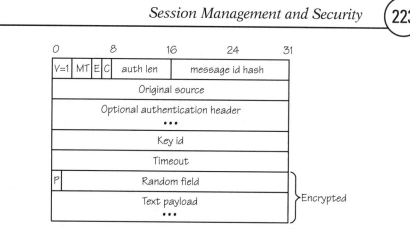

FIGURE 8.7   Encrypted SAP data packet.

modified session description. But in such cases, to prevent unauthorized modifications, it's been recommended that the modified announcement contain an authentication header that's signed by the same key as the original session announcement. An alternative approach is that neither the original announcement nor the modified announcement contains an authentication header, but both originate from the same host.

Sessions can be deleted in much the same way, by sending a SAP session deletion packet, with the verification procedures as used for session modification. Sessions can also be deleted via either explicit or implicit timeouts. In the first case, the session description includes timestamp information which specifies both a start and an end time for the session. In the second case, when no end time is explicitly included in the description, it's expected that a session announcement message will be received periodically. If this periodic message is not received within a certain time (30 minutes or 10 times the announcement period, whichever is greater), then the announcement will be deleted.

SAP not only includes mechanisms for ensuring the integrity of session announcements (using the msg id hash) and encrypting announcements, but it also supports authenticating the origin of an announcement. Session announcements can be encrypted with either a symmetric or an asymmetric algorithm.

If a session modification announcement is received that contains a valid authentication header but which is not signed by the original creator of the session, then the session must be treated as a new session. This is in addition to the original session, unless the originator of one of the session descriptions can be authenticated using a digital certificate that has been signed by a trusted third party.

The Session Initiation Protocol (SIP)

SDP and SAP can be used together to provide a general mechanism for announcing multicast sessions to potential participants; these announcements can either be restricted to a well-defined group (via TTLs and administrative scoping) or be disseminated across an entire internetwork. As a pair of protocols, they fulfill the need to post announcements of sessions either to directory applications or Web pages. But another protocol, SIP, is needed when a session is formed by issuing invitations to specific users.

SIP can be used for something as simple as contacting someone via an IP telephony application using unicast data or for more complex sessions like a multi-party multicast conference using video and a whiteboard application.

SIP can be used to reach both persons and robots; for example, it might be used to invite a media storage device to record an ongoing conference or to invite a video-on-demand server to play a video as part of a conference. SIP does not directly control these devices, however—that's left to protocols like RTSP. SIP can also invite participants to conferences with or without resource reservation. SIP itself does not reserve resources, but it may relay information to the invited system to enable the system to reserve the appropriate resources (using RSVP, for example).

Figure 8.8 presents a schematic example of how SIP can be used to invite a user to view the audio recording of a previously scheduled multi-

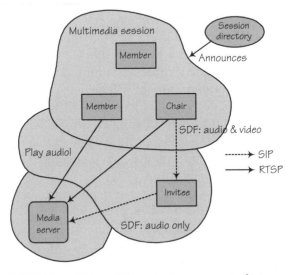

FIGURE 8.8 Using SIP to invite a user to listen to a recorded session.

media session. In this case, after the session was announced via the local session directory and started (the first cloud of users), the chair of the session uses SIP to invite another user to listen to the recording of the session that was placed on a media server via RTSP.

Once negotiation between the chair and the invitee is completed, the invitee, who is given parameters for the audio portion only, issues a SIP request to the media server to play the audio stream.

One basic assumption in SIP's design is that a location server at the user's home site either knows where the user resides, knows how to locate the user, or at least knows of another location server that can find the user. (SIP does not define how these servers get this information, however.) SIP also transparently supports name and redirection services, allowing the implementation of telephony services such as selective call forwarding, conditional and unconditional call forwarding, and so on.

SIP recognizes two types of location servers: the proxy server and the redirect server. A proxy server acts as both client and server for the user, accepting requests intended for one address and relaying them to the user's current (or preferred) address so that a proper connection can be initiated.

The protocol exchanges for the INVITE method are shown in Figure 8.9 for a proxy server. The proxy server accepts the INVITE request (step 1), contacts the location service with all or parts of the address (step 2), and obtains a more precise location (step 3). The server then issues a SIP INVITE request to the address returned by the location service (step 4). It then returns the success result to the original caller (step 6). All requests have the same call-ID.

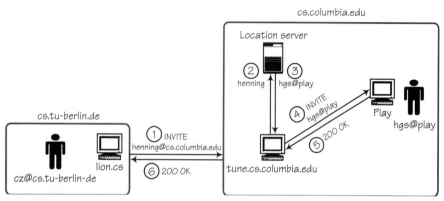

FIGURE 8.9 Reaching a caller via a SIP proxy server.

Another type of server, the redirect server, does not forward invitations to the intended recipient; instead it furnishes information back to the caller as to other locations where the recipient can be reached. Just as with the proxy server in Figure 8.9's example, a redirect server accepts the INVITE request and contacts the location service as before; but, instead of contacting the newly found address itself, returns the address to the caller. The caller would issue a new request, with a new call-ID, to the address returned by the first server.

SIP can use either UDP or TCP as a transport protocol. UDP has performance advantages over TCP, but TCP clients are easier to implement (no retransmission timing code needs to be written, for example). Also, using TCP allows SIP server functionality to be added to HTTP servers with very little extra code. (A number of SIP's commands are taken directly from the HTTP command set.) Proxy servers can be designed with the capability to serve as UDP-UDP or UDP-TCP proxy servers to handle conversions between the traffic types, such as required by a firewall.

All SIP messages are text-based and use HTTP v1.1 conventions, except for the additional ability of SIP to use UDP. When sent over TCP or UDP, multiple SIP transactions can be carried in a single TCP connection or UDP datagram. Within a SIP message, URLs are used to indicate the source and intended destination of a request, redirection addresses, and the current destination of a request. Normally, all these fields will contain SIP URLs. When additional parameters are not required, the short form SIP URL can be used unambiguously. A SIP URL may also be embedded in Web pages or other hyperlinks to indicate that a user or service may be called. Much of the message syntax is identical to HTTP version 1.1.

Conference or call setup is a multistep procedure. In the first step, the requesting client tries to ascertain the address where it should contact the remote user agent or user agent proxy. If the address is not location-specific, the requesting client would use DNS to look up the domain part of the user address. As long as the user address of the invitee is found, subsequent steps of the call setup follow a request-response protocol. For example, an SDP session description would be transmitted to the invitee and the user agent or conference server would reply either that the request was successful or unsuccessful, might send a progress report, or note that further action is required. The defined SIP requests are shown in Table 8.8.

A successful SIP invitation consists of two requests, INVITE followed by CONNECTED. The INVITE request asks the callee to join a particular conference or establish a two-party conversation. After the callee has agreed to participate in the call, the caller confirms that it has received that agreement by sending a CONNECTED request. If the call is rejected

TABLE 8.8 SIP Requests

Message Type	Contents, Usage
INVITE	Indicates that the user or service is being invited to participate in the session. The message body contains a description of the session the callee is being invited to.
CONNECTED	Confirms that the client has received a successful response to an INVITE request.
BYE	Used to abort the call attempt.
REGISTER	Informs a SIP server of the address (a Request-URI) for a user or service.
UN-REGISTER	Cancels an existing registration established for the Request-URI identifying a user or service.

or otherwise unsuccessful, the caller does not send a CONNECTED request.

The INVITE request typically contains a session description (which might be written in SDP format) that provides the called party with enough information to join the session. For two-party calls, the request contains a session description detailing the media types and formats that the caller is willing to receive, and where it wishes the media data to be sent. If the caller wishes to accept the call, it responds to the invitation by returning a similar description listing the media that the callee wishes to receive. The latter listing must be a subset of the description in the invitation. When a call is set up in this fashion, the session description doesn't have to refer to an immediate connection, but may refer to some time in the future; actual transmission of data does not start until the time indicated in the session description.

After receiving and interpreting a request message, the recipient responds with a SIP response message. The status codes used in these responses are given in Table 8.9. The first digit of the status code defines

TABLE 8.9 SIP Status Codes

Code	Name	Meaning
1xx	Informational	Request received, continuing process.
2xx	Success	The action was successfully received, understood, and accepted.
3xx	Redirection	Further action must be taken in order to complete the request.
4xx	Client Error	The request contains bad syntax or cannot be fulfilled at this server.
5xx	Server Error	The server failed to fulfill an apparently valid request.
6xx:	Global Failure	The request is invalid at any server.

the class of response; the last two digits do not have any role in categorizing the response.

A sample Invite request might look like the following:

```
C->S: INVITE schooler@vlsi.cs.caltech.edu SIP/2.0
Via: SIP/2.0/UDP 239.128.16.254 16
Via: SIP/2.0/UDP 131.215.131.131
Via: SIP/2.0/UDP 128.16.64.19
From: mjh@isi.edu (Mark Handley)
Subject: SIP will be discussed, too
To: schooler@cs.caltech.edu (Eve Schooler)
Call-ID: 62729-27@oregon.isi.edu
Content-type: application/sdp
Content-Length: 187


v=0
o=user1 53655765 2353687637 IN IP4 128.3.4.5
s=Mbone Audio
i=Discussion of Mbone Engineering Issues
e=mbone@somewhere.com
c=IN IP4 224.2.0.1/127
t=0 0
m=audio 3456 RTP/AVP 0
```

In this example, the Via fields list the hosts along the path from invitation initiator (the first element of the list) towards the invitee. In the example, the message was last multicast to the administratively scoped group 239.128.16.254 with a TTL of 16 from the host 131.215.131.131. The request header states that the request was initiated by mjh@isi.edu. The Via header indicates that this was initiated from the host 128.16.64.19. schooler@cs.caltech.edu is being invited; the message is currently being routed to schooler@vlsi.cs.caltech.edu. In this case, the session description is using the Session Description Protocol (SDP), as stated in the Content-type header. The header is terminated by an empty line and is followed by a message body containing the session description.

A sample Redirect request could look like this:

```
S->C: SIP/2.0 302 Moved temporarily
Via: SIP/2.0/UDP 131.215.131.131
Via: SIP/2.0/UDP 128.16.64.19
From: mjh@isi.edu
To: schooler@cs.caltech.edu
Call-ID: 62729-27@128.16.64.19
Location: sip://239.128.16.254;ttl=16;transport=udp
Content-length: 0
```

In this example, the proxy located at 131.215.131.131 is being advised to contact the multicast group 239.128.16.254 with a TTL of 16 and UDP transport. In normal situations, a server would not suggest a redirect to a local multicast group unless, as in the previous situation, it knows that the previous proxy or client is within the scope of the local group.

A sample Negotiate reply (with a "606 Not Acceptable" reply) would look like this:

```
S->C: SIP/2.0 606 Not Acceptable
From: mjh@isi.edu
To: schooler@cs.caltech.edu
Call-ID:62729-27@128.16.64.19
Location: mjh@131.215.131.131
Warning: 606.1 Insufficient bandwidth (only have ISDN),
606.3 Incompatible format,
606.4 Multicast not available
Content-Type: application/sdp
Content-Length: 50
v=0
s=Lets talk
b=CT:128
c=IN IP4 131.215.131.131
m=audio 3456 RTP/AVP 5 0 7
m=video 2232 RTP/AVP 31
```

In this example, the original request specified 256 Kbps total bandwidth; the reply states that only 128 Kbps is available. The original request specified GSM audio, H.261 video, and the wb whiteboard tool. The audio coding and whiteboard are not available, but the reply states that DVI, PCM, or LPC audio could be supported in that order of preference (payload types are DVI = 5, PCM = 0, and LPC = 7 as specified in RFC 1890). The reply also states that multicast is not available. In such a case, it might be appropriate to set up a gateway and re-invite the user.

Conference Control

As I mentioned earlier, network-wide session management can be applied to a number of multicast sessions, but another form of management, conference control, is often needed to control discussions and interactions among individuals forming a group. This is especially necessary considering the dynamic and widespread nature of the Internet—without a means for selecting the next speaker or polling participants, most any conference would quickly become chaotic.

The tasks that comprise conference control can be classified as follows:

Application control. Applications need to be started with the correct initial state, and the knowledge of their existence must be propagated across all participating sites. Control over the starting and stopping can either be local or remote.

Membership control. Who is currently in the conference and has access to what applications.

Floor management. Who or what has control over the input to particular applications.

Network management. Requests to set up and tear down media connections between end-points, and requests from the network to change bandwidth usage because of congestion.

When it comes to controlling conference participation on a network, there are basically two models for conference control—lightweight sessions and tightly coupled conferencing.

Lightweight sessions are multicast-based multimedia conferences that lack explicit session membership and explicit conference control mechanisms. Typically a lightweight session consists of a number of many-to-many media streams using RTP and RTCP over IP multicast. The only conference control information available during the course of lightweight sessions is that distributed in the RTCP session information (i.e., an approximate membership list with some attributes per member; see Chapter 6).

Tightly coupled conferences may also be multicast-based and use RTP and RTCP. In addition, they have an explicit conference membership mechanism and may have an explicit conference control mechanism that provides facilities such as floor control.

The International Telecommunications Union has devised a sophisticated system for controlling tightly coupled conferences based around its H.261 video codec systems and ISDN networks, incorporating the T.120 protocols, using Multipoint Control Units (MCUs) and a Multicast Communication Service, that depends a great deal on the reliable and constant bit rate nature of ISDN.

No standard mechanism for performing tightly coupled conference control currently exists in the Internet community, although a protocol called the Simple Conference Control Protocol (SCCP) has been proposed. The SCCP is designed for tightly coupled conferences with a designated moderator who must give permission for new members to join. In addition to floor control, the protocol addresses media management, management of the set of members, and assignment of a special moderator role to one participant. The protocol assumes consistent state between participants but does not address the issue of how this state is kept consistent when running over unreliable transport protocols like IP and UDP. It assumes that the underlying multicast transport provides reliable consistent delivery of data with globally ordered messages.

On the other hand, the IETF has devised a more loosely coupled framework based around the use of IP multicast which can be used for control of local systems as well as wide-area multicast sessions. Loosely coupled conferences put less constraints on the protocols used, but must scale to much larger numbers and be very tolerant of loss and network segmentation. Within this framework, a system like the Conference Control Channel Protocol (CCCP) can be used to build various types of control applications such as floor management, coupling control of the media applications with the control applications (see Figure 8.10). This is usually claimed to scale to large numbers of participants better than the MCU-based approaches.

The main idea behind CCCP is to provide a control mechanism that's independent of the applications and services involved. This approach allows the same media tools and same conference control mechanism to

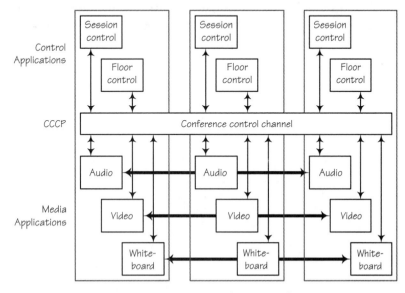

FIGURE 8.10 A conceptualization of CCCP.

be used for both tightly and loosely coupled conferences, while allowing conference control policy to change as needed.

Summary

Either symmetric or asymmetric cryptographic methods can be used to encrypt data, but both depend on proper distribution of the keys involved. In a multicasting session, this can prove to be a rather complex undertaking—no method has yet proven to be satisfactory for all situations.

For session management, users need a better way to learn of available multicast sessions than what was first available on the MBone. The combination of the Session Description Protocol (SDP) and the Session Announcement Protocol (SAP) offers a standardized way of describing sessions and their media requirements, as well as the dissemination of this information to prospective participants.

Coupling the Session Initiation Protocol (SIP) with SDP provides a different means of session management by allowing session originators to invite participants to private conferences.

Once multicast conferences are started, some means of controlling speakers, polling participants, and negotiating media is needed to keep conferences from becoming chaotic and unproductive. Various protocols are being worked on, with most leaning towards a lightweight session (or loosely coupled) model that seems to scale well and fit the usual Internet-distributed framework.

9

Application Software

Wide-area multicasting as pioneered on the MBone has long followed the traditional Internet philosophy—the free development and sharing of tools for use of the Internet. Many of the applications developed for multicasting fit in this category (i.e., they've been freely distributed for use on the MBone). Some fall in the "for research use only, use at your own risk" category. But the recognition that IP multicasting is becoming more important for efficient use of intranets and the Internet, coupled with the desire to transmit more multimedia traffic on the Internet, has led to an increasing number of commercial applications becoming available as well.

In 1997, the IP Multicasting Initiative surveyed over 100 users of IP Multicast technology. Within that group, the most frequently cited use of multicasting (more than 60 percent) was for audio and video distribution (or webcasting, as some call it). About 40 percent of the respondents used multicasting for collaboration and conferencing, while about 30 percent used the technology for delivering information (push technologies) on their networks. Much of this multicast traffic has been limited to corporate intranets rather than over the Internet. That's highly likely to continue over the next few years for three reasons: (1) Businesses depend greatly on internal distribution of information to function; (2) intranets allow corporations better control of their net traffic; and (3) ISPs have only lately begun to create the infrastructure to routinely support multicasting on the Internet. (See Chapter 10 for more details on this last point.)

When it comes to classifying the various multicasting applications, it's difficult to define unique classes that don't overlap. Many applications have more than one capability or purpose, so they can cross over the lines between application classes. For the purpose of this book, I've decided to classify the multicasting applications in the following categories—Multimedia Distribution, Conferencing Applications, Collaborative Applications, Information Distribution (including push technologies), Announcement Tools, and Diagnostic Tools. The following sections are not an exhaustive list of all tools that are currently available for multicasting; we'll take a look at the more important ones, and only list some of the lesser tools. (In each section, I'll be discussing the commercial products first, followed by the freeware or shareware applications.)

As has been common with many of the past developments concerning Internet applications, you'll find that many of the available multicast tools are designed for use on the Unix operating system only. More applications for MS Windows are becoming available, especially among the commercial apps, with a few available for use on the Macintosh.

Multimedia Distribution

This category of software focuses on the delivery of multimedia data over multicast networks. That data might be either a single stream of data, such as a video or audio stream, or a synchronized set of streams. Table 9.1 lists the applications that fall into this category.

The distribution of multimedia information has a wide variety of uses. First, there's basic business communication needs such as broadcasting the latest stockholders' meeting or the CEO's speech to employees. Previous video and audio recordings can also be stored and retransmitted to departments as needed. Distance learning, or training, is another application—there are multicasting programs that provide the means for users to interact with the speaker and distribute more than one type of related media at the same time (lecture slides plus the

TABLE 9.1 Applications for Multimedia Distribution

Application	Developer	Media	Platforms	Source
IP/TV	Precept Software Inc.	video, audio	Windows95, Windows NT	www.precept.com
NetShow	Microsoft Corp.	video, audio	Windows95, Windows NT, Unix, Mac	www.microsoft.com/netshow
StarCast	Starlight Networks	video	Windows	www.starcast.com
RealAudio	RealNetworks	audio	Windows95, Windows NT, Mac (Unix)	www.real.com
RealVideo	RealNetworks	video	Windows95, Windows NT, Mac	www.real.com
VCR, MVoD	University of Mannheim	video	Unix	
mMOD	Lulea University of Technology	video	Windows95, Windows NT 4.0, Unix	mates.cdt.luth.se/software/mMOD
ICAST	ICAST Corp.	video, audio	Windows95, Windows 4.0	www.icast.com
imm	University of Hawaii	video	Unix	mice.ed.ac.uk/mice/archive/imm.html

instructor's video, for example). If more feedback is required, though, collaborative applications, which we'll cover in another category in this chapter, might be better tools in such situations. Much of the use of streaming media on the Internet has been driven by entertainment uses, such as transmitting broadcasts of music, sports events, live concerts, and so on.

Codecs

It would be nice if there was only one standard for representing audio and video data, but there isn't. Many different ways of compressing multimedia data have been designed, either to handle different types of losses during transmission or for the bandwidths of various transmission media (modems vs. ISDN vs. satellites vs. LANS, for example). Codec is a short term for encoder-decoder, the hardware or software that takes a specific media type and uses digital algorithms to reduce its size. Occasionally, you'll see me use the term transcoding; it's related to codecs because transcoding involves translating from one codec to another, usually on-the-fly.

IP/TV

IP/TV is a commercial product developed and sold by Precept Software Inc. and also offered by Cisco. It's designed to deliver TV-quality full-motion video to desktop PCs running Windows95 or Windows NT. The IP/TV system consists of three components—IP/TV Program Guide, IP/TV Server, and the IP/TV Viewer.

The Program Guide is used for controlling the video programs you've created for distribution. With the Program Guide, you can schedule video programs and include repeat capabilities for multiple program start times. Each program includes the program name, start time, repeat showing time, encoding scheme, bandwidth or frame rate limits and frame size, password (optional), and a brief description of the content.

The IP/TV Viewer is used for both checking scheduled video programs and viewing a video. The listing window (Figure 9.1) displays information about each channel or program that's available within a given period (week or month, for example). A pop-up menu can be used to display more details on a selected program (Figure 9.2).

IP/TV also includes a feature called SlideCast that's good for distance learning, training, and other presentations that use graphics or slides. The SlideCast feature enables a program viewer to simultaneously view presenters giving their presentations as well as view any PC-based demonstration materials, such as viewgraphs. The IP/TV server can capture both the pre-

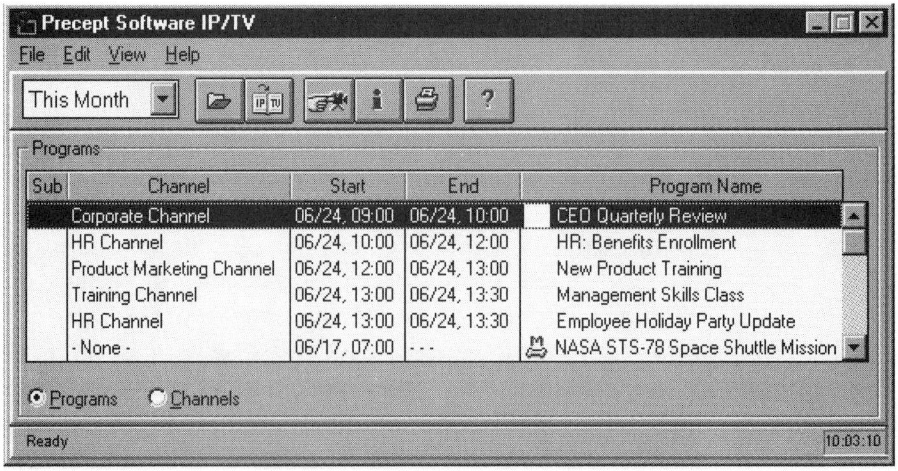

FIGURE 9.1 Channel listing window.

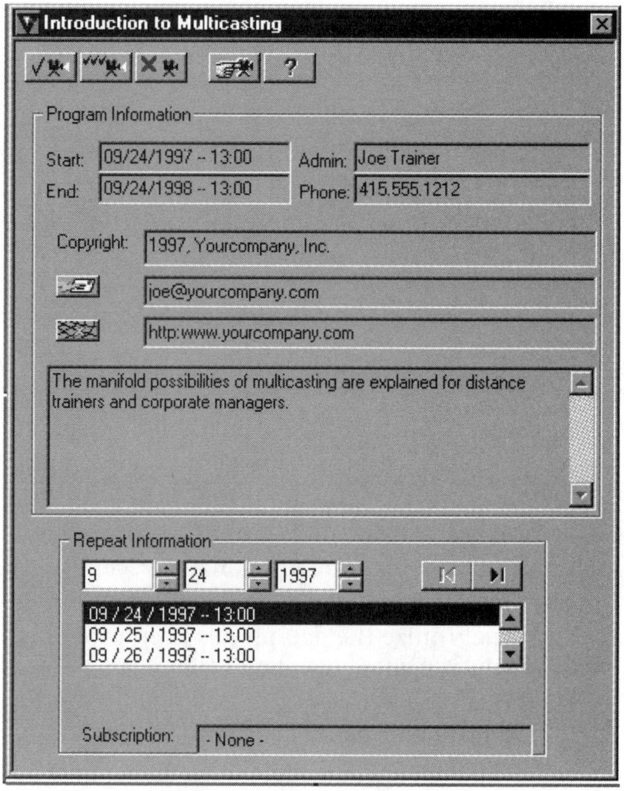

FIGURE 9.2 Program pop-up.

senter being videotaped and the slides or overheads from the associated presentation. When a presenter wants to illustrate a key point using a slide, the IP/TV server takes the actual slide (from **MS** PowerPoint, for example) and displays it directly on the user's screen. SlideCast can also be used in automated mode with audio only if there is insufficient bandwidth for a video transmission.

Another IP/TV feature that's useful for distance learning and training as well as interactive conferences is the Question Manager, which enables viewers to submit questions to speakers via the Viewer. Questions are typed into a Viewer window; the software allows the presenter, or a moderator, to receive and sort the questions by time received or subject, for instance.

The IP/TV Server can be used with any Windows-compatible video hardware or software codec. It enables playback of video for Windows format files, such as AVI or MPEG files. The standard codec included with the server for video compression is an H.261 codec; IP/TV also works with several hardware compression/expansion boards.

With version 1.6, IP/TV has also added the SmallCast feature, which extends the reach of video programs to WANs that have not upgraded to IP Multicast. SmallCast sends multicast content inside unicast packets for tunneled transmission over private WANs, much like tunnels are used to create the MBone. A remote server then multicast-enables the content for local distribution over the LAN.

NetShow

NetShow is Microsoft's application for distributing streaming media, either in unicast or multicast situations. NetShow uses a special format, the Advanced Streaming Format (ASF), for describing streaming files before they're transmitted over the network; all content has to be converted to ASF for transmission and reception via NetShow. ASF is a set of rules for content creation and identification, describing how to organize and synchronize the data; it has been proposed to the IETF as a profile for use with RTP. Microsoft includes tools for creating ASF files as part of the NetShow server package.

Like IP/TV, Netshow uses the concept of a channel to establish communications between a NetShow server and the multicast clients (Figure 9.3). When users connect to a NetShow channel via the NetShow player or a Web page in which the feed is embedded, they will receive whatever is being played at that time. A channel can be populated with programs, much like television. Programs can be live feeds or played from a tape at a specific time.

The NetShow player allows users to play audio, illustrated audio (synchronized sound and still images), and full-motion video files. The NetShow player on Windows is an ActiveX control with a helper application that embeds the ActiveX control in it.

The NetShow server is designed to run on Windows NT 4.0 and above, and can deliver both live and on-demand content. A NetShow Real-Time Encoder is included with the server for delivering live content. On-demand content has to be stored on the server's hard drive. A number of codecs are supported.

User control of received data differs in the unicast and multicast cases. NetShow doesn't accept feedback from users while multicasting a program. But if you use NetShow to unicast a program to users, they're able to pause the program or skip forwards and backwards in the stream.

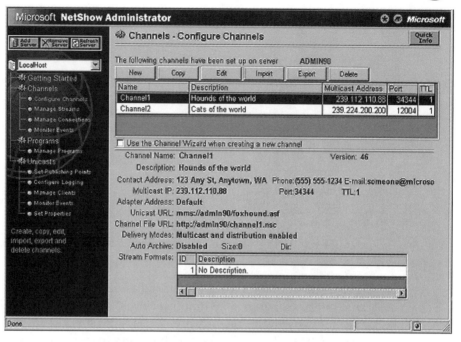

FIGURE 9.3   NetShow channel configuration.

StarCast

StarCast, from Starlight Networks, is not only designed to use IP multicasting, but is also aimed at working well over satellite networks, supporting real-time transmission of full-screen, 30 frames-per-second MPEG-1 video.

StarCast uses a bandwidth reservation protocol to prevent contention between streaming and bursty data traffic. When a new video sequence is to be transmitted, the protocol checks to see that the server is not overloaded and can handle another stream. Then, the protocol checks the total video traffic on the network segment that's directly attached to the server, guaranteeing that some bandwidth remains for use by bursty data services. The protocol will deny the stream's access to the network if either the server or the local network segment is in danger of becoming overloaded. Traffic shaping is also used to limit the video transfer rate and help guard against packet loss.

StarCast consists of three components—the Multicaster, the Recaster, and the Viewer. The StarCast Multicaster is the interface for directly capturing video and/or audio information and multicasting it on an intranet, or multicasting previously recorded video. The Recaster takes digital media from a satellite communications system and multicasts the content

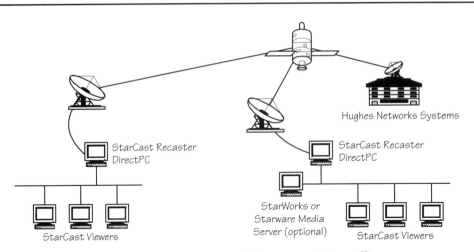

FIGURE 9.4 Using StarCast Recaster with the DirectPC satellite system.

across an intranet. Lastly, the StarCast Viewer is the PC client that displays the multicast media data that it receives, in conjunction with MPEG decoding hardware or software. The system supports MPEG-1 video as well as Intel's Indeo format and browsers from both Netscape and Microsoft. Future support for RSVP and RTP is planned.

As I mentioned earlier, StarCast has aimed much of its effort at satellite transmissions. To help smooth the transition of using IP multicasting with satellite networks, StarCast has allied with Hughes Network Systems (HNS) to combine multicasting with DirectPC links (see Figure 9.4). In this case, the StarCast Recaster serves as the interface between the satellite system and the corporate intranets. Feeds from the HNS DirectPC satellite service can either be directly multicast to an intranet or stored on a StarCast server for later playback.

RealAudio and RealVideo

RealAudio and RealVideo have become one of the more popular multimedia clients distributed on the Internet; according to RealNetworks, Inc., more than one million copies have been downloaded by users. Both are designed to deliver streaming media over the Internet to PC clients and can be used either in unicast or multicast modes. Players are available for all major platforms (i.e., Windows, Mac, and UNIX and can be used with Netscape and Microsoft browsers as well as ActiveX and Java).

The first client developed by RealNetworks was RealAudio, designed for streaming audio only; RealVideo came later to handle streaming video.

Since then, RealNetworks has been working to integrate all of its streaming work into a single framework called RealMedia that supports many different data types, including text, audio, animation, video, 2D and 3D images, MIDI, and other presentations. RealMedia uses different plug-ins on both the server and the client to handle a wide variety of data types.

RealMedia servers run on Windows NT and UNIX systems, and clients receive data via RTSP. Another protocol, RTSL, or Real Time Session Language, has been proposed to define relations between streaming data and synchronize playback of multiple data types, much like the ASF specification that Microsoft's defined.

VCR and MVoD

A VCR-like application for use on the MBone has been designed and developed by Wieland Holfelder at the University of Mannheim, Germany. This application uses a VCR interface to control recording and playback of sessions sent over the MBone. VCR stores these sessions by synchronizing different media streams based on information provided by RTP. It also allows indexing and random access within recorded sessions. A command language enables limited programming features (e.g., to schedule recordings or playbacks at a later point of time).

One limitation to the VCR tool is that it was designed as a single-user application and cannot be accessed from remote sites. The successor to the VCR project is the MBone VCR on Demand (MVoD) service which offers interactive remote recording and playback of multicast videoconferences (see Figure 9.5). The MVoD server includes an interface to SAP to learn about ongoing MBone sessions. Users running the MVoD client can then choose to play back the recorded session at their convenience via either multicast or unicast.

Timestamps in the RTP and RTCP packets allow the MVoD service to perform intermedia (e.g., two audio streams) and intra-media (e.g., an audio and a related video stream) synchronization without needing to know the actual payload of the RTP data packets.

mMOD

The multicast Media-on-Demand, or mMOD, system developed at Lulea University of Technology in Sweden, is similar to VCR and MVoD. MMOD consists of two programs; the VCR and the Web controller.

The VCR program is a standalone program for recording IP packets either at the UDP level or the RTP level. If the packets are recorded at the

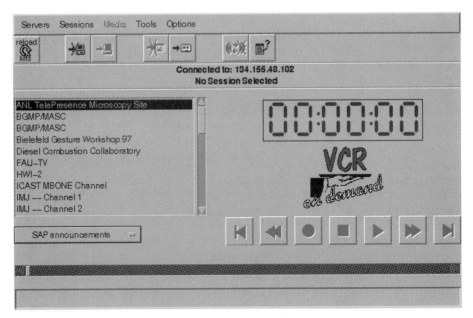

FIGURE 9.5   Sample MVoD client screen.

UDP level, they are stored without parsing or rearrangement. The program is designed to store data when an unknown format is transmitted. Recording at the RTP level means that the VCR program parses the RTP header of each incoming packet and checks for duplicates and out-of-order packets. Playback using UDP-recorded packets includes any duplicate or lost packets while RTP playback will try to reorder the packets and send them in the order based on their original timestamps (or the sequence number in the RTP header).

The Web controller program that acts as the interface to the mMOD system uses a Web browser. Available sessions are listed on an HTML page; information about known sessions is retrieved either from the sdr cache or mSD, a tool for viewing session directories with a Web browser. When a user selects a session for playback, an HTML form is used to determine the playing parameters (such as destination and unicast/multicast).

Other Tools

The commercial ICAST system consists of three parts—the Broadcaster, the Viewer and the Guide—that can be used to multicast audio, video, and text streams. The Guide is a real-time directory of all available programs. A standalone Viewer is available to display multimedia programs, while plug-in Viewers can accomplish the same task within either Netscape or Microsoft Web browsers. The Broadcaster application is the control application, used for scheduling and broadcast of the programs, selection of an encoding standard, frame rate, and bandwidth.

Imm, or Image Multicaster Client, is a client program which receives multicasted images and is designed to reassemble images multicasted as UDP packets from the server program called *immserv*.

Conferencing Applications

While it may seem more logical to lump together conferencing applications with groupware applications that often include videoconferencing as part of their feature set, I've chosen to separate the two classes since many collaborative apps often have a different design goal (i.e., to share workspaces and exchange data other than real-time multimedia). The conferencing applications listed in Table 9.2 include only those apps that focus either on providing real-time multimedia links (either audio or video, or both) between group participants or on the control of conferences. Others are included in the next section on collaborative applications.

Two of the most popular video tools for use on the MBone are Network Video, *nv*, by Ron Frederick of Xerox PARC, and the INRIA videoconferencing system (*ivs*) by Theirry Thurletto of INRIA in Sophia Antipolis, France.

The Xerox PARC Network Video tool, *nv*, is a video-only application that uses a custom coding technique designed specifically for the Internet, allowing it to run faster than an H.261 codec. In most respects, nv has been obsoleted by vic, except that nv can send video of the user's screen, whereas vic can only send video from an external device (e.g., a video cam-

---

Conferencing Standards

The H.323 conferencing standard developed by the International Telecommunication Union has become an important step in making desktop conferencing easier and more interoperable. Previous ITU conferencing standards like H.320 dealt with specific media like Basic Rate ISDN, but H.323 is aimed largely at packet networks. H.323 uses UDP for handling audio and video media, and TCP for handling data. Conferences rely on RTP to keep the audio and video streams synchronized.

TABLE 9.2   Conferencing Applications

Application	Developer	Platforms	Source
Conferencing			
nv	Xerox PARC	Unix	mice.ed.ac.uk/mice/archive/nv.html
ivs	T. Thurletto, INRIA	Unix	zenon.inria.fr/rodeo/ivs/
Rendez-Vous	INRIA	Unix	zenon.inria.fr/rodeo/rv/
vat	Lawrence Berkeley Labs	Unix	mice.ed.ac.uk/mice/archive/vat.html
NeVoT	H. Schulzrinne	Unix	www.fokus.gmd.de/step/nevot/
FreePhone	INRIA	Unix	www.inria.fr/rodeo/fphone/
vic	Lawrence Berkeley Labs	Unix	www-nrg.ee.lbl.gov/vic/
NVAT	NEC Corp.	Windows95, Windows 4.0	www1.meshnet.or.jp/~mms-eizo/nvat/index-e.html
Rat	University College, London	Unix	www.cs.ucl.ac.uk/staff/vhardman/rat_project/
Conference Control			
confman	University of Hannover, Germany	Unix	www.rvs.uni-hannover.de/products/confman/
confcntlr	Lawrence Berkeley Labs	Unix	www-itg.lbl.gov/mbone/confcntlr/
TelePort	LUTCHI Research Centre	Unix	pipkin.lut.ac.uk/~ben/PHD_Public/teleport.html

era). The INRIA Video Conferencing System, ivs, relies exclusively on H.261 for video compression, which allows it to work with the large installed base of H.320 video codecs. Ivs includes PCM and ADPCM audio codecs as well as an H.261 codec for compression, making it easier to participate in videoconferences with minimum hardware (a video camera and frame grabber, for instance).

Rendez-Vous is being developed as a follow-on product to ivs; it is an experimental tool that uses RTP to transmit video via either unicast or multicast. It supports MPEG-1 and -2 reading and transcoding; the H.261 video standard is used for transmission, making it compatible with vic. The system includes dynamic video and audio rate control to match the available bandwidth. One of its design goals was to support testing of layered coding and transmission of video and audio flows, the use of Forward Error Correction for video and audio, and use over both wireless and satellite links.

Another audio conferencing tool is the visual audio tool, or *vat*, written by Steve McCanne and Van Jacobsen of Lawrence Berkeley Laboratory.

The vat user interface displays the names of all conference participants, highlighting the name of the current speaker. Vat supports GSM, PCM, LPC4, and IDVI audio standards.

Another audio tool is network voice terminal, *NeVoT,* by Henning Schulzrinne of Columbia University. The tool runs over RTP and supports DES-based voice encryption as well as the recording and playback of .au and AIF/AIFC format audio files. NeVoT can also be configured for use with the vat audio packet format, making it interoperable with vat sessions.

FreePhone is an audio conferencing tool that can be used to manage both multiple unicast and multicast sessions. It supports RTPv2 and includes a redundancy mechanism to packet reconstruction that provides improved audio quality when the packet loss rate is high. Since FreePhone supports RTPv2, it's compatible with rat and vat. (An RTPv2-compatible version of NeVoT is due out, which will also make the two applications compatible with each other.) A screen shot showing a sample FreePhone session is shown in Figure 9.6. Many of the audio conferencing tools discussed in this section have similar graphical interfaces.

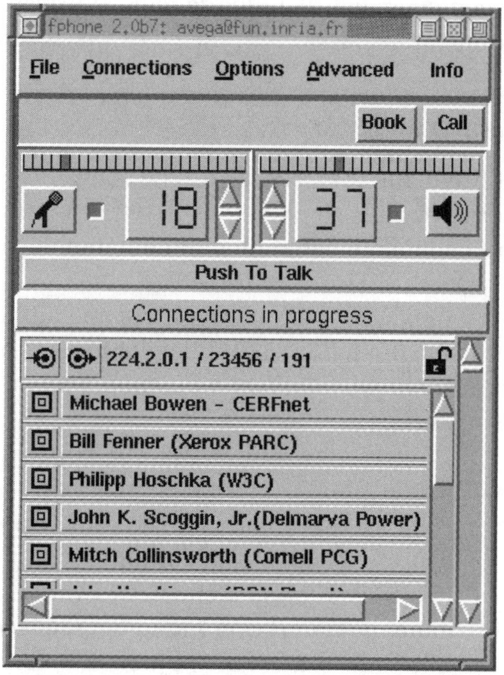

FIGURE 9.6 Example FreePhone session window.

Vic is a video conferencing tool written at Lawrence Berkeley Labs. The LBL approach has been to create a modular set of tools for handling MBone sessions, so vic handles video, while other tools handle other data types—vat for audio, wb for whiteboard, and sd for session directories. Vic uses RTP for media communications and includes a "robust H.261" video encoder and voice-activated video switching; the encoder combines nv's robustness to losses with the higher compression gain and codec compatibility of H.261. In voice-activated switching, a viewing window can be configured to follow the speaker, (i.e., it uses cues from *vat* to switch the viewing window to whichever source is speaking).

NVAT (Network Video Audio Tool) is another teleconferencing tool that supports multicast; in this case, the tool is designed for use with Windows95 and Windows NT. It uses the Video for Windows API for video capture and ACM for audio, simplifying compatibility with hardware that comes with the appropriate drivers. The current version supports RTPv1, but a future version with support for RTPv2 is planned.

Rat, or the Robust Audio Tool, is yet another multicasting tool for audio conferences. Developed at the University College in London, it uses techniques such as redundancy and waveform substitution to achieve robust transmissions in the face of packet losses.

Conference Control Tools

Since many conferences can be composed of related media and require a series of tools, applications have been written to control all of the tools needed for a given multicast conference. These include *Confman, Confcntlr, mmcc,* and *TelePort.*

Confman is a tool to initiate and administer online conferences using *vat, vic, nv,* and/or *wb*. While planning a conference, Confman lets you choose the partners, the start time, and the MBone tools to be used in the conference (see Figure 9.7).

Confman recognizes two different conference types—closed and multicast. Closed conferences are those between two or more participants using unicast distribution of the data. Multicast mode conferences are self-explanatory; if access to the multicast conference has to be restricted, the only choice is to encrypt the data. In such cases, Confman can be used to distribute the encryption key to the selected participants.

Confcntlr is another multicasting tool developed at Lawrence Berkeley Labs. This one is intended to allow easier access to, and control of, video conferencing. Confcntrl was developed for use with vic and vat,

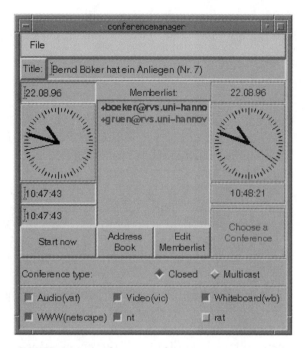

FIGURE 9.7   Confman conference manager tool.

and offers a graphical user interface to set controls for audio and video signals as well as starting and stopping conferences.

TelePort is a tool designed to control vic, vat, and wb while offering users some awareness of what the other members of a conference are doing. Using a *door/office* metaphor, TelePort lets users know how busy workgroup members are, whether they can be interrupted, who they are talking with, and whether they're available for collaboration. In contrast to mmcc, which resides on a well-known multicast address and acts as a global call manager, TelePort can reside on any multicast address. TelePort sessions can be announced using sdr.

Collaborative Applications

Rather than focus on the delivery of multimedia data to a number of clients, collaborative software concentrates on coordinating interactions between members of a group. Many of these applications use a whiteboard metaphor, where group members can share drawings or other images, or post comments on a displayed file (a drawing or word processor file, for example). The collaborative applications are listed in Table 9.3.

CU-SeeMe

Cu-SeeMe started out as a videoconferencing application, but has since added other functions. Cu-SeeMe includes a PhoneBook interface for keeping track of correspondents (i.e., conference members) and offers both whiteboard and chat functions for multiuser collaboration. It supports H.323 standards for videoconferencing, including H.263 for a video codec and T.120 for the whiteboard, which supports text and graphics. Both ActiveMovie and Video for Windows are supported, as is the Motion JPEG (M-JPEG) video codec (for use over ISDN and LAN connections).

Up to 12 participant windows can be viewed at the same time (see Figure 9.8). Connections can be made either via unicast or multicast technologies.

MeetingPoint is another conferencing product from White Pine, designed to support CU-SeeMe. Meeting Point is the server component of its client/server videoconferencing system. Although it's designed to offer a central meeting point for conferences using either unicast or multicast, it can also use IP multicasting to transfer traffic between MeetingPoint servers in order to reduce the bandwidth requirements. MeetingPoint is the successor to White Pine's Reflector software.

TABLE 9.3   Collaborative Applications

Application	Developer	Platforms	Source
CU-SeeMe	White Pine Software Inc.	Windows95, Windows NT, Mac	www.cuseeme.com
mStar	Lulea University of Technology	Windows95, Windows NT, Unix	mates.cdt.luth.se/software/
TeleDraw	University of Stuttgart, Germany	Unix, Windows95, Windows NT, Mac	WWW.Uni-Stuttgart.De/RUS/Projects/ MERCI/MERCI/TeleDraw/Info.html
wb	Lawrence Berkeley Labs	Unix	ftp://ftp.ee.lbl.gov/conferencing/wb/
nt	University College, London	Unix	mice.ed.ac.uk/mice/archive/nt.html

FIGURE 9.8 Sample CU-SeeMe screen.

NOTE A reflector is conference server software that delivers multimedia group interactions across IP networks. A conference server is the server program in a client/server videoconferencing solution. Reflectors can be set up to provide multiple conferences on the same system and some may serve as gateways between unicast/broadcast traffic and multicast traffic.

mStar

I mentioned earlier the *mMOD* system developed at the Lulea University of Technology for playing recording video sessions on demand. That same group has developed the *mStar* environment for distributed teamwork over multicast networks. The mStar system includes: *mWB,* a multicast whiteboard tool; *mChat,* a text-based group chat program; *mVote,* a distributed voting tool; and *mWeb,* a program for sharing WWW objects. The package

FIGURE 9.9 The mDesk toolbar.

is written in Java and has been successfully used on both Unix and Windows systems.

A basic building block of mStar is *mDesk,* or the multicast desktop. This application is used as the central locality for the user to access the different tools, or agents, of the mStar system (Figure 9.9).

The mVote tool allows users to create new issues, vote about these issues, and view a summary of the voting (Figure 9.10). When audio might not be available, users can exchange comments and chat with one another using the text-based tool, mChat. The whiteboard tool, mWB, allows users to draw together and share images and text documents (Figure 9.11).

Another tool, mWeb, allows users to distribute World Wide Web pages and other objects defined by URLs among a workgroup. It also allows users to synchronize their browsers to display the same page. mWeb can be configured to follow the selections made in a running browser, so that one user controls the link selection and all other members follow the links selected by the sender without any interaction on their part.

TeleDraw is another whiteboard application for multiparty sessions, although this one is focused on object-oriented drawing. TeleDraw can be run either as a stand-alone application using a Java runtime system or as an applet within a Java-enabled Web browser. Since it uses Java, TeleDraw is a cross-platform application, running on Unix, MS Windows, and Macintosh systems. Additionally, it supports the recording and replay of TeleDraw sessions using a proprietary protocol. TeleDraw supports RTPv2 and can run on top of TCP or over UDP for either unicast or multicast sessions. Plans are to add support for the T.126 protocol to improve interoperability with other conferencing/whiteboard applications.

The original collaborative app for the MBone was *wb,* which is still one of the most popular tools for multicast sessions. McCanne and Jacobsen at Lawrence Berkeley Labs in California wrote wb (whiteboard),

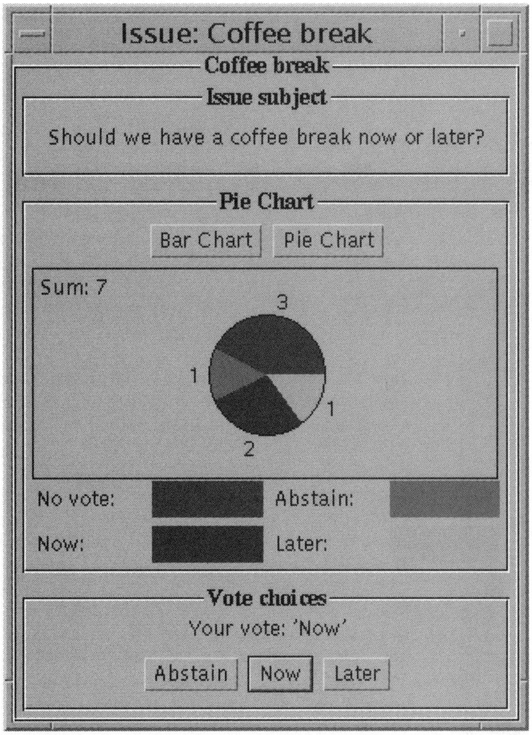

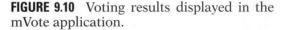

FIGURE 9.10 Voting results displayed in the mVote application.

which provides a shared drawing space and can be used for presentations over the MBone. Wb can import slides in PostScript and the speaker can add small annotations during the presentation.

Not all collaborative applications focus on diagrams and drawings. For collaborative work that's aimed at text only, *nt* is a shared text editor for multicast sessions.

Information Distribution

As opposed to the multimedia distribution applications we described earlier, the applications in this section focus on delivering other types of data, such as stock quotes and other financial data, to client workstations. Thus, they may be more concerned with carefully controlled timed delivery of data or reliable multicasting (eCast is one such example). If you're looking to experiment with push technologies over multicast, these are the applica-

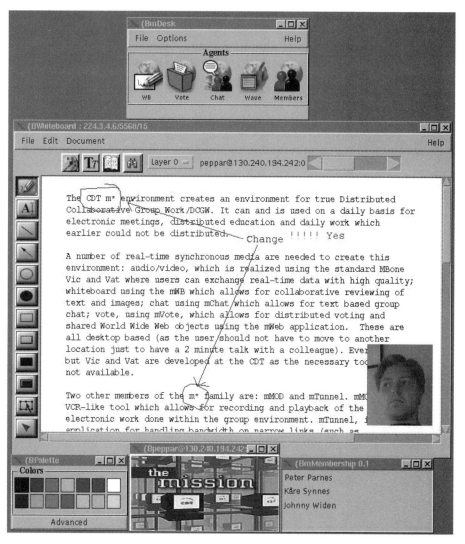

FIGURE 9.11 Sample mWB work area.

tions designed for that job. This section also includes applications that have been written to multicast Web pages. Table 9.4 lists the Information Distribution Applications.

The distribution of information over IP networks via either unicast or multicast has received a great deal of attention since the introduction of PointCast and other applications that have been categorized as *push technologies.* Actually, the approach is more correctly called a *publish-and-subscribe method,* as sketched in Figure 9.12. A server or information

TABLE 9.4　Information Distribution Applications

Application	Developer	Platforms	Source
TIBnet	TIBco	Unix, Windows95, Windows NT	www.tibco.com
Velociti	Vitria Technology, Inc.	Unix, Windows95	www.vitria.com
BackWeb	BackWeb Technologies, Inc.	Windows95, Windows NT, Unix, Mac	www.backweb.com
MultiCast	StarBurst Communications, Inc.	Windows95, Windows NT, Unix	www.starburstcom.com
WebCanal	INRIA	Unix, Windows	webcanal.inria.fr
eCast	Lucent Technologies	Windows	www.bell-labs.com/projects/e-cast/
mMosaic	G. Dauphin, ENST	Unix	sig.enst.fr/~dauphin/mMosaic/
MCM	J-C Touvet, INRIA	Unix	ftp://ftp.edelweb.fr/pub/MCM/

broker has the responsibility for collecting information and categorizing it (steps 1 and 3 in the figure). Clients subscribe to the different information categories (channels) according to their interests (step 2). When appropriate information is received by the broker, it transmits that information to the clients who subscribed to that channel (step 4). Although many of the programs that have been written to "push" information on networks continue to use unicast methods, a significant few offer multicast transmission to reduce the network load.

TIBnet

The products from Tibco probably comprise the most advanced system of tools for disseminating information via networks, either via broadcasts or multicasts. Tibco's applications rely on true information push using a publish-and-subscribe model. Subscribers indicate the subjects on which

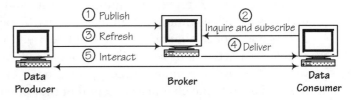

FIGURE 9.12　The publish-and-subscribe method for disseminating information.

they wish to receive data, then listen to the network for messages containing that subject; when new information on a subject is created or received by the server, that information is transmitted over the network. A key link between the server and subscribers is the subject-oriented approach in its TIB/Rendezvous product—with subject-based addressing, the server inserts a subject in the message and clients receive data by checking for messages with a particular subject.

TIB/Rendezvous also supports a request/reply model to handle queries, transactions, and equipment control on the network. While traditional request/reply interactions involve only one requester and one server, Tibco's system also supports broadcast request/reply transactions in which multiple servers can respond to a request. Either broadcast or multicast addressing can be used for these situations.

Tibco developed its own reliable multicast protocol, which is a derivative of Tibco's Reliable Datagram Protocol that can work on a variety of networks. The TIBnet architecture includes an LDAP-based subject name server for controlling and managing the use of subjects within a network along with proxy functionality for corporate firewalls to ensure security and provide subject filtering for incoming multicast channels. In this system, rather than have users poll for information, TIBnet follows an event-driven approach. When an event happens, it is propagated across the network to all interested subscribers (either a user or an application). The content is sent multicast and is filtered by interest along the way through the network, not only by the IP Multicast address, but also by subject within the multicast group.

Velociti

Like TIBnet, Vitria's *Velociti* is designed as an event-driven publish-and-subscribe system for delivering information; Velociti, however, uses CORBA as its fundamental base technology. Velociti allows one of four quality-of-service values to be assigned to each channel for message delivery. The QoS values range from best-effort to transactional.

In addition to providing multiple security and administrative domains as well as multiple naming domains, Velociti includes support for caches and replica channels. Caches can be used to tune performance over a wide-area network by redistributing published information that's been transmitted over a remote source channel to the LAN. Replica channels are similar to cache channels, except that they persistently log all events; they therefore can be used to provide some fault tolerance.

BackWeb

BackWeb is another information push system, but one that's not designed specifically for using IP Multicast. Deliverable content can include software executables, Java applets, Web-based content, audio and video files, as well as standalone applications. To help distribute the network load that's often been associated with push technologies, BackWeb includes support for BackWeb proxy servers which can store frequently downloaded information. Channel filtering and lookouts can be programmed into the proxy servers to further restrict traffic. Clients exist for Windows95, Windows 3.11, Windows NT, and the Mac.

Turning back to multicasting, BackWeb supports multicasting by using Tibco's multicasting technology. BackWeb offers a BackWeb-TIBCO connection and the TIB/Rendezvous software for multicasting data from BackWeb servers. This system supports only Windows95 or Windows NT.

StarBurst MultiCast

StarBurst Communications offers a system called *StarBurst Multicast* that's aimed at corporate file distribution over multicast networks using reliable multicasting. MultiCast uses StarBurst's MFTP protocol (see Chapter 6), which uses multiple passes to guarantee that all clients receive all file blocks; after the initial transmission, the subsequent passes contain only the missing blocks that the clients have requested (via NACKs returned to the server).

Prior to sending files, the Multicast server multicasts a message to a group of predetermined recipients, informing them that data will be transferred at a particular time. The recipients then register to receive the information.

The Multicast server can run on various forms of Unix as well as Windows95 and Windows NT. The Multicast client is available for Unix, OS/2, Windows95, and Windows NT.

WebCanal

WebCanal, from INRIA, is a system that's been designed to push information to other users. A special channel, the directory channel, is dedicated to announcements about the available information channels. Users can tune into this channel to get to an available channel without connecting to a central server.

WebCanal uses SAP and SDP for session announcements and a variation of SRM (Simple Reliable Multicasting, see Chapter 6), called LRMP (Lightweight Reliable Multicast Protocol) for transmitting the data. LRMP was designed as an extension to RTP/RTCP and only allows the sender to send repair packets. Another protocol, MIDP or Multipoint Information Distribution Protocol, was created to handle how information is described and published via WebCanal, including reliable delivery and security.

The WebCanal system includes a series of Java-based applications—WebCaster, WebConf, WebTuner, Mtalk, and two diagnostics tools, LrmpMon and RtpDump. WebCaster is the channel publishing application used on a server to create channels and publish documents on those channels. WebConf is a conferencing application which allows users to share Web pages via multicast. Another client application is WebTuner, which allows a user to subscribe to multiple channels and receive the information of interest. *Mtalk* is another client application for multicast chatting between users on the network.

In WebTuner, users see not only the channels to which they've subscribed, but also the individual objects making up the contents of the channel. One view of this is a tree-based view, as in Figure 9.13.

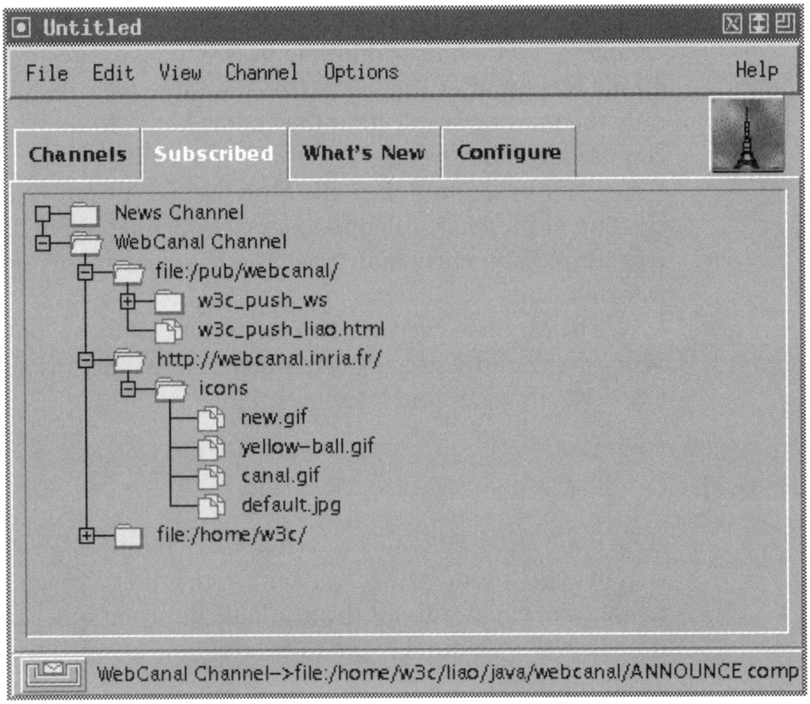

FIGURE 9.13 Tree view of subscribed channels.

Users can also apply various filters to channels. These filters can be for the scope of the multicast, a channel's category, the audience, or payment status (Figure 9.14).

e-Cast

e-Cast, from Lucent Technologies, is one of the few reliable multicasting products that's currently available. Lucent has started out offering a developer's toolkit for its RMTP multicasting protocol (see Chapter 6 for a description) and GlobalCast is also marketing the protocol, along with its other reliable multicasting protocols, as part of the GlobalCast API and

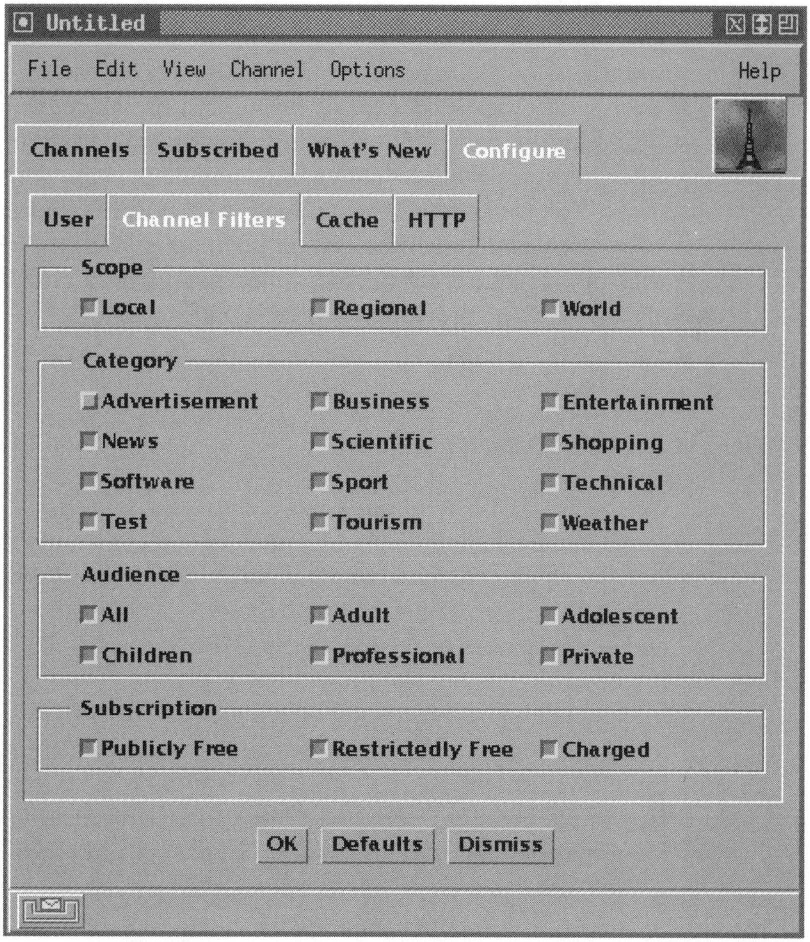

FIGURE 9.14 Channel filter configuration window.

developer's kit. The first product from Lucent using RMTP is a file transfer application that works with Unix, Windows95, or Windows NT.

Other Tools

With the ever-increasing interest in the Web as a primary means of sharing information on the Internet, some projects have aimed at combining multicasting with the Web. These include programs for multicasting HTML pages and imbedded objects to other Web browsers, as well as replicating the contents of Web servers.

mMosaic has been based on one of the original Web browsers, NCSA Xmosaic. It can multicast any embedded object—XPM, JPEG, GIF, PNG, MIDI data, and so on—to other browsers, along with the cursor and scrollbar positions.

MCM, or Multicast Mosaic, was developed by Jean-Christophe Touvet and is a tool specifically for multicasting HTML slides. Initially designed for use with the NCSA Mosaic browser, it has since been upgraded to work with other browsers. The system follows a master-slave architecture where the master packs all the slides into a single package for multicasting to the slaves. The package is repeatedly multicast until all intended recipients have received the package. When the master loads a Web page, only the URL of this page is multicast to the slaves, whereupon that slide is displayed from the previously received package.

Session Announcement Tools

In Chapter 8, we spent quite a bit of space discussing the protocols that have been designed to describe multicast sessions and announce those sessions to other prospective participants. Only a few tools have been written to handle session announcements, but these have thus far proven adequate and seen the bulk of the use on the MBone (especially sd and sdr). Table 9.5 lists the Session Announcement Tools.

The session directory tools include *sd* (session directory) by McCanne and Jacobsen and *sdr*. Sd and sdr both offer a convenient way of announcing multicast sessions. Sdr performs similarly to sd, but it uses a later version of the Session Description Protocol (SDP), making sd and sdr incompatible. Sdr uses the concept of plug-ins to allow it to control, and launch, other multicast applications, such as vat and confcntlr.

The Multimedia Conference Control tool, or *mmcc*, is a session orchestration tool for point-to-point as well as multipoint teleconferences.

TABLE 9.5　Session Announcement Tools

Application	Developer	Platforms	Source
sd	Lawrence Berkeley Labs	Unix	mice.ed.ac.uk/mice/archive/ sd.html
sdr	University College, London	Unix	mice.ed.ac.uk/mice/archive/ sdr.html
mmcc	USC Information Sciences Institute	Unix	mice.ed.ac.uk/mice/archive/ mmcc.html
multikit	Live Networks, Inc.	Unix, Windows95	www.lvn.com/multikit/

A caller can explicitly invite others to participate in a conference, and the program alerts them to accept or decline. Mmcc can also distribute a cryptographic key for confidential sessions. Note that sdr was designed to replace mmcc.

Although *multikit's* first use is as an SDP browser, it also offers an extensible framework for experimenting with multicast-based protocols. One interesting feature is its support for a positional view of a directory. Positional views allow directory entries (or other objects) to be located at a particular set of coordinates in the view, thus allowing the creation of active maps that display updated information, such as the display of earthquake epicenters shown in Figure 9.15. (LiveGate, another interesting product from the same company, is a server program that lets non-MBone-connected computers access and participate in MBone sessions.)

Diagnostic Tools

Although multicast networks can be more complex to monitor and maintain, the number of tools for doing this is rather small. The essential tools are included with the public-domain distribution files for the mrouted DVMRP router software; only a few other tools have been written and distributed. Table 9.6 lists the diagnostic tools.

StreamWatch, from Precept Software Inc., is a commercial tool for monitoring RTP and IP Multicast traffic on a network (Figure 9.16). A Program View window lists all current or scheduled video programs, either from sdr, the IP/TV program Guide, or a local file. A User View window lists all users viewing a given program at any time. Data stream information can be gathered via RTCP, including the level of jitter, number of packets received and lost, amount of bandwidth consumed, and type of data compression used. Data collected in StreamWatch can be stored in an

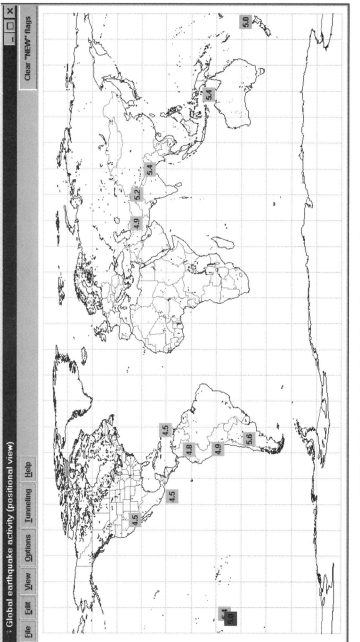

FIGURE 9.15 Positional display of earthquake epicenters.

TABLE 9.6 Diagnostic Tools

Application	Developer	Platforms	Source
StreamWatch	Precept Software Inc.	Windows95, Windows NT	www.precept.com
mconfig		Unix	
mrdebug		Unix	
mlisten		Unix	www.cc.gatech.edu/computing/ Telecomm/mbone/
mview	MERIT	Unix	www.merit.edu/~mbone/mviewdoc/ Welcome.html
multiMON	Communications Research Centre, Canada	Unix, Windows95[1], Windows 4.0[1]	www.merci.crc.doc.ca/mbone/ MultiMON/

Note:[1] client only

ODBC-compatible database and then used in conjunction with a bill-back accounting procedure if desired.

Some of the common configuration and management tools include *mconfig, mrdebug, mlisten,* and *mstat.* Mconfig displays the MBone configuration of an SNMP-capable multicast router and allows appropriate users

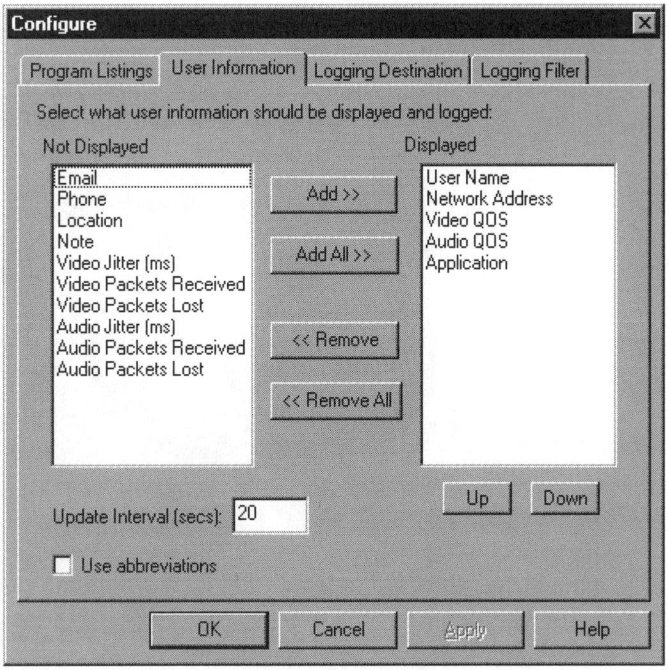

FIGURE 9.16 Sample StreamWatch screen.

to modify the configuration. Mrdebug allows the user to display the multi-cast routes taken by a message in a given network. Mstat is a utility for querying statistics from a remote multicast router using SNMP. All distributions of mrouted, the standard MBone multicasting router software, include the mrinfo, mtrace, and map-mbone utilities. The SNMP-capable mrouted distributions also include the mconfig, mrtree, and mstat.

Mlisten is a tool developed at Georgia Tech for the collection and processing of MBone membership information; it can be used to generate information about join/leave statistics, connection times, and multicast tree sizes.

Mview can be used to maintain a database of information about each router, subnet, and link in a multicast network. Data can be collected via other utilities such as mrinfo, mtrace, mstat, and mrtree. The program can then be used to produce PostScript maps of a network area, display a map of a partial packet distribution tree for a specific host group, or to monitor packet rates at a set of SNMP-capable nodes.

MultiMON was designed to monitor multicast traffic on local network segments in order to assist a network administrator in managing the traffic on an intranet. The program can be used to graphically display the breakdown of multicast traffic by application type (Figure 9.17) or to display information about individual sessions.

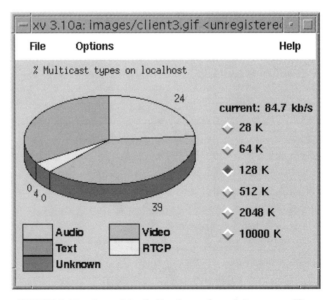

FIGURE 9.17 Graphical display of multicast traffic.

Summary

Both free and commercial programs for using multicasting are now available for a variety of platforms. Many of the programs are aimed at the UNIX operating systems, but more are being ported to **MS Windows**. Most of the commercial applications are aimed at **MS Windows** as well.

You can use these multicasting applications for tasks as simple as broadcasting live presentations or recorded videos to an audience to more complex tasks like collaborating on a design project or selectively disseminating time-crucial data via a publish-and-subscribe system (push technologies). If anything, multicasting suffers from a dearth of enterprise-class management and diagnostic tools.

10

The MBone and Other
Multicast Networks

Although a great deal of interest in IP Multicasting is due to the convergence of increasing interest in IP networks and advances in multimedia, an experimental network, the Multicasting Backbone or MBone as it is more popularly known, is largely responsible for proving that all this can work in the real world.

I'll be covering the basic history and some of the details of the MBone in this chapter to give you a flavor of how this multicasting network works. Even if you're interested in business uses of multicasting, the MBone can serve as a good training ground for learning about multicasting, its applications and network management.

Since 1997 was a watershed year in multicasting as the first ISPs started rolling out commercial services utilizing IP Multicasting on the Internet, the last part of this chapter reviews what @Home, BBN Planet, Digex, MCI, and UUnet have planned for multicasting.

The MBone

In the early 1990s, wide-area multicasting was a relatively new concept that hadn't been tried in any major effort on the Internet. Experimentation with multicasting technology started on DARTNET, a small-scale experimental network financed by DARPA in the late 1980s. Stephen Deering, one of the primary architects of wide-area multicasting on the Internet, started work on IP multicasting in 1988 and submitted his thesis on wide-area multicasting in 1991. That changed in 1992 when the Multicasting Backbone, or MBone, was conceived. Back then, Internet routers didn't include support for multicasting, so special routing software, the *mrouted* daemon, was developed for certain Unix workstations. These special multicast routers were linked together as a subnet, or overlay, atop the Internet.

The first live audio was broadcast from several sessions of the March 1992 meeting of the IETF in San Diego to participants at 20 sites on three continents spanning 16 time zones. The IETF site and most of the remote sites ran a program called vat, the Visual Audio Tool. For the IETF audiocast, the broadcasters used 64-Kbps PCM audio data produced directly by the audio device support that's built into Sparcstations.

By the Seattle meeting of the IETF in 1994, both audio and video were multicast on the MBone to 567 hosts in 15 countries; a map of the main MBone participants prepared by Steve Casner that year is shown in Figure 10.1.

NOTE   The two-letter codes in the figure are the common Internet codes for identifying countries; for example, US = United States, JP = Japan, FR = France, NL = Netherlands.

Estimates of the MBone's size generated in March 1997 are that it covers over 3400 subnets in more than 25 countries.

Architecture and Implementation

The MBone is currently a combination of mesh and star topologies. The main *backbone* of the MBone is a mesh of links among the backbone networks and regional MBone nets. Most regional multicasting networks attached to the MBone take on the form of a star. The MBone is composed of separated networks that support multicasting (see Figure 10.2); these networks form islands of multicast capabilities in the midst of the rest of the Internet. On each of these islands, there is a host that is running the *mrouted* multicast routing daemon. In order to enable transmission of multicast traffic between these island networks, a technique was

Major MBONE Routers and Links

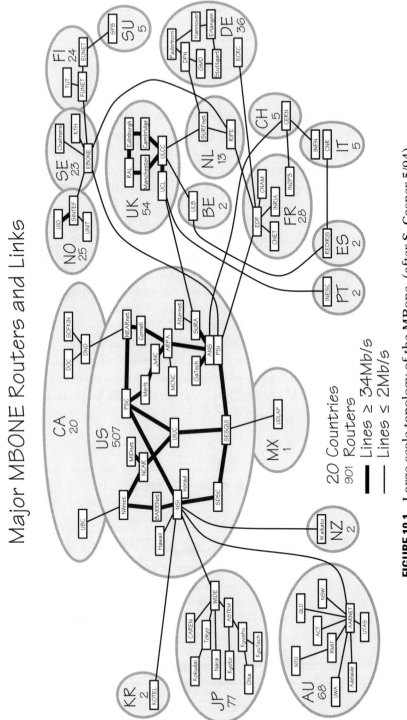

FIGURE 10.1 Large-scale topology of the MBone. (after S. Casner 5/94)

developed to pass the datagrams through unicast tunnels that connect the islands.

MBONE TUNNELING

Each tunnel has a *metric* and a *threshold*. The metric is the cost associated with sending a datagram on the given interface or tunnel and is used for routing packets among different tunnels; the threshold is used to limit the distribution scope for multicast datagrams (i.e., how far through the Internet a datagram travels). Table 10.1 lists the common recommended metrics for multicasting on the MBone.

As an example of how the metrics are used to select tunnels, let's suppose that we have three MBone sites, M1, M2, and M3, connected as in Figure 10.3. The primary tunnels (those with greater bandwidth) are defined as M1-M2 and M2-M3, while a backup tunnel is M1-M3. To reflect that the backup tunnel M1-M3 cannot provide as much bandwidth as the two primary tunnels, the metrics could be set to 1 for the primary tunnels and to 3 for the backup tunnel.

When M1 gets a multicast packet from one of its clients, it will compute the cheapest path to each of the other M sites. The tunnel M1-M3 has a cost of 3, whereas the cost via the other tunnels is (1+1) = 2. Therefore, the tunnel M1-M3 is usually not used; it would be used if any of the other tunnels broke.

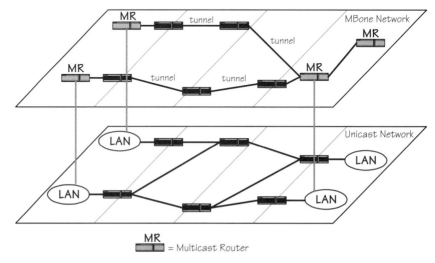

FIGURE 10.2 MBone islands and tunnels.

TABLE 10.1 Multicasting Metrics

Situation	*Metric*
Backup tunnels	1
LAN, or tunnel across a single LAN	1
Any subtree with only one connection point	1
Serial link, or tunnel across a single serial link	1
Multi-hop tunnel	2 or 3
Sum of metrics on primary path	1

A tunnel's threshold is the minimum TTL (see Chapter 2) required for a multicast datagram to be forwarded to the given interface or tunnel. It is used to control the scope of the multicast datagrams (Table 10.2).

A multicast router will only forward a multicast datagram across one of its interfaces if the TTL field in the IP header is greater than the TTL threshold assigned to the interface. For example, a multicast datagram with a TTL of less than 16 is restricted to the same site and would not be forwarded across a router interface to other sites in the same region.

Once tunnels are configured, they will be treated just like any other kind of link in the global network infrastructure. But tunnels are not simple links. For instance, if a tunnel's cost is set to 1 (the usual default), just like a direct link between two routers, it will be treated as a direct link even though the tunneled packets are in fact relayed several times by unicast routers. This may result in strange choices, like preferring a routing path through a long tunnel. To avoid these distortions, the underlying unicast routing structure for a tunnel should be investigated before assigning tunnel metrics.

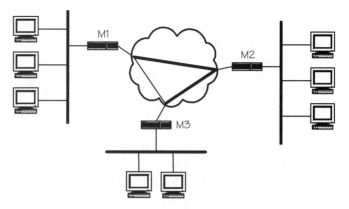

FIGURE 10.3 Using a metric to select tunnels.

TABLE 10.2 TTL Thresholds

TTL	Restriction
0	Same host
1	Same subnet
15	Same site
63	Same region
127	Worldwide
191	Worldwide, but with limited bandwidth
255	Unrestricted

CONVERTING MULTICAST PACKETS

All multicast packets have to be converted to unicast packets before they can be transmitted across a tunnel. Two different encapsulation techniques have been tried for tunneling multicast datagrams on the Internet. The first used an IP option called Loose Source and Record Route (LSRR); this was implemented in versions of mrouted released before March 1993. (This method also remains an option in the new software for backward compatibility with nodes that have not upgraded.) In this mode, the multicast router modifies the packet by appending an IP LSRR option to the packet's IP header (see Figure 10.4). The multicast destination address is moved into the source route and the unicast address of the mrouted router on the other side of the tunnel is placed in the IP Destination Address field.

LSRR lists the routers that should be used along the path between a source and a destination, but it does not limit the number of hops between those routers; in other words, other routers can process the packet in between the listed routers. One problem that was noted during use of LSRR was that multicast tunnel packets using the IP Loose Source and Record Route option can divert packets to a slower processing path in some router architectures. Therefore, a different encapsulation technique was devised.

Using the encapsulation technique, a multicast router that wants to send a multicast packet across a tunnel will prepend another IP header, set the destination address in the new header to be the unicast address of the multicast router at the other end of the tunnel, and set the IP protocol field in the new header to a value of four (which means that the next protocol is IP). The multicast router at the other end of the tunnel receives the packet, strips off the encapsulating IP header, and forwards the packet as appropriate.

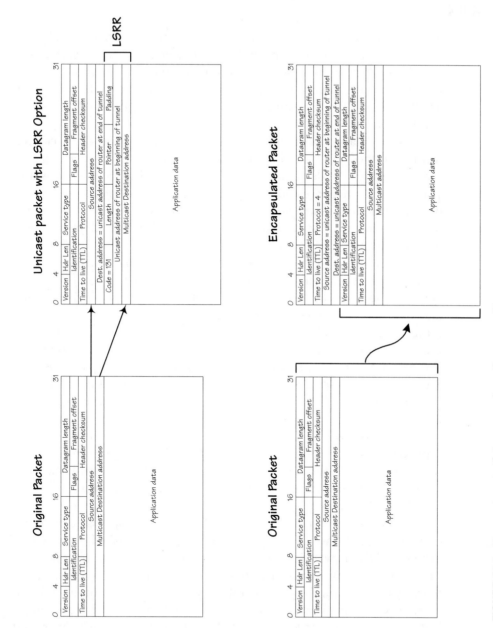

FIGURE 10.4 Preparing multicast packets for tunneling.

ROUTING ON THE MBONE

Since the MBone and the Internet have different network topologies and different information to relay among the routers, the multicast routers used in the MBone run a separate routing protocol to determine how to forward multicast packets. The majority of the MBone routers currently use the Distance Vector Multicast Routing Protocol (DVMRP); some also use Multicast OSPF (MOSPF).

As we detailed in Chapter 5, DVMRP is a very simple distance vector routing protocol. The multicast routers exchange distance vector updates that contain lists of destination, or rather potential sources, and distances. The distances are expressed as hop counts and the sources are combinations of IP addresses and subnet masks. The DVMRP updates are sent not only over the multicast-capable interfaces, but also over all the tunnels that start from the multicast router.

DVMRP is used by the MBone routers to compute the *reverse paths* used by the reverse-path forwarding algorithm to determine paths between the multicasting source and members of the multicast session (see Chapter 5 for more details). When an mrouted process receives a multicast packet from an interface or a tunnel, it will check in the DVMRP routing table whether that interface or that tunnel is on the shortest path from the source. If this is not the case, the packet is dropped. Otherwise, it is forwarded toward all multicast-capable interfaces and all tunnels for which the local router is the previous hop from the source.

Since DVMRP is slow propagating changes in network topology, any rapid changes in the network are a problem. For example, routers which no longer have multicast group members might still receive multicast traffic or some group members might lose part of a transmission if a link in the MBone is disabled.

Since both group membership and the MBone topology can change dynamically, the multicast delivery tree has to be refreshed periodically. When the MBone was first set up, there was no pruning of the multicast routing tree to remove inactive routers. Every multicast datagram was sent to every mrouted on the MBone if it passed the threshold limit. Only truncated broadcasting was supported (i.e., the only pruning was done at the leaf subnets) where the local mrouted would transmit a datagram onto the local network if there was a local host that had joined the multicast group. As the MBone grew, this became a problem, so reverse-path multicasting (RPM) was supported, starting with version 3.0 of mrouted. (Refer to Chapter 4 for details on RPM.)

A Sampler of MBone Uses

Since the original IETF meeting audiocast, there have been quite a few different events on the MBone. Much of the MBone's use has focussed on audio and video broadcasts and conferences, not only to prove that this can be done on a packet-switched network like the Internet, but also to give examples of the value that can be gained by adding audio and/or video to an application. This has included typical conference broadcasts covering topics like supercomputing, the semi-annual IETF meetings, scientific visualization, as well as videocasts of U.S. House and Senate sessions and live satellite weather photos.

Perennial favorites are the Space Shuttle missions; the NASA select TV cable channel is broadcast onto the MBone during flights. When you consider how far the pictures of the astronauts travel along the way and across many different technologies, it's amazing that the system works! But it does.

The MBone has shown its value in education as well. The Jason/Medea project first used the MBone to transmit experimental data from the research vessel Laney-Chouest during exploration of the Sea of Cortez in 1993 in collaboration with the Woods Hole Oceanographic Institution in Massachusetts. Both scientists and students alike could receive this data via the MBone. For example, this data was distributed to over 100,000 students in various schools around the country, ranging from kindergarteners to 12th graders. The Jason Foundation has expanded this approach to a regular schedule of scientific expeditions that bring along student reporters/assistants and transmit information back to schools around the United States. Support materials include teacher's lesson plans and pointers to other information on the Web.

As a forerunner of some of the entertainment based on streaming video and audio now being run on the Internet, the MBone has been used to broadcast both live and recorded music. For example, on November 18, 1994, the Rolling Stones multicast 25 minutes of their live concert in the Dallas Cotton Bowl over the MBone. Another MBone service, Radio Free VAT, serves as a community radio station where DJs sign up for air time via an automated server.

Now let's take a look at what you need to do if you want to use the MBone—this includes both receiving a multicast session or transmitting a session of your own.

Using the MBone

If you're just getting your feet wet in multicasting and want to experience multicasting before your intranet is enabled for multicasting, or you just want to see what people can do with multicasting, the MBone is a good place to start. We'll cover some of the important steps in connecting to the MBone as receiver/session participant, then cover the steps for setting up a multicast session of your own for the MBone.

First, here's some background. The MBone is largely run by consensus, with the MBone community both managing the MBone topology and the scheduling of multicast sessions to minimize congestion. For instance, when a new site announces itself to the MBone mail list using one of the sublist addresses given in Table 10.3, the nearest potential providers decide who should establish the most logical connection path to minimize regional loading of the Internet.

Event scheduling is largely handled by using another electronic mail list, rem-conf@es.net. Advance announcements of events are sent to this mail list to prevent scheduling conflicts and overloading of the MBone.

There are a lot of people who have already gone through the trials of setting up a multicast router or modifying OS kernels, and so on, in order to connect to the MBone; much of this information has been freely shared in the traditional spirit of the Internet. A good starting point is the MBone FAQ (Frequently Asked Questions), which can be found at http://www.cs.columbia.edu/~hgs/internet/mbone-faq.html, ftp://genome-ftp.stanford.edu/pub/mbone/mbone-connect. Another source of MBone information is the Web site at http://www.mbone.com/ and http://www.cl.cam.ac.uk/mbone/.

I've already mentioned the rem-conf mailing list as the source of conference announcements, but it's also used for general discussions about the MBone. Another mailing list that's a source of MBone-related information is mbone@isi.edu; this list focuses on network configuration and tool development. If you want to review the archives of the rem-conf mailing

TABLE 10.3 Mailing Lists for MBone Engineering Issues

Region	Mailing list
Australia	mbone-oz-request@internode.com.au
Canada	canet-mbone-request@canet.ca
Japan	mbone-jp-request@wide.ad.jp
Korea	mbone-kr-request@cosmos.kaist.ac.kr
Singapore	mbone-sg-request@lincoln.technet.sg
UK	mbone-uk-request@cs.ucl.ac.uk
Europe	mbone-eu-request@sics.se
N. America	mbone-na-request@isi.edu
Other	mbone-na-request@isi.edu

list, a good source is http://www.mbone.com/lists/ which has organized the archives by month and offers some searching capabilities.

Remember, though—you don't have to set up a multicast router in order to get a feel for what can be done with the MBone and multicasting. For instance, you can use your Ethernet LAN along with conferencing tools like *vat* or a whiteboard tool like *wb* to see how things work before you connect to the MBone. Once you're convinced that there's value to using multicasting applications and the MBone, then you'll want to move on to WAN multicasting by linking to the MBone to prove its capabilities. That step will mean either installing mrouted on a workstation or configuring an existing router for multicast support.

CONNECTING TO THE MBONE

If you're going to use the MBone, you'll need a multicast feed; make sure that your network provider can supply such a feed. Not all ISPs offer MBone connections to their customers. In fact, the number that do so is pretty small, even among the larger nationwide ISPs; the MBone Web site tries to maintain a list of active ISPs at http://www.mbone.com/mbone/contacts.html.

If you're planning to connect a network to the MBone, you might have to set up a workstation running a version of the mrouted daemon. An alternative is to use a commercial router that supports DVMRP, MOSPF, or PIM. If you're going to use mrouted, one of the best sources for all the latest versions of mrouted (as well as other MBone software) is http://mice.ed.ac.uk/mice/archive/.

One advantage to setting up mrouted is that you can make changes or upgrades to the multicast router without affecting the unicast routers handling the mission-critical daily traffic on your network. Whichever course you take, though, you should either be very familiar with your network's configuration or working with one of your company's network administrators to guard against mistakes that could affect the regular network or MBone connections.

If you're a network provider participating in the MBone, the multicast router has to handle at least three tunnels—one incoming, and two outgoing, since you're a branch on a tree. On the other hand, if you're just a participant (or a leaf on the tree, if you recall our discussions of delivery trees in Chapter 4), then you'll just need a single tunnel.

A special network configuration's been suggested for running mrouted as a provider. Figure 10.5 is a sketch of this suggested setup. First, note that two different routing devices are attached to the network: one for unicast traffic, the other for MBone traffic. Since the MBone node will most likely support at least three tunnels, the workstation running mrouted should have multiple network interfaces.

The configuration sketched in Figure 10.5 allows the computer running mrouted to connect with tunnels over the external Ethernet and the physical backbone network, and connects with tunnels to the lower-level mrouted machines over the internal Ethernet, which splits the load of replicated packets.

JOINING A MULTICAST SESSION

Participating in a multicast session depends on two things—the computer you're using and the nature of the content that the session is transmitting.

Not all Unix OS kernels support IP Multicast, so patches often have to be applied to your workstation's OS in order to make them compatible with the MBone (or any other IP Multicast net). But many other, newer versions of Unix OSes support multicasting—BSD/386 version 1.1 and above, DEC OSF/1 version 2.0 and above, IRIX version 4.0 and above, and Solaris version 2.1 and above, all include kernel support for multicasting. Windows95, Windows NT 4.0, and the Macintosh (using Open Transport) also support IP Multicast out-of-the-box.

All of the popular tools used on the MBone, like sd, sdr, vat, vic, nv, and so many of the others that I mentioned in Chapter 9, were originally written for Unix workstations. Some of these tools have been ported over to MS Windows. A good source for the software, along with installation instructions and users' manuals, is http://www.tascmad.mcg.gla.ac.uk/mbonepcs.html. A few tools exist for the Mac, although they're pretty hard to find and haven't been updated in some time (aside from CU-SeeMe). At a minimum, plan on using sd or sdr, vat and nv, and perhaps wb.

It may seem pretty obvious, but before you join a multicast session, you need to know of its existence. For the moment, tracking announcements via the rem-conf@es.net mailing list is probably the best way of

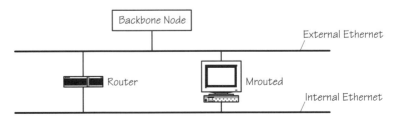

FIGURE 10.5 Router-mrouted setup for local network.

staying on top of things. There are also two Web sites, one at http://www.cilea.it/MBone/browse.htm and another at http://www.msri.org/computing/mbone/ (the latter run by MSRI, the Mathematical Sciences Research Institute, Berkeley, CA) that maintains an up-to-date list of announced MBone sessions (see Figure 10.6). Users looking to join a particular multicast session can browse this site for more information about a session.

Actually participating in a session is pretty straightforward. Since the session directory applications running on the MBone—sd and sdr—are based on a TV Guide model, you can view the list of currently available multicast sessions (Figure 10.7a), select one for more information (Figure 10.7b), then click Open to start. The necessary tools (vat and nv, for instance) are then launched on your workstation and you're receiving the data for that session.

The audio quality of MBone broadcasts is usually quite good, but don't expect to see movie-quality video via the MBone. The video resolution is comparable to some conference room systems, but the frame rate is low; typical frame rates are one to two frames per second when a large

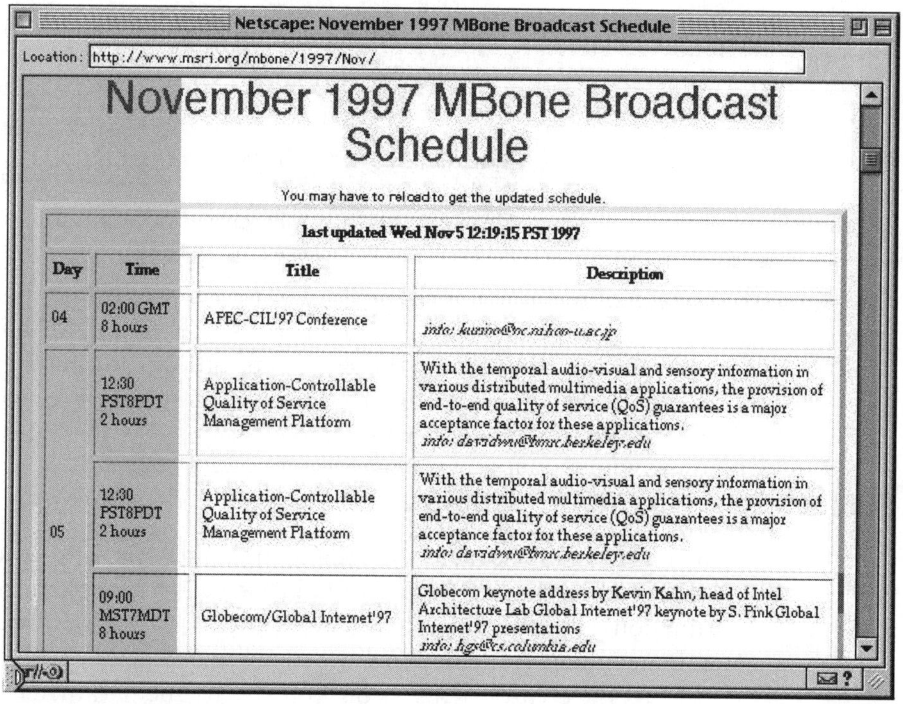

FIGURE 10.6 Web-based schedule of MBone events.

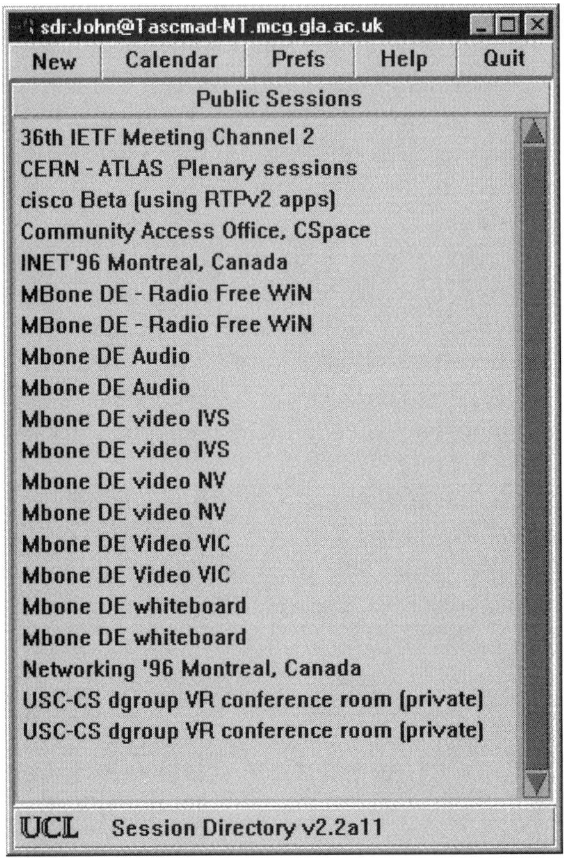

FIGURE 10.7a   Sample sdr session window.

portion of the image is changing, and four to five frames per second when the image is mainly stationary. (Remember, we're talking about the MBone here; if you were running the same apps on your intranet, you could devote more bandwidth to the session and tools like Precept's IP/TV will provide up to 30 frames-per-second video.)

SETTING UP A MULTICAST SESSION

If you're planning to multicast data on the MBone, first remember that the MBone in its present form should be viewed as a single resource, so coordination with other broadcasts is important. Only in a few places can the MBone handle more than one video channel together with audio.

As the creator of a session, you specify the parameters for a session (required programs and encodings, scope limits, session duration); sd (or

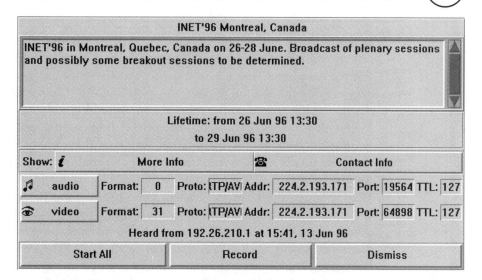

FIGURE 10.7b   sdr information window for INET'96 session.

sdr) generates a random multicast address and port numbers which are included in the session description and then periodically announced, using the same scope (time-to-live value) as the data session itself. When setting a TTL value for the multicast session, you should base your selection on the type of data you plan to broadcast (see Table 10.4).

Typical traffic during an IETF multicast is 100 to 300 Kbps, so use 500 kbps as an upper-limit for bandwidth planning. Assume that at most you'll be able to support a maximum of five simultaneous voice conversations with a maximum bandwidth of 64 Kbps apiece. Typically, audio is carried at 13 to 64 Kbps, video at up to 128 Kbps. The design bandwidth must be multiplied by the number of tunnels passing over any given link since each tunnel carries a separate copy of the packet.

TABLE 10.4

Application	*TTL*	*Threshold*
IETF channel 1 low-rate GSM audio	255	224
IETF channel 2 low-rate GSM audio	223	192
IETF channel 1 FCM audio	191	160
IETF channel 2 FCM audio	159	128
IETF channel 1 video	127	96
IETF channel 2 video	95	64
Local event audio	63	32
Local event video	31	1

Multicast sessions require a fair amount of planning; the global announcement and the propagation time of the announcements make the directory approach less suited for spontaneous, small-group discussions. For the time being, there is no explicit way to notify the intended audience except by e-mail, although new protocols like SIP (Chapter 8) are being developed for invited conferences. Event scheduling is usually handled by the mailing list rem-conf@es.net. If you wish to conduct an MBone event, you can announce it on the list, then wait for others to object. Assuming there are no objections, you can then use sd or sdr to advertise the event. Another way to manage MBone schedules is to use http://www.cilea.it/ MBone/book.htm to reserve transmission time on the MBone.

If you need some assistance in debugging your MBone connection, double-check the MBone FAQ and archives of the mailing lists. Another document worth reading is an Internet Draft named the Multicast Debugging Handbook, draft-ietf-mboned-mdh-00.txt, by Dave Thaler of the University of Michigan and Bernard Aboba of Microsoft; it can be found at the usual IETF sites, including ds.internic.net and other mirror sites.

Depending on the content that you plan to multicast, the bulk of your time may be spent preparing for the session. For instance, preparing a pre-recorded video for transmission involves choosing data compression codecs to minimize the bandwidth requirements, along with making the actual recording and setting up the server to transmit the video. On the other hand, setting up a video or audio conference usually involves just making sure that the intended participants have the right hardware (a video camera and microphone at each workstation, for instance) and software. Multimedia workstations and PCs have become more mainstream and prices for small video cameras have dropped quite a bit, so the hardware issues may well be moot in many cases.

MBone Issues

The technology behind the MBone has evolved since the first audiocast in 1992. Pruning has been implemented and the source-routing version of tunnels was replaced with encapsulation. But the primary routing software, mrouted, was designed to run on workstations, which have limited I/O capabilities and thus can become subject to traffic congestion problems, particularly with higher-bandwidth applications.

Even though the MBone has been used for regular broadcasts of events like the IETF meetings, it should still be viewed as an experimental network, aimed primarily at gaining experience with multicasting protocols, session announcements, and so on. A *real* implementation of multicasting that can be used on a daily basis by many participants requires the removal of tunnels and integration of multicast routing with standard IP routing. We're already seeing some commercial router manufacturers including support for multicast routing protocols in their products, with more on the way, so multicasting beyond the MBone is becoming a more likely reality—see the next section of commercial multicasting networks.

There are a few problems surrounding security. Since IP multicast datagrams can be received by anyone within TTL range of the sender, the sender has to encrypt the data if privacy is desired. One way to handle this is end-to-end encryption, but an infrastructure is required for distribution of cryptographic keys and that's only now being developed; it's still at an awkward stage for regular use (see Chapter 8).

Also, the use of UDP for transmitting multicast datagrams carries a security problem with it. For example, a host receiving audio on port 3456 at a certain multicast address will also unwittingly receive (possibly malicious) NFS packets sent to the same multicast address and a different port.

Protocols for session announcement and description are being developed to make it easier (and more secure) for managing sessions. A security extension is being written for SAP to allow for private announcements of sessions, including authentication of the session initiator and encryption of the announcement.

All this will make the MBone and other multicasting networks easier and more secure to use. Now let's turn to the recent efforts that ISPs have developed to provide multicasting services to their business customers.

Other Multicasting Networks

It has only been since the middle of 1997 that Internet Service Providers (ISPs) have moved from providing MBone access to widespread support of multicasting (at least for business customers).

UUNet/UUCast

UUNet Technologies, Inc. set up a new IP Multicast service, UUCast, in late 1997. The system uses Cisco 4700 routers and the PIM routing protocol for the network. UUCast is offered in a variety of different stream sizes, ranging from 5 Kbps to 128 Kbps so that customers can select either low-end streams for ticker information or similar datacasting or higher-end streams for audio and video applications.

Initial infrastructure limits are set at sending a single audio or video stream to 250,000 simultaneous subscribers (in the U.S. only), but plans are to increase that limit to 1 million simultaneous users sometime in 1998.

Customers of UUCast receive a unique multicast group address for each data stream and the customer premise router is configured with a virtual point-to-point connection to the multicast router located in a UUNet POP (point-of-presence) (see Figure 10.8).

UUNet also plans to offer hosting services for live events in conjunction with UUCast, using NetShow to use the multicasting infrastructure. Unlike the RealNetwork (see next section), content can be broadcast using any multicast software, not just RealPlayer.

MCI

In the summer of 1997, MCI Communications Corp. and RealNetworks created a network for multicasting streaming data called RealNetwork. It is initially designed with nine major distribution points on MCI's Internet backbone (see Figure 10.9); each distribution point includes two or three RealMedia *splitters* (similar to a mirror or cache server) to distribute the load by serving content to consumers from whichever of the nodes is closest. Initial estimates are that the system will be able to serve 50,000 simultaneous connections for a live webcasting event; plans are to increase the system to handle 150,000 streams by the time this book is printed.

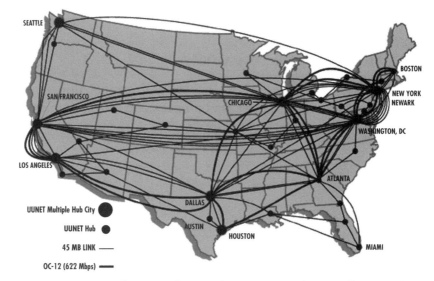

FIGURE 10.8 Large-scale map of UUNet's U.S. network (not all POPs shown).

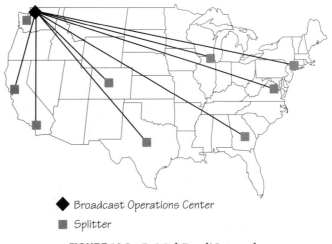

◆ Broadcast Operations Center

▧ Splitter

FIGURE 10.9 Initial RealNetwork.

RealNetwork has a Broadcast Operations Center (BOC) in Seattle which offers a turn-key encoding and uplink service for customers. Content can be delivered via a dedicated Internet connection, satellite downlink, magnetic media, tape, or telephony and stored on a local access server. The BOC takes care of encoding the feed into the proper format using RealAudio or RealVideo encoders if necessary.

Once live streams are encoded, they are routed to a RealServer for delivery to the network splitters. RealServers are located on network segments that have direct access to the Internet backbone over high-bandwidth connections; these servers do not serve end users. Their sole responsibility is to output their feeds to the splitter relay sites located within the internetMCI backbone (see Figure 10.10).

All hosted content is distributed to end users through the splitter sites. A splitter site consists of a specially configured cluster of RealServers. These RealServers perform the splitting and retransmission of live streams to the end users. Splitters can also serve cached on-demand content that's been distributed from the BOC file servers.

Multicast is used for delivering live content wherever possible. If multicast is not available, a unicast stream will be used. All on-demand material is always delivered via unicast methods.

BBN ProVision

BBN Planet, now a part of GTE Internetworking, created a pilot network to provide RSVP and multicasting services in 1996. The pilot network pro-

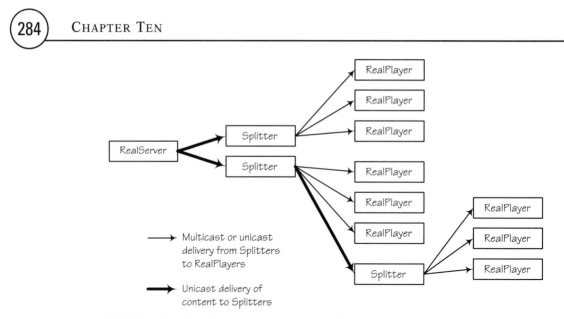

FIGURE 10.10 Feeding content from RealServers to splitters and end users.

vides "bandwidth-on-demand" using the RSVP support and smart queue-ing features that are provided in Cisco IOS version 11.2. The trial was conducted on a separate 1.544-Mbps IP network.

By late 1997, BBN ProVision was being used to provide proprietary multicasting services to about 100 corporations. One of the companies, the Worldwide Broadcasting Network, Inc., or WBN, is now using ProVision as the basis for its 451F multimedia search and retrieval service for business customers.

DIGEX

Like MCI, DIGEX has decided to couple support for streaming media with multicasting on its network. It's using the RealMedia software from Real Networks; the service they offer is called Live Event. In DIGEX's case, DIGEX runs the Live Event servers and businesses lease DIGEX's services. Content is prepared and hosted on Windows NT servers at the DIGEX facilities; DIGEX charges the customers only for the number of RealMedia streams required to broadcast their event.

@Home

The @Home Network started their test of multicasting with cable modems in Fremont, California in the autumn of 1997. The trials have been aimed at delivering streaming audio and video content at rates of 128 Kbps to

256 Kbps to homes. Since it's focused on the home market, the trial is mainly concerned with delivering entertainment-related content such as the @Home Movie Preview Channel. Since @Home has licensing arrangements with many other providers of video content, it's felt that many other content providers will also offer streaming video over the multicast network starting sometime in 1998. The network trial uses the RealMedia software from Real Networks for delivering the data streams.

Issues Facing ISPs

Aside from those ISPs that offer MBone connectivity, there is no interoperability between the multicasting networks that ISPs have formed. It's not that multicast traffic cannot be exchanged between the different networks; it's more a question of setting and standardizing policies for the routing of multicast traffic, including such issues as charges, advertising trees, and so on.

As I mentioned in Chapter 5, hierarchical routing protocols for multicasting are relatively new and have yet to be standardized. The ability to perform policy-based routing between autonomous systems or between areas in much the same way as it's performed for unicast traffic is a fundamental requirement for Internet-wide multicasting between ISPs, but the work on understanding the issues and setting standards for this work has just started.

In the absence of standards allowing the ISPs to interoperate with multicast traffic, customers of these services will have to provide both unicast and multicast services unless you can guarantee that all the intended recipients are served by the same ISP.

Summary

As the relatively young granddaddy of wide-area IP multicasting networks, the MBone is still growing and offering a wide variety of conferences and other applications that use multicasting. The MBone is a good way to get your feet wet with multicasting, particularly for testing both standard and new applications before you use them in-house on an intranet on a routine basis.

Commercially provided multicasting services just started to become available in 1997. In the absence of standardized policies for exchanging multicast traffic though, each multicast ISP stands as an island onto itself. But that will change before long, both because standards work on these issues has already started and demand for the services continues to grow.

11

Implementation Strategies and Issues

Throughout this book, we've concentrated on how multicasting is implemented within the TCP/IP protocol suite (i.e., from the IP protocol layer up through the application protocol layer). Aside from discussing how IP multicast addresses are converted to Ethernet multicast addresses, we've said nothing about the network plumbing (i.e., the network infrastructure that underlies the IP protocol suite).

IP has the beauty of being able to work with just about any physical network—satellite, frame relay, SMDS, ATM, Ethernet, and async, for example. But using IP multicasting with each of these physical networks isn't always straightforward or easy. When you're planning to convert your own corporate network to support IP multicasting, you have to be aware of how well multicasting works with your network infrastructure and what constraints your network media might put on its use.

This chapter sets out to briefly describe each of the major physical network types and then explain how IP multicasting fits with the network technology. We'll be covering the following network technologies: Asynchronous Transfer Mode (ATM), satellite, frame relay, switched multimegabit data services (SMDS), and dial-up connections (i.e., ISDN and modems). In addition, we'll also cover the options that are available for using multicasting with VLANs, which is an increasingly popular networking technology that emphasizes switches in place of routers.

Asynchronous Transfer Mode (ATM)

Unlike IP, ATM is a cell-switching technology. Rather than use routers for forwarding data packets, ATM networks are built around switches that move fixed-sized 53-byte cells (see Figure 11.1) to their destinations. (Each cell has a 5-byte header and 48 bytes of payload.) Cells are transported through a switch based on the connection identifier in the cell header. ATM supports transmission rates up to 622 Mbps and can be scaled to support gigabit speeds via the use of multiple channels.

ATM networks are connection-oriented (i.e., a connection must be set up before messages can be sent; see Chapter 2). Two different types of connections are supported—permanent virtual circuits (PVCs) and switched virtual circuits (SVCs), with PVCs being the most common type thus far. PVCs are intended to be a relatively permanent part of your network infrastructure, lasting on the order of months or years, while SVCs are set up dynamically as needed and are likely to be disabled immediately afterward.

NOTE   PVCs have traditionally been the ATM circuit of choice, but SVCs are becoming more popular.

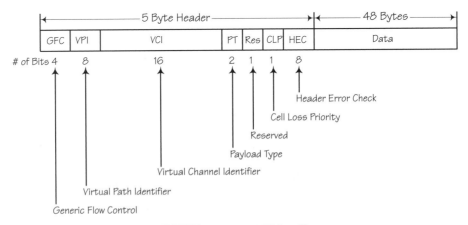

FIGURE 11.1   An ATM cell.

When a virtual circuit is established, a specific physical route is selected between the source and the destination, and all the switches along that path make table entries so they can route packets accordingly. Once a virtual circuit is set up, all messages for that connection follow the same path to the destination. The virtual connection is dedicated to the source and the destination and cannot be shared by anyone else. However, more than one virtual connection can run over a single physical link.

ATM also has built-in support for quality of service. This QoS support is on a per-connection basis and is not dynamic (i.e., cannot be changed during the duration of the connection), unlike RSVP. Furthermore, ATM's routing algorithm, PNNI (Private Network-to-Network Interface), includes QoS information with routing information, allowing network nodes to use this information to establish paths for the required QoS. This contrasts with RSVP, which depends on routers to honor RSVP QoS requests, but the IP routing algorithms have not yet been designed to pick routes based on QoS. Proposals for mapping RSVP QoS classes to those of ATM so the two networks can interoperate are still in progress.

ATM defines a number of functional interfaces in a network. The one of primary concern to us is the UNI, or User-to-Network Interface, which defines the protocols and procedures that enable an ATM host to connect to an ATM switch. The current UNI protocols are UNI 3.0/3.1.

Connections can be point-to-point or point-to-multipoint. As you might expect, point-to-point connections are used when data is exchanged directly between only two ATM hosts. In ATM, a point-to-multipoint connection is defined as a logical connection between a single root node (i.e., a host) and multiple leaf nodes. The point-to-multipoint connection is similar to a simple delivery tree in IP Multicast. When the root node sends data, a copy is received by all leaf nodes, but leaf nodes cannot communicate directly with each other.

ATM QoS Classes

ATM includes support for QoS via four network service classes: CBR (Constant Bit Rate), VBR (Variable Bit Rate), ABR (Available Bit Rate), and UBR (Unspecified Bit Rate). CBR acts like a leased line, providing a tightly constrained delay with a fixed bandwidth. VBR constrains the delay, but allows the bandwidth requirements to vary. ABR uses complex feedback mechanisms to control losses. UBR is essentially a best-effort delivery attempt, offering no QoS guarantees.

A method called Classical IP and ARP over ATM was the first implementation of IP over ATM. It was perhaps the most natural suggestion, since it positions ATM as a replacement for the wires or LAN segments connecting two hosts on the same subnet. IP routers are still required to interconnect two or more IP subnets, thus limiting ATM to intra-subnet connectivity. A series of RFCs were created by the IETF to define the workings of Classical IP and ARP over ATM.

RFC 1483 defines two techniques for encapsulating routed and/or bridged IP packets in ATM AAL5 cells. (AAL5 is the ATM standard for supporting the transport of Variable Bit Rate (VBR) traffic and signaling messages. An AAL, or ATM adaptation layer, is a collection of protocols that provide services to higher layers in the protocol stack by adapting user traffic to a cell format.) PVCs set up between two routers as defined in RFC 1483 are an effective technique for utilizing ATM, offering the advantages of higher bandwidth and support for IP as well as other protocols.

Another RFC, RFC 1577, defines the classical IP and ARP over ATM protocol. RFC 1577 limits connectivity to point-to-point connections between two ATM-attached IP hosts on the same *Logical IP Subnetwork* (LIS). Since IP communications on any subnet operates over two types of addressing (i.e., IP and whatever data link protocol is in use), a dynamic binding or mapping between the IP address and the media-specific address is needed. For shared media like Ethernet, this is done via ARP (see Chapter 2). The equivalent functionality for ATM under RFC 1577 is called ATMARP. The classical IP model defined in this document defines an ATMARP server, whose primary purpose is to maintain a table of IP and ATM mappings; there must be at least one ATMARP server for each LIS.

Two other documents, RFC 1626 and RFC 1755, are also part of the package defining classical IP and ARP over ATM. RFC 1626 defines how IP clients can negotiate a different size for the MTU (Maximum Transmission Unit) than the default of 9180 bytes. RFC 1755 defines the UNI 3.1 signaling procedures that are used in implementations of classical IP and ARP over ATM.

As I mentioned earlier, ATM supports point-to-multipoint virtual circuits between a single sender and multiple receivers. But, in UNI 3.1, the root (i.e., the sender) is responsible for adding the leaves, which is the opposite of the receiver-oriented approach of IP Multicast. Also, ATM has no knowledge of the IP layer or class D addresses, and a mapping between the host group address and the ATM addresses of group members is required. This is accomplished by the Multicast Address Resolution Server (MARS).

Before we see how **MARS** operates, we need to discuss how a set of ATM hosts can participate in an ATM-level multicast. There are two models for supporting such a multicast. The first involves a *VC mesh*, (i.e., an ATM host that establishes a point-to-multipoint VC with other ATM hosts that are members of a specific multicast group; see Figure 11.2). If all hosts on the cluster wish to transmit and receive within the same multicast group, then there will be one point-to-multipoint VC originating from each host, thus the use of the word mesh.

The second model uses a Multicast Server, or MCS. In this case, an ATM host sends data directly to the MCS over a virtual circuit that, in turn, retransmits the data to the members of the multicast group over a point-to-multipoint VC (see Figure 11.3).

Although both models achieve the same result, there are tradeoffs to each. For instance, a VC mesh requires more VCs (in most cases, many more), requiring more buffers, switch control blocks and signaling overhead. But a VC mesh offers optimal performance. On the other hand, it's relatively easy to manage an MCS; fewer VCs are required to support a multicast group with an MCS. But performance can be an issue and latency may be higher for this setup than with a VC mesh. Also, the MCS can be a single point of failure.

Let's return to the discussion of MARS. MARS is similar to a ATMARP server, but it supports multicast address resolution. IP Multicast senders can query the MARS whenever a multicast address needs to be resolved with the ATM addresses of the members of an IP host group.

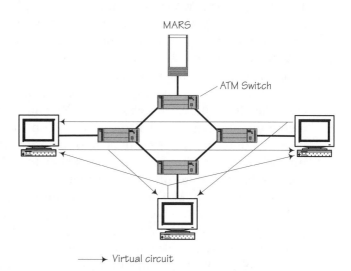

FIGURE 11.2 A VC mesh.

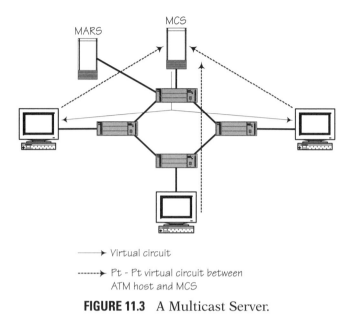

> Virtual circuit

------> Pt - Pt virtual circuit between
ATM host and MCS

FIGURE 11.3 A Multicast Server.

ATM hosts (or routers) that participate in an ATM-level multicast and share a MARS define a *cluster*. This cluster is mapped to a single LIS, although it's been proposed that MARS support a cluster that spans multiple LISs. Clients who wish to participate in a multicast group establish a point-to-point VC with the MARS and register with the MARS (see Figure 11.4) by sending a MARS Join message to the *all nodes* group address (224.0.0.1). The MARS then adds the client as a leaf on its ClusterControl VC, which is a point-to-multipoint VC that is established between the MARS and all multicast-capable cluster members. Clients can leave a host group by issuing a MARS Leave message to the MARS.

An MCS can also be used to multicast data in MARS cluster. In this case, the MCS will register with the MARS and the MCS becomes a leaf on a point-to-multipoint VC called the ServerControl VC.

The IETF has not been alone in trying to define standards for running IP over ATM. The main standards body for ATM, The ATM Forum, has also been working on protocols that integrate multiprotocol networks (not just IP) with ATM. One of the early efforts was LAN Emulation (LANE) which can run network layer protocols, including multicast, transparently over ATM. But LANE has a high amount of protocol overhead and functions best as a single subnet solution. MPOA, or Multiprotocol Over ATM, takes the ATM solutions to the next level, expanding on LANE, clas-

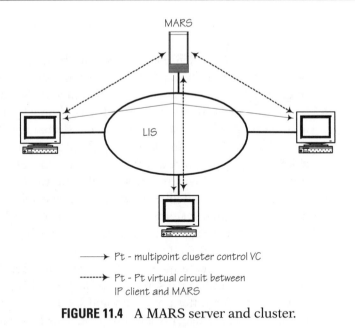

FIGURE 11.4 A MARS server and cluster.

sical IP over ATM, NHRP (Next-Hop Routing Protocol), and MARS by incorporating all these pieces into a single architecture. MPOA became an ATM standard in 1997, so implementation and deployment on networks is still largely in the fledgling stage.

Satellite Networks

Satellite technology is a wide area network technology that is inherently broadcast in nature (i.e., every host on the network can see every packet that is sent, regardless of the source or destination). Satellite network services can be purchased from several major providers to deploy a Private Virtual Network for your enterprise. Typical speeds range from 9600 bps to 24 Mbps in the forward direction with lower-speed back channels. Round trip latencies of over 500 ms are common with geostationary satellites, although planned future services using Low Earth Orbit Satellites, such as Teledesic, are supposed to offer lower latencies and higher speeds.

In order to support multicasting on a satellite network, which is inherently a broadcast medium, each site's LAN should be connected to a satellite receiver via a multicast router. Since each site will receive the signal broadcast from the satellite, the multicast receiver either forwards or blocks the received data depending on whether hosts on the LAN belong to the host group.

In general, satellite networks work best for implementing multicast delivery trees that have a single source and do not require a large amount of feedback. That's because, even though some satellite networks (such as VSAT) can be bidirectional, the return channel, or back channel, operates at a lower speed than the main broadcast channel. To cope with this, systems like StarBurst MultiCast (see Chapters 6 and 9) uses a negative acknowledgment system, which keeps return traffic to a minimum, to promote reliable multicasting over satellite networks.

Two types of satellite networks can be used for multicasting. There are unidirectional systems, such as those used for broadcasting television signals, and there are bidirectional systems, of which VSAT (Very Small Aperture Terminal) is the most common.

For a unidirectional satellite network to operate with TCP/IP protocols and multicasting, a separate back channel is needed. Some satellite service providers offer unidirectional satellite services with a terrestrial back channel to the central uplink site. This land-based back channel can take many forms, such as the Internet, frame relay, ISDN, or modems.

A number of carriers offer VSAT data services for local as well as global coverage (Figure 11.5). In a VSAT network, the central site (the *uplink*) sends data to the satellite which in turn beams the signal to the earth where any VSAT terminal within the satellite beam may pick up the

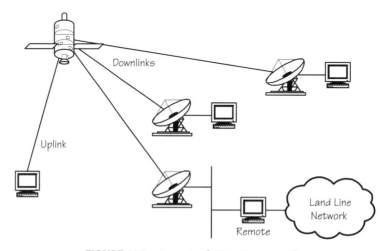

FIGURE 11.5 A typical VSAT network.

signal. In the reverse direction, the VSAT terminal sends a lower-speed signal to the satellite which is then directed to the central uplink site.

Many-to-many multicast applications such as conferencing are not easily accommodated on satellite networks—your remote sites are only tied to the central uplink site rather than to each other. In the case of a VSAT network, conferencing would require that transmissions from one VSAT site to another VSAT site be routed through the central uplink site. Satellite networks are thus most appropriate for such multicasting applications as broadcasting of software upgrades and large files, such as inventory reports.

Frame Relay Networks

Frame relay service provides virtual leased lines to the customer. Much like X.25, frame relay is a packet-switching protocol that connects two LANs over a public packet-switched network.

Frame relay is a WAN protocol that operates at Layer 2 of the OSI model. Unlike conventional packet-switching services such as X.25, frame relay uses statistical multiplexing to load data from multiple sources at the customer site on a single line to the frame relay network. The paths, or virtual circuits, are defined through the network. However, bandwidth is not allocated to the paths until actual data needs to be transmitted. The bandwidth is dynamically allocated on a packet-by-packet basis. Frame relay also provides multiple logical connections within a single physical connection.

In frame relay networks, error recovery functions are left to the endpoint devices running higher-layer protocols, (i.e., the workstations and PCs). Out-of-band control signalling is used, which means that call-control signals are carried on a connection that's separate from that used for the data; this reduces the switching complexity of the network and the amount of network processing needed.

The format of a frame in frame relay (see Figure 11.6) is a very simple one, designed to keep processing requirements to a minimum. The

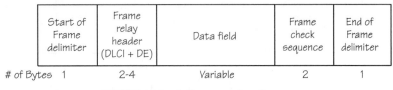

Start of Frame delimiter	Frame relay header (DLCI + DE)	Data field	Frame check sequence	End of Frame delimiter
# of Bytes 1	2-4	Variable	2	1

FIGURE 11.6   A frame relay frame.

main purpose of the frame relay frame is to encapsulate a frame from a LAN. The frame format does not allow flow control and error control to be performed since there are not any sequence numbers.

Frame relay networks (see Figure 11.7) are connection-oriented, where a Permanent Virtual Circuit (PVC) provides an end-to-end data path between the sender and receiver. To create your network, each frame relay site requires a router with a frame relay WAN port and frame relay assembler/disassembler (FRAD—Frame Relay Access Device), which is usually installed by your carrier.

Frame relay addresses are called Data Link Connection Identifiers (DLCIs). In a frame relay network, routing is accomplished by forwarding frames across a Permanent Virtual Circuit (PVC). Each PVC has an assigned DLCI value; frame relay's statistical multiplexing allows the creation of multiple PVCs on the same physical connection, and DLCIs are used to distinguish one PVC from another. The combination of a UNI and a DLCI on that UNI defines a PVC endpoint.

Customers can lease a PVC between two points or can lease multiple PVCs between a sender and multiple receiving sites, thus enabling multicast. Virtually all carriers, such as AT&T, provide flat rate pricing for frame relay based on a fixed Committed Information Rate (CIR)—that is the data rate for which bandwidth is reserved for that user. Data exceeding the burst are discarded. Bursts of data higher than the CIR may also be transferred successfully, based on the size of the burst accommodated by the system (determined by the Discard eligibility parameter in each frame). All of these parameters are negotiated with the carrier when you order your services. The bandwidth of a frame relay connection can range from 56 Kbps over switched 56 or ISDN lines to 1.544 Mbps over T1 lines.

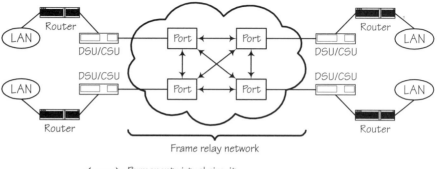

FIGURE 11.7 Frame relay network.

IP multicasting can be deployed over frame relay services in two different ways: either by designing a series of PVCs to distribute multicast traffic to other sites or by using the multicast server method defined for frame relay.

In the first case, you can set up appropriate PVCs between a sender and its receivers, hard-wiring the delivery tree, as it were. This results in a star configuration, with the sender at the center of the star and all receivers located exactly one hop away from the sender (see Figure 11.8). This configuration does not reduce the bandwidth requirements since the multicast replication occurs at the source and is more like unicast multipoint communications, only each PVC carries the traffic to a single site.

A better approach for selecting PVCs—one that does use bandwidth more efficiently—is to create a hub-and-spoke design with a router overlay (see Figure 11.9). In this configuration, select remote sites act as hubs which then distribute the data to other remote sites (the spokes) in the nearby area. Although this results in more hops to get to a particular location, it distributes the replication of multicast packets in the network to the multiple hubs rather than concentrating the process at the central site.

The second approach for deploying IP multicasting over frame relay is to use a service called *multicast frame relay*, specified by the Frame Relay Forum in a 1994 Multicast Implementation Agreement. This service provides multicast at the frame relay layer, rather than at the IP layer.

Since frame relay is a connection-oriented protocol, special implementations are required for many-to-many multicast services. The standardized frame relay multicast service relies on a multicast server. This multicast server is responsible for subscription and unsubscription of

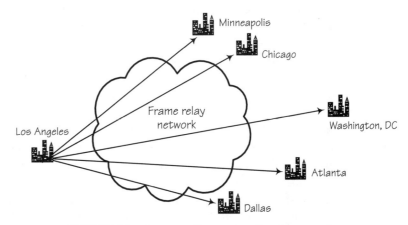

FIGURE 11.8   Star configuration for frame relay.

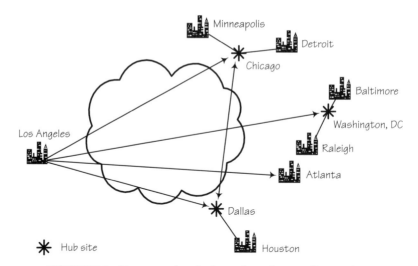

FIGURE 11.9   Frame relay hub-and-spoke configuration.

members as well as the delivery of data units to the members of an active group. In the frame relay multicast model, multicast servers can either be centralized or distributed.

There are three types of multicast services that have been defined for frame relay—one-way, two-way, and N-way. All require a one-to-many mapping of source to destination; each requires the service provider to interpret the meaning of multiple destinations.

In a one-way multicast model (see Figure 11.10), multicast traffic originates from the root. The root has point-to-point frame relay connections (PVCs) to all leaves in the multicast group. The root also has a one-way multicast connection to the multicast server; this connection is called the Multicast Data Link Connection Identifier, or MDLCI. The multicast server accepts frames from the MDLCI and delivers them to each leaf member; frames arrive as though they were delivered on the individual PVCs and the DLCI in each received frame reflects the source of the message, not the MDLCI.

Two-way multicast service provides duplex communications channels (see Figure 11.11). In this model, each member of the multicast group has a point-to-point frame relay connection to the multicast server. One participant is defined as the root and the rest are designated as leaves. Two-way transmission is only allowed between the root and the leaves; data cannot be transferred from one leaf to another. In Figure 11.11, workstation A is the root and workstations B, C, and D are the leaves. The multicast server

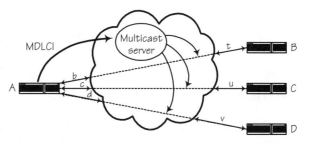

FIGURE 11.10 One-way multicast service model.

will accept a frame from station A on the MDLCI, then transmit it to each
of the leaf members. Leaves may return data via the same DLCI. For example, station C will send frames to station A on DLCI c and they will arrive
on station A's MDLCI, a.

In an N-way multicast service model, all transmissions are duplex
ones and all are multicast. Multicast group members are defined as peers.
Any data received by the multicast server is transmitted to all the members
of the active multicast group.

One-way multicasting is best used where the end stations are
routers or bridges, while two-way multicasting is useful where the root
does not need to communicate individually with the leaves and the number of leaf stations prohibits the establishment of individual PVCs
between the root and each leaf. The *N*-way multicast service is good for
applications that require all participants to acquire the same data, such
as videoconferencing.

The formal *multicast services over frame relay* specified by the Frame
Relay Forum are not yet widely available. Hence, if you currently subscribe to frame relay service, you and your vendor will likely need to archi-
tect your own multicast topology. Multicast frame relay is a relatively
static configuration, since the service provider must set up the DLCIs.

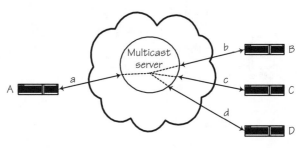

FIGURE 11.11 Two-way multicast service model.

However, because of flat-rate pricing, the user is not penalized if extra traffic is generated at the frame relay layer.

Switched Multimegabit Data Service

Switched Multimegabit Data Service (SMDS) is a combination of the features of a shared-media LAN and ATM (see Figure 11.12). It is based on the IEEE 802.6 protocol which defines the transmission of ATM cells over a shared bus. It is a connectionless high-speed terrestrial service that was originally developed by Bellcore to enable local exchange carriers to provide high-speed connectivity between LANs in a metropolitan area. SMDS can transfer data at rates of between 1.544 Mbps and 44.736 Mbps over T1 and T3 circuits.

Like ATM cells, each SMDS cell consists of a 48-byte payload and a 5-byte header. Since SMDS is a connectionless service for shared-media networks, it requires a more detailed addressing scheme than ATM. Thus, SMDS cells are not identical to ATM cells; they use an 8-bit access control field while ATM uses the 4-bit generic Flow Control Field.

Network addresses are basically telephone numbers. They consist of a 4-bit code followed by the standard components of a telephone number: country code, area code, and subscriber number. The customer may be assigned a special number to represent a list of SMDS telephone numbers—any packet sent to that number is delivered to all members on that

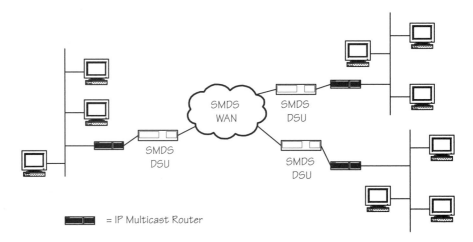

FIGURE 11.12 Example SMDS network.

list. Since all packets sent on the network are available for reception by all nodes, SMDS appears as a wide-area shared LAN and can support multicast natively.

SMDS is designed to accommodate bursty traffic. As long as the average data rate remains below an agreed-upon value, SMDS will make a best-effort attempt to deliver traffic to the correct destination.

Even though it's easy to deploy IP Multicast over SMDS, there are some cautions. Just as on a LAN, IP Multicast traffic is broadcast over the SMDS cloud. This would be acceptable to the user as long as the multicast traffic does not interfere with other traffic. But SMDS carriers typically tariff the service based on SMDS traffic as measured by an SMDS switch inside the network, which means that they will charge the user for traffic inside the SMDS network cloud that he does not receive, which isn't acceptable to most customers.

One possible solution is to create a number of multicast groups at the SMDS level and map particular host groups to them. However, this means that the host groups would have to be relatively static as SMDS groups; therefore, the dynamics of host group formation that's a part of IP multicasting would be lost.

Dial-Up Connections

In many ways, dial-up modems and ISDN (Integrated Services Digital Network) have little in common other than the copper wires they use, but it's convenient to talk about them in the same section when it comes to multicasting. That's mainly because individual ISDN circuits and dial-up modems essentially constrain you to a single architecture when you're designing your multicast networks. The router at your site that serves your ISDN or modem lines (see Figure 11.13) is the center of a star network. The PCs at the end of the modem or ISDN lines are leaf nodes and all multicast traffic destined for them must pass through the router.

In the past, it might have been inconceivable to use dial-up modems for IP multicasting, but the growth of individual use of the Internet, accompanied by technologies like 56-Kbps modems and streaming multimedia clients for PCs, is driving the usage of IP Multicasting over dial-up lines. The continuing increase in the numbers of telecommuters and mobile professionals also makes it important to consider supporting multicasting over dial-up connections. For the moment, this means

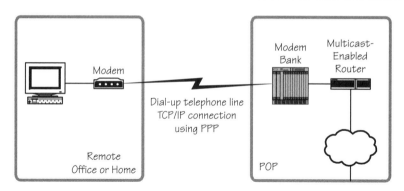

FIGURE 11.13   Sample dial-up network.

focusing on ISDN and dial-up modems, but it won't be long before xDSL (Digital Subscriber Line) technologies and cable modems provide other connections for individuals while they're on the road or working at a remote site.

ISDN is a service that's composed of two types of channels—bearer channels and signaling channels. ISDN providers combine these two channel types to create two different types of ISDN service offerings: the Basic Rate Interface (BRI) and the Primary Rate Interface (PRI).

Bearer, or B, channels do one thing—they carry data. B channels are 64-Kbps circuit-switched channels of the same type that handle a regular telephone voice call, although they're all digital. The signaling, or D, channel, is separate from the B channels to provide out-of-band signaling for call setup, teardown, and control.

There are two basic types of ISDN service. The Basic Rate Interface consists of two 64-Kbps B channels and one 16-Kbps D channel; the Primary Rate Interface consists of 23 B channels plus one 64-Kbps D channel. In Europe, PRI consists of 30 B channels plus one 64-Kbps D channel.

ISDN can offer two different types of connections, depending on your needs. If you're supporting a single remote user with an ISDN connection, then a terminal adapter (TA) and PPP for that PC or workstation should suffice. On the other hand, if the remote site wants to connect more than one computing device on a network, (i.e., it wants to connect its LAN to the network at the main office), then an ISDN router is called for.

Handling the ISDN lines at the corporate site isn't too difficult—you can use either a regular router with an ISDN interface or a dedicated ISDN router. Just make sure that the corporate ISDN router supports the same features as the SOHO (Small Office-Home Office) ISDN routers that are most likely installed at the remote sites. At the remote sites, you'll need to be sure that the ISDN router supports IGMP.

The sharpness and smoothness of video over ISDN is suitable for many multimedia applications. However, users connected via ISDN still need to be selective and choose multicast transmissions whose bandwidth can handle their connection (usually 64 or 128 Kbps). Multicast session guides should include bandwidth requirements to help host group members select the appropriate media encoding to participate; for instance, some users of ISDN may well have to select lower-grade video to participate in a conference or even select audio only if there are too many participants, leading to too many video feeds for the bandwidth of the ISDN line. This is even more important for smaller-bandwidth modem connections.

Many individuals or remote locations have connections to a private network using dial-up to the nearest network point-of-presence (POP) or directly to a corporate modem server. The remote host may be permanently assigned an IP address or it may be dynamically assigned. Dynamically-assigned addresses shouldn't cause a problem for receiving multicast data as long as the connection stays up during the session; if the user has to reconnect due to loss of the signal, then it's unlikely he'll receive the same IP address as he had in the previous connection, which will not match the original IGMP membership request. If you're also planning to use some of the multicasting protocols mentioned in Chapter 6 for reliable delivery or group control, then you may have to alter the use of dynamically assigned addresses. Some ISPs offer static address assignments, which solve the previous problem; another approach is to use DHCP (Dynamic Host Configuration Protocol) servers to assign fixed IP addresses to dial-in lines.

LAN Switches and Multicasting

Network architectures have changed over the past few years as fast, relatively inexpensive switches have become available. But switches in general do nothing to extend the benefits of multicasting to the nodes they serve. Most switches, especially the low-cost per-port switches, are strictly Layer 2 devices that look solely at MAC addresses, ignoring IGMP messages and flood multicast traffic out of all ports (see Figure 11.14).

There are currently only three possible solutions to use multicasting efficiently with switches—IGMP snooping, VLANs, and proprietary protocols.

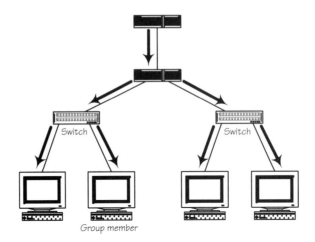

FIGURE 11.14 Multicasting in the presence of switches.

In *IGMP snooping*, higher-end switches can do some Layer 3 decoding and register multicast addresses by listening (snooping) on routine IGMP queries and report messages between hosts and routers. They also snoop on multicast routing protocols to identify the router ports.

Snooping is very processor-intensive because every multicast packet must be classified and analyzed. Higher-layer headers, such as the IP header, need to be analyzed to distinguish IGMP reports from data packets. Analyzing each packet not only puts a processing burden on the switch's CPU, it also introduces latency in packet transmissions. Since routers can run different multicast routing protocols, snooping also has to be done on a number of higher-layer protocols, further adding to the cost and complexity of these low-end switches.

The second approach is to use Virtual LANs (VLANs) to restrict broadcast and multicast traffic by logically grouping hosts in broadcast domains. Although flooding can be contained to a VLAN once it's defined, VLANs do not scale well because flooding increases as the membership of a VLAN grows. Furthermore, inter-LAN connectivity still requires routers, which defeats the purpose of using the higher-speed switches.

LAN switches that support VLANs can be used to effectively control broadcast traffic without resorting to routers. However, the challenge is to configure VLANs so that those LAN stations that normally communicate with each other belong to the same VLAN, while minimizing the size of VLANs and hence minimizing the size of network broadcast domains.

Many VLAN technologies have been implemented using proprietary protocols, making it difficult to mix and match products. However, work by the IEEE of the 802.1 class of protocols for VLANs is progressing; for instance, the IEEE 802.1Q standard defines changes to the Ethernet frame type, enabling VLAN information to be transmitted across a network. As these protocols are approved as standards and implemented in commercial products, VLAN product interoperability will improve.

Another protocol that's important to the support of IP Multicast on VLANs is the IEEE's P802.1p (Draft Standard for Traffic Class and Dynamic Multicasts Filtering Services in Bridged LANs). This standard defines the Generic Attribute Registration Protocol (GARP) and the GARP Multicast Registration Protocol (GMRP).

GARP is a Layer 2 transport mechanism that lets switches and hosts propagate useful information throughout the switching domain. When a host wants to receive a multicast, it uses GMRP to send a join message to the neighboring switch. Upon receiving the request, the switch sets a filter in its forwarding database and exchanges membership information with neighboring switches, much as routers do when they exchange routing tables. When a sender starts multicasting, the switch receives a packet with the specified group MAC address in the destination field, executes a hardware lookup, and forwards the packet to the receiver. Processing at the switch is considerably less than that required for either IGMP snooping or VLANs.

The third solution is to use a vendor's proprietary technology to link switches with routers to handle multicast traffic. For example, Cisco routers, using the Cisco Group Management Protocol (CGMP), can send MAC-address information to Cisco switches telling them which ports various multicast group traffic should be forwarded to (see Figure 11.15).

Deploying IP Multicasting

If you're planning to deploy IP multicasting support on your corporate network, it's always best to do so in gradual stages, just like for any other new technology. You can start with a localized, isolated test LAN, then work up to a few subnets, and then eventually use WAN links to get a broader base for multicasting.

As you start deploying multicasting, it's wise to start simple and set up a pilot project on a single LAN. This will enable you to determine just what kind of reduced bandwidth requirements you can gain from multicasting and also test the necessary software without interfering with, or even crashing, your production network.

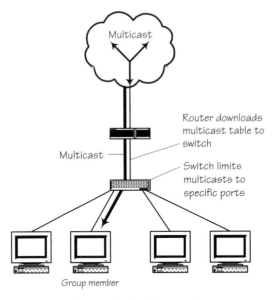

FIGURE 11.15 CGMP.

Once you're satisfied with your LAN-based tests, you can deploy the application to your local intranet (i.e., not over WAN links). Make sure that all your routers support multicasting.

Eventually, you may have to deploy multicast support in stages, especially if your network is geographically dispersed. If so, you can always use tunneling to link up the LANs supporting multicasting. Many routers now support multicast routing protocols, including DVMRP, MOSPF, and PIM, but recall that DVMRP is essential for creating tunnels.

If you're going to create tunnels over WAN links, bear in mind what bandwidth your multicast sessions will use. The MBone works without noticeably degrading the rest of the Internet's traffic (on most occasions) because bandwidth is limited to 500 Kbps. Since you (supposedly) have control over the bandwidth requirements of your intranet, you may choose to use more bandwidth for multicast sessions such as videoconferencing. In such situations, the total bandwidth you require will be less than if you used unicast traffic, only but recall that even a single video channel might eat up a lot of a WAN link's bandwidth.

Another issue that shouldn't be overlooked is that of network security. As I've mentioned in previous chapters, almost all multicasting traffic is carried in UDP packets. Many of the multimedia applications that use multicasting will send data to a host using one or more different UDP streams, which presents a challenge to packet-filtering firewalls, which are relatively common.

In order to accommodate incoming UDP streams, a standard packet filtering firewall must open one or more *high ports* (numbered greater than 1023) for the incoming connections. This can be a security issue because a high port might be open for internal network use, such as by a database server. In this situation, outside hackers can probe the network to find the address of the internal host that has the service open on the high port. This is one of the reasons why many sites choose to explicitly disallow all UDP traffic from crossing the firewall. One possible solution to this dilemma when you're running multicast traffic is to use newer firewalls that use *smart filters*, i.e., they attempt to add state to UDP by maintaining a list of UDP packets that have crossed the firewall interface and check inbound packets for corresponding outgoing UDP packets. The wide variety of firewalls makes the subject too complex to do it justice here and is best covered in other books; a good source of more information on network security and firewalls is *Internet Security for Business* by Terry Bernstein et al., (John Wiley and Sons, 1996).

Summary

Some care has to be exercised when you're planning to deploy IP multicasting on your network. Knowledge of your network's physical infrastructure is crucial, especially for your WAN links, since different physical media support multicasting differently.

The details of ATM support for IP Multicasting have been gradually refined and two services, the MCS, or MultiCast Server, and MARS, or Multicast Address Resolution Server, have been standardized for use with multicasting on ATM networks.

Satellite networks are another good way to multicast over WANs, particularly when only unidirectional multicasting is required. A low-bandwidth back-channel can be used to provide feedback from the host group members or with a reliable multicast protocol, but many-to-many multicasting is not compatible with satellite networks.

Frame relay networks are also useful for multicasting, although the design of the frame relay network depends greatly on the capabilities offered by your service provider and the nature of the multicasting application.

The growing interest in the use of switches instead of routers on networks has led to increased deployment of VLANs. VLANs can be used to restrict multicast traffic within the boundary of a domain, but switches can still cause problems with multicast traffic. Many less expensive and older switches simply flood multicast data onto their ports, defeating the purpose of multicasting. Quite a few newer switches can filter multicast traffic and the IEEE P802.1p standard has been developed to further simplify how a switch handles multicast traffic.

Future Directions

At the risk of sounding trite, IP Multicast has a promising future ahead of it. But, even though the MBone has been around for quite some time (in Internet years, at any rate), IP Multicast is still at an early stage of development when it comes to commercial use.

Many of the important protocols for multicast routing, reliable multicast, and multimedia transport have been developed only recently and have not yet seen widespread deployment. As a close to this book, let's take a look at how IP Multicast will develop over the near-term, what network uses it will impact, and what it will be impacted by.

The Evolving Multicast Infrastructure

The growth of the MBone since its inception in 1992 to include over 3400 subnets in more than 25 countries should be enough to convince many that interest in using multicasting has been growing, and growing quickly. Despite that growth, until 1997, the only way to use IP Multicast on the public Internet was to use the MBone.

Now that's changed as some of the major national Internet Service Providers rolled out multicasting services of their own last year. Admittedly, these services may have restricted uses in mind (streaming media, for example), but it's a start. Considering that the greatest fraction (60 percent) of the companies surveyed by the IP Multicast Initiative in 1997 were using multicasting for audio and video distribution, the ISPs' initial concentration on streaming multimedia makes sense. For the consumer market, distributing news and entertainment via multicasting may well prove to be the first major uses of multicasting on the Internet.

But these new commercial multicast networks pose problems of their own. As I mentioned in Chapter 10, these services only offer multicast delivery to clients of their networks. If you want to become a member of a particular host group, but just happen to be served by a different ISP, you'll not receive the session as multicast data, but via unicast methods.

Various issues have to be solved before this approach evolves to one that's ISP-independent. First, protocols for interdomain multicast routing have to be standardized by the IETF and deployed by the ISPs (see Chapter 5 for details on the latest proposals).

Second, and just as important, inter-provider policies have to be developed. Unfortunately, the usual approaches to defining provider policies for unicast traffic cannot be adapted to multicast traffic in a straightforward way. Peering agreements between ISPs are often settled between ISPs who can exchange similar volumes of traffic, and a lot of work is put into keeping the traffic flows in both directions even. Charging an ISP for differences in incoming versus outgoing volumes is a relatively simple issue. But that all changes with multicast traffic. Suppose that a single packet crosses the boundary from ISP A into ISP B, then triggers duplication into 100 or 1000 packets for distribution to host group members within ISP B's network (see Figure 12.1). How do you track the multicast packets within the domain? What kind of settlement algorithm is appropriate? These questions have yet to be answered. This thorny issue is being studied by the IETF and NANOG (North American Network Operators Group) so we should see some initial attempts at solutions before the year's end.

Even as more commercial multicast services become available, the MBone will continue, supporting its usual variety of conferences and experimental uses. It'll continue to be important to maintain an experimental network like the MBone for trying new protocols and applications for multicasting. Some of this work may well be transferred to the Internet II as it's built, but that won't happen immediately.

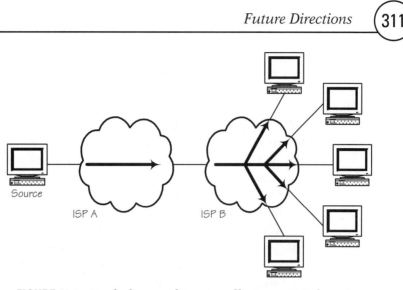

FIGURE 12.1 Exploding multicast traffic in an ISP domain.

Intranet Deployment

Even though businesses are already using the commercial multicasting services like BBN Pro Vision for business tasks other than distributing streaming multimedia, it's highly likely that intranets will prove to be "where the action's at" for multicast deployment over the next few years.

The deployment of IP Multicast within corporate networks is, in some ways, easier than on the Internet. That's mainly because your company controls the network. As long as you can prove that there's a business advantage (and even better, monetary gain) to the in-house use of IP Multicast, then you should be able to budget for the installation of multicast-capable equipment on your intranet.

Deployment may prove to be even simpler than you originally anticipated. Many newer routers, for instance, already include multicast routing protocols like DVMRP, MOSPF, and PIM; in such cases, it's just a question of configuring the routers to use multicasting. And the TCP/IP stacks in operating systems like Windows NT 4.0 and Windows95 include support for IGMP and multicasting.

What may prove to be more of an issue is what bandwidth you'll be able to allocate to multicasting. Multicasting is supposed to be a way to use bandwidth more efficiently, but the new multicasting applications you intend to support may well require more bandwidth and perhaps put constraints on network latency and jitter that didn't exist before. If you're moving towards use of multimedia and videoconferencing, for instance, deployment of multicast support may have to be accompanied by support for RSVP and quality of service.

Very few corporate networks use only one physical network medium. That's especially true if MANs (Metropolitan Area Networks) and WANs (Wide Area Networks) are involved. As I indicated in Chapter 11, every major network medium can be configured to support IP multicasting, and a great deal of effort has been expended to improve the standards that support multicasting on networks like frame relay, ATM, and satellites. This past year has seen many of these efforts become standards and commercial implementation of these standards is now starting to take off. Some interoperability issues may come up (they inevitably do at this stage of development), but you'll see the variety of available products increase significantly over the next one to two years.

With the plumbing part on its way to solution, multicasting software is poised to start taking off as well. Many of the applications I covered in Chapter 9 are the result of academic research projects. But more commercial multicast apps started to appear in 1997 and, thanks to the promotional efforts of the IP Multicast Initiative, more developers are becoming aware of the value of developing multicast applications. Again, your choices will only increase with time. And keep your eye on what the research groups are doing—don't forget that the Web browser and companies like Netscape grew out of the efforts of academic research projects.

But business use of multicast applications can place more stringent constraints on these applications than consumer or academic use. Mission-critical services may have to depend on reliable multicast protocols; we've seen just how complex that issue can be in Chapter 6. But, by early 1998, the market had enough commercially available packages for reliable multicasting that most initial business needs can be met. Even in 1997, large corporations like General Motors and Toys-"Я"-Us were routinely using satellite networks and reliable multicasting to distribute software and inventory updates on their corporate networks.

Expect the patterns of corporate use of multicasting to change over the next few years. The 1997 survey by the IP Multicast Initiative, which I mentioned earlier, indicated that current corporate use focuses on using multicasting for audio and video distribution, collaboration and conferencing, and delivering information (publish-and-subscribe or push technologies) on their networks. It seems likely that applications for transferring large files, such as software updates and inventory reports, will increase in popularity in the corporate sphere; some corporations have already been doing that (often over satellite networks) and some significant strategic alliances were made in 1997 between legacy software firms and companies providing multicast file distribution technologies using reliable multicast protocols. I'd also expect that, as collaborative and workflow applications are written to use multicasting more, they'll become just as important as streaming multimedia, if not more so. And, as the uses for information dissemination with publish-and-subscribe systems mature, multicasting will increase in usage.

Ties with Other Protocols

One of the reasons that IP networks and particularly the Internet have proven to be so successful is the modular way that the protocols have been designed. Even though many of the protocols have been designed by different groups, they work well together. IP Multicast is a part of that effort, and its continued growth and implementation on IP networks will likely be impacted by developments of other protocols, particularly IPv6 and RSVP.

Just like the MBone, there's a test network for IPv6 that's called the 6bone. But IPv6 has not yet been widely implemented on other networks. To some degree, that's because various details of IPv6 implementations have not been settled. Also, some of the important features (aside from the larger address space that IPv6 provides) can be implemented in IPv4, though perhaps not as easily.

The currently strong ties between IP Multicast and multimedia implies that developments in IP Multicast and the Integrated Services Architecture, especially RSVP, will affect each other. In fact, RSVP has largely been focused on multicast sessions since its inception. Even though RSVP support is now included in some routers, its deployment is rather limited. It'll take some time for network managers to get a feel for how well RSVP works and what effects it'll have on router resources and network traffic.

Challenges for the Future

IP Multicast has the ability to impact two significant uses of the IP networks: (1) reducing the bandwidth required for multimedia and video-conferencing and (2) simplifying the resources needed for distributing information. In many cases, the technologies for these uses are relatively recent and are only slowly becoming mainstream on the Internet as well as intranets.

But streaming multimedia, videoconferencing, and publish-and-subscribe data distribution aren't the only network applications that will come to depend on multicasting more and more.

One area that I've not covered in the book, but is receiving quite a bit of study in some circles, is that of distributed simulations. This includes battle simulations being studied by the U.S. Department of Defense (DoD) as well as other academic work on multiparty games using the MBone. (For instance, MiMaze is a multiplayer maze game that's been designed for use on the MBone.) In the IETF, the Large Scale Multicast Applications Working Group (LSMA) is focusing on the needs of these applications, which require real-time or near-real-time communications. The DoD goals are to use IP multicast for simulations using 10,000 simultaneous groups for upwards of 100,000 simulation processes (virtual entities) in a global-sized WAN by the year 2000. The work on Distributed Interactive Simulation (DIS) has expanded to incorporating VRML (Virtual Reality Markup Language) and Java.

In the past, many network applications were designed solely for one-to-one communications. That's now changed as more users have connected to networks and useful work can be done electronically between members of a team or among groups of people. Whenever it's necessary to exchange information between more than a few systems, IP multicasting has the opportunity to reduce bandwidth requirements and provide the infrastructure for further application development. This doesn't only apply to procedures like collaborative work using groupware applications or entertainment like multiuser games, but also exchanging information between controllers on the factory floor or replicating servers. Over the next few years, you'll not only see new uses of multicasting, but also the ability to use IP multicasting over practically any network media, including not just land-based and satellite networks, but also wireless systems (see Figure 12.2).

Many of the companies using IP multicasting might well be classed as working on the "bleeding edge." Certainly, IP multicasting is not yet in any shape to be used by everyone on all IP networks. But that will change with time. In order to see a wider-spread deployment of IP multicasting, certain issues need to be resolved. I've already mentioned the issues of inter-domain routing and ISP-related policies earlier in this chapter, so let's move on to other issues.

For one, there needs to be further development of reliable multicasting. Too many protocols for reliable multicasting exist. The situation is too complex to guarantee that we'll converge on only one protocol for reliable multicasting, but we need to settle on just a handful to make implementation simpler. To that end, the IRTF (Internet Research Task Force) has

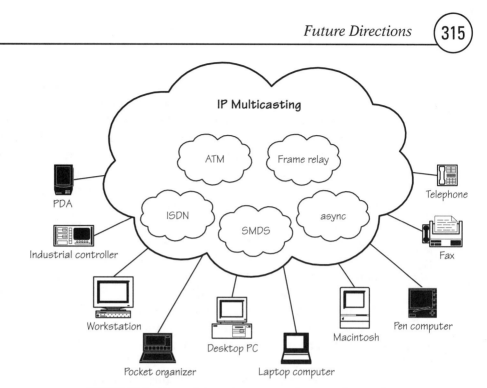

FIGURE 12.2 IP multicasting everywhere and anywhere.

formed a research group in 1997 to guide the development of standards for reliable multicast.

Maintaining the security and privacy of multicast sessions will be extremely important for many commercial applications. But the infrastructure required for distributing encryption keys is just evolving and isn't well-suited in its current form for multicast sessions. Small groups can use the

The IRTF

We've said a lot about the efforts of the IETF, or Internet Engineering Task Force, which is responsible for developing standards and best practices for the Internet. Another important group is the Internet Research Task Force, or IRTF. The IRTF is composed of a number of small research groups which are focused on long-term study of special topics related to Internet protocols. The IRTF's mission is to promote research of importance to the evolution of the future Internet. The IRTF is managed by the IRTF Chair in consultation with the Internet Research Steering Group (IRSG); the IRTF Chair is appointed by the Internet Architecture Board (IAB). For more information, visit http://www.irtf.org.

current technologies and infrastructure, but we'll have to wait for better methods to use encryption on a large scale. If you're planning to encrypt multicast data for private sessions, don't assume that the problem will be solved by network layer security, such as via IPSec; other methods will have to be used until IPSec is widely deployed. Again, this will be more easily accomplished within an intranet since there's some modicum of control and policy-setting for both senders and receivers; this will eventually extend to business partners using an extranet, but routine use that changes from day-to-day is further down the road.

I've said a lot about quality of service in this book, not only for delivering interactive multimedia, but also for real-time delivery of other types of information such as stock quotes, other financial information and manufacturing data. Quality of service has not been widely offered on commercial IP networks and really only began to attain visibility in 1997. Despite the increased press coverage of QoS issues, it still remains to be seen when you'll need special QoS classes for your network traffic and how they'll be provided. At this point, we're all still in the early stages of the learning curve.

Session announcement and control is another issue that needs more work to simplify the use of multicasting outside of research environments and bring it into the mainstream. The work of the mmusic working group is a good first step in standardizing session descriptions and announcements, but directories and tools have to be put into place to enable anyone to easily use the information as it becomes available. Not only will we see more "TV Guides" for multicast sessions become available, we'll also see conference announcements tied to LDAP directories; plus we'll probably have agents that scan the Internet for announcements of interest to us.

In case you haven't noticed, the business world has become more mobile. Not only do we have home offices and satellite office facilities for workers that frequent more than one location, but cellular modems and other wireless technologies coupled with laptops mean that workers expect to be able to use their networks from just about any location, at any time. The old paradigm for IP networks was that an IP address was associated with a fixed geographic location, your desktop computer for instance, but that's changing. The standards for Mobile IP are still being worked out and, along with them, are proposals for handling multicast traffic to mobile nodes. Eventually, you'll be able participate in multicast sessions as either a sender and/or a receiver regardless of your location and network link.

Lastly, multicast management has to improve. Tools are needed to expose the underlying group forwarding topology, group memberships, compliance with requested transmission properties, and source reachability. Various SNMP MIBs (Management Information Bases) have been proposed for multicast routers, but these need to be integrated with standard network management tools. Troubleshooting tools need to be able to handle source-to-member and member-to-source modes, as well as account for multicast policy, once it's been defined.

Keeping Up

None of the technologies I've described in this book are "written in stone." Even if the specification of protocols and their deployment follows a relatively deliberate path, the development of Internet-related technologies often seems to follow an unbelievably fast pace. Keeping up with some of these technologies can be a full-time job.

Once you've finished this book, you'll want to keep track of developments in IP multicasting since so many new possibilities are likely. A good starting point is the IP Multicast Initiative (http://www.ipmulticast.com). You may also want to track events in various IETF Working Groups, particularly those shown in Table 12.1.

TABLE 12.1 Important IETF Working Groups

Group name	Acronym	Web Site
Audio/Video Transport	AVT	http://www.ietf.org/html.charters/ avt-charter.html
Integrated Services	INTSERV	http://www.ietf.org/html.charters/ intserv-charter.html
Integrated Services over Specific Link Layers	ISSLL	http://www.ietf.org/html.charters/ issll-charter.html
Inter-Domain Multicast Routing	IDMR	http://www.ietf.org/html.charters/ idmr-charter.html
Large Scale Multicast Applications	LSMA	http://www.ietf.org/html.charters/ lsma-charter.html
MBone Deployment	MBONED	http://www.ietf.org/html.charters/ mboned-charter.html
Multiparty Multimedia Session Control	MMUSIC	http://www.ietf.org/html.charters/ mmusic-charter.html
Resource Reservation Setup Protocol	RSVP	http://www.ietf.org/html.charters/ rsvp-charter.html
Routing Over Large Clouds	ROLC	http://www.ietf.org/html.charters/ rolc-charter.html

If you're interested in tracking what Internet Drafts are available on a subject, a good source is http://www.ietf.cnri.reston.va.us/lid-abstracts .html, which groups current Internet Drafts by working group. Don't forget to review the drafts listed under individual submissions, since many early proposals are listed there rather than under a working group.

Good luck and have fun!

Glossary

AAL (*ATM Adaptation Layer*)   A group of protocols that takes data traffic and frames it into a sequence of 48-byte payloads for transmission over an ATM network.

AAL5   An ATM Adaptation Layer designed to support connection-oriented traffic at variable bit rates.

ACK (*Acknowledgment*)   A message that confirms receipt of a transmitted packet.

Adaptive Application Software   This expects a consistent quality of service (QoS) at any point in time, but can adjust its operation to adapt to changes in the actual QoS that's provided; synonymous with tolerant application.

Addressing   A network function for identifying various components of the networks, such as hosts, nodes, routers, etc., but assigning them unique numbers called network addresses.

All Hosts Group   A special multicast address used to reach all of the multicast hosts that are directly connected to the same network as the source host (address = 224.0.0.1).

Area   A group of networks and routers that use the same interior proto-col to route packets both within the group and among other groups.

ARP (*Address Resolution Protocol*)   A TCP/IP-based protocol used in routing for converting IP addresses into physical network addresses.

AS (*Autonomous System*)   A collection of networks and routers con-trolled by a single administrative authority; most commonly used in inter-domain routing, where an AS describes a self-connected set of networks that share a common external policy for connectivity.

Asynchronous   When applied to communications, an approach for syn-chronizing signals between sender and receiver on a per-byte basis; start and stop bits are used as delimiters.

ATM (*Asynchronous Transfer Mode*)   An asynchronous architecture for framing and transmitting data. ATM includes fixed-length data cells of 53 bytes, consisting of a 5-byte cell header and a 48-byte payload.

Authentication   In cryptography, the process of verifying the identity of the sender of a message as well as proof that the message has not been altered.

Backbone Networks   Very high-speed networks used to interconnect WANs, MANs, and LANs.

Best-Effort Delivery   A class of data delivery in which there are no abso-lute delivery guarantees and no specific traffic parameters.

Border Router   A router located on the edge of an AS (Autonomous System); it uses BGP (Border Gateway Protocol) to exchange routing information with another administrative routing domain.

BRI (*Basic Rate Interface*)   An ISDN service specification that provides two 64-Kbps B-channels and one 16-Kbps D-channel, all on the same physical link.

Broadcast   In networking, a process that forwards a data packet to all nodes of the network even if only a few of the destinations are intended recipients.

Cipher Text   Data that has been encrypted. Despite the use of the word "text," any digital data can be encrypted into cipher text.

Circuit Switching   A networking method in which information is carried over a dedicated path that connects the source to the destination through several network nodes. A logical channel for the connection is established at each of the physical links before data is transmitted.

Class D Address   The set of IPv4 addresses reserved for multicasting; the first four bits in a Class D address are 1110.

Codec (*Coder-decoder or encoder-decoder*)   A communications device (hardware or software) that converts an analog media type (e.g., voice, video) and converts the data into a digital stream or vice versa.

Connectionless   When referring to a communications service, a service where packets are transferred from a source to a destination without requiring a preestablished connection.

Connection-Oriented   A communication service where an initial connection between the source and destination must be established before transmission of any data.

CRC (*Cyclic Redundancy Check*)   A bit-error detection technique that appends parity (redundancy) bits to the packet based on a mathematical algorithm. If, upon receipt of the packet, the receiver calculates the same parity bits as the ones received with the packet, the packet does not contain errors.

CSU/DSU (*Channel Service Unit/Data Service Unit*)   A customer premise (CPE) device which is used to provide the interface for circuit data services, which includes the physical framing, clocking, and channelization of the circuit.

Datagram   The packets that IP transfers; datagram consists of a datagram header and the data area.

DE (*Discard Eligible*)   A bit field defined within the frame relay header which indicates that a frame can be discarded within the frame relay switch when the local queuing load exceeds a configured threshold.

Dense-Mode Routing   A multicast routing protocol that's designed to deal with network topologies where many of an internetwork's subnets contain at least one host group member. Dense-mode routing algorithms use the flood-and-prune technique, sending and storing explicit prune states in response to excess data packets.

DHCP (*Dynamic Host Configuration Protocol*)   A protocol which can be used on end-system computers to automatically obtain an IP host address, subnet mask, and local gateway information. A DHCP server dynamically supplies this information in response to the host's broadcast requests.

Distance-Vector Routing   A routing protocol where the shortest-path computation is based on periodic exchange of an array of distances from a given node to every other node in the network. This array is called a distance vector.

DLCI (*Data Link Connection Identifier*)   A numerical identifier assigned to the local end of a frame relay virtual circuit.

DNS (*Domain Name Service*)   A TCP/IP-based service that provides translations between TCP/IP domain names and IP addresses.

DVMRP (*Distance-Vector Multicast Routing Protocol*)   A multicast routing protocol that uses a distance vector to determine the network topology. The most common routing protocol used for the MBone.

EGP (*Exterior Gateway Protocol*)   A routing protocol that allows gateways attached to different networks to exchange routing information.

FCS (*Frame Check Sequence*)   Any mathematical formula that derives a numeric value based on the bit pattern of a transmitted block of data and uses that value at the receiver to determine if there are any transmission errors.

FEC (*Forward Error Correction*)   An error correction technique where no retransmissions are made; the receiver is responsible for correcting any errors in the packets by using the parity bits.

Flooding   In routers, forwarding a received packet on all interfaces except the one on which it arrived.

Forwarding Table   *See* Routing Table.

FRAD (*Frame Relay Access Device*)   A device which operates natively at the data-link layer of frame relay. The device frames and transmits traffic over a frame relay network; at the receiving end, a FRAD extracts the traffic from the frame and places it on the local media.

Frame Relay   A high-speed, connection-oriented packet-switching technology that provides efficient, reliable packet delivery over virtual circuits. The basic transport unit is called a frame and carries both routing and user information.

Hash   *See* Message Digest.

Header   The front portion of a packet that contains protocol, layer, and control information.

Hierarchical Routing   Dividing the network into a number of individual routing domains, where each routing domain executes its own routing protocol. Another protocol, or another instance of the same protocol, is used for routing between the individual domains.

Hop   Crossing a router from one subnetwork to another.

Hop Limit Field   In IPv6, the name of the field that replaces the function of IPv4's TTL field; *see* TTL.

Host   An end-point system attached to a network; it either sends or receives messages.

Host Group   A set of network hosts sharing a common identifying multicast address; all members of a host group receive any data packets addressed to this multicast address.

HTML (*HyperText Markup Language*)   A document formatting language used to format content which is presented in Web pages on the World Wide Web.

HTTP (*HyperText Transfer Protocol*)   A TCP-based application-layer protocol used for communicating between Web servers and Web clients.

ICMP (*Internet Control Message Protocol*) An network-layer protocol in the TCP/IP suite that provides feedback on errors and other information that relates to IP packet handling.

IGMP (*Internet Group Management Protocol*) A protocol that allows a router to discover which hosts on its LAN are interested in participating in which multicast groups.

Integrated Services Architecture The system designed by the Integrated Services Working Group of the IETF for the transport of audio, video, real-time, and regular data traffic within a single network infrastructure. The architecture consists of five components: QoS requirements, resource-sharing requirements, allowances for dropping packets, provisions for usage feedback, and a resource reservation model.

Inter-Area Multicast Forwarder In MOSPF, an area border router that is responsible for forwarding group membership information and multicast datagrams between areas.

Interface In routing, the connection between a router and one of its attached networks. An interface has state information associated with it, which is obtained from the lower-level protocols and the routing protocol itself. An interface is sometimes also referred to as a link.

Intolerant Application Software that requires either absolute or statistical guarantees of the network's performance.

IP (*Internet Protocol*) The network layer protocol in the TCP/IP suite. It is a connectionless protocol which includes extensions for host and subnetwork addressing, routing security, as well as fragmentation and reassembly.

IPv4 (*Internet Protocol version 4*) The version of the Internet Protocol that is most widely deployed today.

IPv6 (*Internet Protocol version 6*) The version of the Internet Protocol that has been proposed as the successor to IPv4. IPv6 has a larger address field (128 bits as compared to IPv4's 32-bit field).

ISDN (*Integrated Services Digital Network*) A protocol reference model intended to provide ubiquitous, end-to-end digital service for data, audio, and video.

Jitter The distortion of a signal as it is propagated through a network, where the signal varies from its original reference timing. In packet-switched networks, jitter is the distortion of the inter-packet arrival times as compared to the inter-packet times of the original transmission. The variation in latency.

Join Latency The time taken to forward the membership request to a router on the delivery tree of a host group.

LAN (*Local Area Network*)   A local communications environment where any connected host can contact any other connected system without the need for a routing protocol.

LANE (*LAN Emulation*)   An ATM specification which defines how to provide LAN-based communications across an ATM subnetwork.

Latency   Network delay; the minimum time that elapses between requesting and receiving data.

Leave Latency   The delay between the time when a host group member issues a Leave request and when multicast traffic from that host group ceases to be received by the former member.

Link State Routing   A routing algorithm in which routers share only the identity of their neighbors, but they flood the entire network with this information.

LIS (*Logical IP Subnetwork*)   An IP subnetwork where all devices have a direct communication path to other devices sharing the same LIS, such as on a shared LAN or point-to-point circuit.

Local Repair   A recovery mechanism for lost multicast packets where receivers may also carry out retransmissions.

LSA (*Link State Advertisement*)   A packet forwarded during the link-state routing process to neighboring nodes which includes information concerning the local node. The information includes the link state of the attached interfaces, or the topology of the network. Used in OSPF.

MARS (*Multicast Address Resolution Server*)   A mechanism for resolving IP and ATM multicast addresses.

MBone   A virtual network layered atop sections of the physical Internet for transmission of IP multicast sessions.

MCS (*Multicast Server*)   A network entity in ATM networks that receives data from an ATM host over a virtual circuit and, in turn, retransmits the data to the members of the multicast group over a point-to-multipoint virtual circuit.

Message Digest   The representation of a chunk of data as a single string of digits created using a one-way hash function; also called a hash.

Mixer   In RTP, a device that combines multiple streams into a single stream, preserving the original format.

MOSPF (*Multicast Open Shortest Path First*)   An extension to the OSPF routing protocol to allow handling multicast routing; it is a link-state multicast routing protocol.

MPOA (*Multiprotocol Over ATM*)   A series of specifications and procedures that enable network layer protocols to operate directly atop ATM and provide end-to-end internetworking between hosts in an ATM and a non-ATM environment.

MTP (*Multicast Transport Protocol*)   A transport-level protocol designed to support reliable multicast transfers. It is a sender-based protocol that utilizes a master entity to order messages from producers and maintain rate control for any data transmissions.

MTU (*Maximum Transmission Unit*)   The maximum allowed data unit that can be transmitted over a particular physical medium.

Multicast   A one-to-many packet forwarding scheme where a single packet is addressed only to the intended recipients and the network replicates packets only as needed.

Multiplexing   A method where multiple input streams of data are combined into a single output stream so they can share a common physical medium.

Multipoint   In communications, one-to-many or many-to-many data transmissions.

Next Hop   Relative to the current router, the next router along the path to network N.

Non-Repudiation   The property of a secure system that prevents anyone from denying that he or she sent a file or data when in fact he or she did.

One-Way Hash Functions   A class of cryptographic functions which encrypt data without using a key. The data is encrypted to a fixed-length string of digits that is assumed to be unique because of its randomness.

OPWA (*One Pass With Advertising*)   A method to allow RSVP control packets that are sent downstream to gather information that may be used to predict the end-to-end QoS. The results (advertisements) are delivered by RSVP to the receiver hosts and to the receiver applications if necessary. The advertisements may then be used by the receiver to construct, or to dynamically adjust, an appropriate reservation request.

OSI (*Open Systems Interconnection*) Reference Model   The 7-layer model created by the ISO that defines basic network functions. Each layer in the model corresponds to one level of network functionality.

OSPF (*Open Shortest Path First*)   An interior gateway routing protocol which uses a link-state protocol coupled with a shortest-path first path selection algorithm.

Packet-Switching   A networking method where data between two end-systems is not sent as a continuous stream of bits, but is divided into small units called packets that are sent one at a time. These packets are multiplexed or allocated different time slots for transmission.

Peer Communication   Entities communicating at the same level in a hierarchy of communications services. Peer communications governed by protocols in a given layer take place as if no other protocols are involved.

PIM (*Protocol-Independent Multicast*)   A multicast routing protocol designed to provide scalable inter-domain routing; it is not dependent on any particular unicast routing protocol. Its specifications include two modes, dense and sparse. The dense mode operates similarly to DVMRP. The sparse mode requires downstream routers with members to explicitly join the multicast delivery tree.

Positive Acknowledgment with Retransmission   A Method for acknowledging receipt of a packet, it requires that a recipient send an acknowledgment message back to the source as it receives data. The sender keeps a record of each packet sent and waits for an acknowledgment before sending the next packet.

PPP (*Point-to-Point Protocol*)   A data-link framing protocol used to frame data packets on point-to-point links, such as modem links.

PRI (*Primary Rate Interface*)   An ISDN user interface specification. In North America, a PRI is a single 64-Kbps D-channel used for signaling and 23 64-Kbps B-channels used for voice or data.

Processing Delay   The time required by a router for looking up routes, changing the header, and other switching tasks.

Propagation Delay   The length of time it takes information to travel the distance of the line.

Protocol   A rule that governs end-to-end or node-to-node communications between peer entities across a network. It includes procedures for establishing, maintaining, and managing those communications.

Public-Key Cryptography   An encryption method that uses a pair of keys—one public and one private. Messages encoded with either key can be decoded by the other. Also called asymmetric encryption.

PVC (*Permanent Virtual Circuit*)   A virtual connection that's established by network management between a source and a destination, and that can be left up permanently.

QoS (*Quality of Service*)   A term used to describe a set of performance parameters that characterize the transmission quality over a given connection.

RARP (*Reverse Address Resolution Protocol*)   IP-based protocol that converts physical network addresses into IP addresses.

Rigid Application   Software that requires either absolute or statistical guarantees of the network's performance; synonymous with intolerant application.

RIP (*Routing Information Protocol*)   An interior routing protocol that uses a distance vector algorithm and is based on hop counts. Essentially historical.

Route Pinning   Specifying that intermediate nodes in a path through a network will not change unless one of the links breaks. A method to ensure that a routing path doesn't change due to changes in traffic or other network conditions.

Routers   A networking device for forwarding packets and for interconnecting two nodes that may belong to either homogeneous or non-homogeneous networks.

Routing   The process of calculating the network topology and finding a path from a source to every destination in the network based on the network layer information contained in packets.

Routing Table   The array in a router that stores the next hops for each destination in the network.

RP (*Rendezvous Point*)   In shared-tree multicast routing algorithms, rendezvous points are used by senders to announce their existence and by receivers to learn about new senders of a group.

RSVP (*Resource ReSerVation Protocol*)   An IP-based protocol used for communicating QoS requirements to intermediate nodes in a network. RSVP uses a *soft state* mechanism to maintain path and reservation state in each node along the reservation path and can be dynamically changed by the requesting host.

RTCP (*Real-Time Control Protocol*)   Part of the RTP specification, this protocol is used to monitor and control RTP data transfers.

RTP (*Real-Time Transport Protocol*)   A protocol, used primarily with IP, that provides sequence numbering and time stamping for the delivery of multimedia data. It is a connectionless protocol that provides end-to-end delivery services.

RTSP (*Real-Time Streaming Protocol*)   An application-level protocol that aims to provide a robust protocol for streaming multimedia in multipoint applications over either unicast or multicast.

SAP (*Session Announcement Protocol*)   A protocol which distributes SDP session descriptions by periodic multicasting of announcement packets to a well-known address (224.2.127.254).

SDP (*Session Description Protocol*)   An application-level protocol that conveys information about multicast sessions, including relevant setup data; a format for session descriptions.

Service Boundary   The interface between adjoining layers in a protocol stack. Data is transmitted from one layer to another through the service boundary, as defined by the lower layer's service definition.

SIP (*Session Initiation Protocol*)   An application-level protocol used to explicitly invite specific users to a session. The protocol can be used either for unicast sessions, such as a call using IP telephony, or multicast sessions.

Sliding Window Technique   A procedure for providing reliable data transfers that relies on positive acknowledgments and transmits a series of packets before it receives an acknowledgment.

SMDS (*Switched Multimegabit Data Services*)   A connectionless, fast packet-switching B-ISDN service based on 53-byte packets. Can be used to interconnect different LANs into a switched public network, or to interconnect WANs and MANs.

Source-Ordered Delivery   Delivery of data packets where the order of the transmission is maintained for each sender. Source-ordered protocols do not make guarantees on the order in which packets from different senders are received by a receiver.

Spanning Tree   A routing structure that defines a subset of the internetwork in which only one active path connects any two routers. A spanning tree has just enough connectivity so that there is only one path between every pair of routers; it is loop-free.

ST-II (*Stream Protocol Version II*)   A sender-based network layer multicasting protocol that provides support for continuous media streams over IP networks; it supports both unicast and multicast traffic.

Streaming Multimedia   Multimedia data where the received streams are smoothly rearranged to resemble the original stream and thus can be reproduced with fidelity.

Subnetwork   A portion of an internetwork where all systems that can directly communicate using homogeneous technologies.

SVC (*Switched Virtual Circuit*)   A logical connection where control signaling is used to set up and tear down the connection dynamically.

Symmetric Encryption   An encryption method where both the sender and the receiver possess the same cryptographic key, which means that both parties can encrypt and decrypt data with that key.

T1   A WAN transmission circuit that carries DS1-formatted data at a rate of 1.544 Mbps.

T3   A WAN transmission circuit that carries DS3-formatted data at a rate of 44.736 Mbps.

TCP (*Transmission Control Protocol*)   A reliable, connection- and byte-oriented transport layer protocol within the TCP/IP protocol suite. TCP packetizes data into segments, provides for packet sequencing, and end-to-end flow control.

TELNET   A TCP-based terminal emulation protocol used in IP networks for connecting to, and logging into, remote systems.

Token Bucket   A traffic-shaping mechanism where the ability to transmit packets from any given flow is controlled by the presence of tokens. In order for packets belonging to a specific flow to be transmitted, a token must be available in the token, otherwise the packet is either queued or dropped. Controls the transmit rate as well as accommodating bursty traffic.

Tolerant Application   Software that expects a consistent quality of service (QoS) at any point in time, but can adjust its operation to adapt to changes in the actual QoS that's provided.

Totally Ordered Delivery   Ensures that all packets are received by all receivers in the same order; this order may follow some global rule.

Translator   In RTP, a device that translates from one payload format to another.

Transmission Delay   The length of time it takes to send the packet across a given medium.

TTL (*Time To Live*)   A field in the IP packet header that specifies how long, in seconds, the datagram is allowed to remain on an internetwork. The TTL value is decremented at each hop; when the TTL equals zero, the packet is no longer considered to be valid.

Tunneling   The process of encapsulating one type of packet (multicast packets, for instance) in another packet type so that the data can be transferred across paths which otherwise would not transmit the data.

UDP (*User Datagram Protocol*)   An IP-based protocol that is connectionless and unreliable, guaranteeing neither packet sequence, delivery, nor acknowledgment of delivery.

UNI (*User-Network-Interface*)   The ATM specification for signaling between a user-based device, such as a router or similar end-system, and the ATM switch.

Unicast   Network communications where a separate copy of the data is delivered to each recipient.

Unordered Delivery   Packet delivery where there are no guarantees on the order in which packets are delivered to the receiver.

VC (*Virtual Circuit*)   An end-to-end connection between two devices which spans a Layer 2 switching fabric (such as ATM or frame relay). A VC may be permanent (PVC) or temporary (SVC).

VLAN (*Virtual LAN*)   A networking architecture which allows end-systems on topologically disconnected subnetworks to appear to be connected on the same LAN.

WAN (*Wide Area Network*)   A network environment where the elements of the network are located at significant distances from each other, and the communications facilities typically use carrier facilities rather than private wiring. Typically, a routing protocol is required to support communications between two distant host systems on a WAN.

Whiteboard   Software for multiparty communications where data can be displayed as text and/or graphics and altered by any participant.

Wild-Card Multicast Receiver   A router that receives all multicast traffic generated in the area in which it's located.

XTP (*Xpress Transport Protocol*)   Actually a series of protocols, including network- and transport-level protocols, for transmitting data on IP networks. XTP supports multimedia distribution as well as real-time embedded systems and includes multicast group management as well as multicast transport facilities.

Resources

Books

Bernstein, Terry, Anish B. Bhimani, Eugene Schultz and Carol A. Siegel. *Internet Security for Business.* New York: John Wiley & Sons, Inc., 1996.

Comer, Douglas E. *Internetworking with TCP/IP,* Vol. I: *Principles, Protocols and Architecture,* 3d ed. Englewood Cliffs, NJ: Prentice-Hall, 1995.

Huitema, Christian, *Routing in the Internet.* Englewood Cliffs, NJ: Prentice-Hall PTR, 1995.

Schneier, Bruce, *Applied Cryptography,* 2nd ed. New York: John Wiley & Sons, Inc., 1996.

Thomas, Stephen A. *IPng and the TCP/IP Protocols.* New York: John Wiley & Sons, Inc., 1996.

Articles

Armitage, G. J. "Multicast and Multiprotocol Support for ATM Based Internets," *ACM Computer Communication Review* 25 (April 1995).

Ballardie, A., P. Francis, and J. Crowcroft. "CBT—An Architecture for Scalable Inter-Domain Multicast Routing." *Proceedings of ACM SIG-COMM.* San Francisco, CA (1993): 85–95.

Casner, S. "Are you on the MBone?" *IEEE MultiMedia* (Summer 1994); 76–79, 94.

Casner, S. and S. Deering. "First IETF Internet Audiocast. *Computer Communications Review* 22,3 (July 1992).

Clark, D. D., S. Shenker, and L. Zhang. "Supporting Real-Time Applications in an Integrated Services Packet Network: Architecture and Mechanism." *Proceedings of ACM SIGCOMM.* Maryland (1992).

Clark, D. D. and D. L. Tennenhouse. "Architectural Considerations for a New Generation of Protocols." *Proceedings of ACM SIGCOMM.* Philadelphia, Pennsylvania (1990).

Deering, S. "Multicast Routing in Internetworks and Extended LANs." *Proceedings of ACM SIGCOMM 88.* (August 1988): 55–64.

Deering, S. and D. Cheriton. "Multicast routing in datagram internetworks and extended LANs." *ACM Transactions on Computer Systems* (May 1990): 85–111.

Deering, S., D. Estrin, D. Farinacci, V. Jacobson, and C-G. Liu, and L. Wei, "An Architecture for Wide Area Multicast Routing." ACM SIGCOMM London, *ACM CCR* 24, no. 4 (October 1994): 126–135.

Eriksson, H. "MBONE: The multicast backbone." *Communications ACM,* 37 (August 1994): 54–60.

Floyd, S., V. Jacobson, S. McCanne, C-G. Liu, and L. Zhang. "A Reliable Multicast Framework for Light-weight Sessions and Application Level Framing." *ACM SIGCOMM* (1995): 342–356.

Handley, M., I. Wakeman, and J. Crowcroft. "The Conference Control Channel Protocol (CCCP): A scalable base for building conference control applications." *ACM SIGCOMM* (1995).

Levine, B. N., and J. J. Garcia-Luna-Aceves. "A Comparison of Known Classes of Reliable Multicast Protocols." *Proceedings of International Conference on Network Protocols* (ICNP-96), Columbus, Ohio (October 29–November 1, 1996).

Macedonia, M. R., D. P. Brutzman. "MBone Provides Audio and Video Across the Internet." *IEEE Computer,* 27 no. 4 (April 1994): 30–36.

Pasquale, J. C., G. C. Polyzos, and G. Xylomenos. "The multimedia multicasting problem." *ACM Multimedia Systems Journal* (forthcoming).

IETF Documents—RFCs

RFC 2216, Network Element Service Specification Template. S. Shenker, and J. Wroclawski. September 1997. (Status: Informational).

RFC 2215, General Characterization Parameters for Integrated Service Network Elements. S. Shenker, and J. Wroclawski. September 1997. (Status: Proposed Standard).

RFC 2214, Integrated Services Management Information Base Guaranteed Service Extensions using SMIv2. F. Baker, J. Krawczyk, and A. Sastry. September 1997. (Status: Proposed Standard).

RFC 2213, Integrated Services Management Information Base using SMIv2. F. Baker, J. Krawcyzk, and A. Sastry. September 1997. (Status: Proposed Standard).

RFC 2212, Specification of Guaranteed Quality of Service. S. Shenker, C. Partridge, and R. Guerin. September 1997. (Status: Proposed Standard).

RFC 2211, Specification of the Controlled-Load Network Element Service. J. Wroclawski. September 1997. (Status: Proposed Standard).

RFC 2210, The Use of RSVP with IETF Integrated Services. J. Wroclawski. September 1997. (Status: Proposed Standard).

RFC 2209, Resource ReSerVation Protocol (RSVP)—Version 1 Message Processing Rules. R. Braden, and L. Zhang. September 1997. (Status: Informational).

RFC 2208, Resource ReSerVation Protocol (RSVP)—Version 1 Applicability Statement Some Guidelines on Deployment. A. Mankin, Ed., F. Baker, B. Braden, S. Bradner, M. O'Dell, A. Romanow, A. Weinrib, and L. Zhang. September 1997. (Status: Informational).

RFC 2207, RSVP Extensions for IPSEC Data Flows. L. Berger, and T. O'Malley. September 1997. (Status: Proposed Standard).

RFC 2206, RSVP Management Information Base using SMIv2. F. Baker, J. Krawcyzk, and A. Sastry. September 1997. (Status: Proposed Standard).

RFC 2205, Resource ReSerVation Protocol (RSVP)—Version 1 Functional Specification. R. Braden, ed., L. Zhang, S. Berson, S. Herzog, and S. Jamin. September 1997. (Status: Proposed Standard).

RFC 2201, Core Based Trees (CBT) Multicast Routing Architecture. A. Ballardie. September 1997. (Status: Experimental).

RFC 2190, RTP Payload Format for H.263 Video Streams. C. Zhu. September 1997. (Status: Proposed Standard).

RFC 2189, Core Based Trees (CBT version 2) Multicast Routing. A. Ballardie. September 1997. (Status: Experimental).

RFC 2149, Multicast Server Architectures for MARS-based ATM multicasting. R. Talpade, and M. Ammar. May 1997. (Status: Informational).

RFC 2121, Issues affecting MARS Cluster Size. G. Armitage. March 1997. (Status: Informational).

RFC 2117, Protocol Independent Multicast-Sparse Mode (PIM-SM): Protocol Specification. D. Estrin, D. Farinacci, A. Helmy, D. Thaler, S. Deering, M. Handley, V. Jacobson, C. Liu, P. Sharma, and L. Wei. June 1997. (Status: Experimental).

RFC 2094, Group Key Management Protocol (GKMP) Architecture. H. Harney, and C. Muckenhirn. July 1997. (Status: Experimental).

RFC 2093, Group Key Management Protocol (GKMP) Specification. H. Harney, and C. Muckenhirn. July 1997. (Status: Experimental).

RFC 2090, TFTP Multicast Option. A. Emberson. February 1997. (Status: Experimental).

RFC 2038, RTP Payload Format for MPEG1/MPEG2 Video. D. Hoffman, G. Fernando, and V. Goyal. October 1996. (Status: Proposed Standard).

RFC 2035, RTP Payload Format for JPEG-compressed Video. L. Berc, W. Fenner, R. Frederick, and S. McCanne. October 1996. (Status: Proposed Standard).

RFC 2032, RTP Payload Format for H.261 Video Streams. T. Turletti, and C. Huitema. October 1996. (Status: Proposed Standard).

RFC 2029, RTP Payload Format of Sun's CellB Video Encoding. M. Speer, and D. Hoffman. October 1996. (Status: Proposed Standard).

RFC 2022, Support for Multicast over UNI 3.0/3.1 based ATM Networks. G. Armitage. November 1996. (Status: Proposed Standard).

RFC 1949, Scalable Multicast Key Distribution. A. Ballardie. May 1996. (Status: Experimental).

RFC 1946, Native ATM Support for ST2+. S. Jackowski. May 1996. (Status: Informational).

RFC 1932, IP over ATM: A Framework Document. R. Cole, D. Shur, and C. Villamizar. April 1996. (Status: Informational).

RFC 1890, RTP Profile for Audio and Video Conferences with Minimal Control. Audio-Video Transport Working Group, H. Schulzrinne. January 1996. (Status: Proposed Standard).

RFC 1889, RTP: A Transport Protocol for Real-Time Applications. Audio-Video Transport Working Group, H. Schulzrinne, S. Casner, R. Frederick, and V. Jacobson. January 1996. (Status: Proposed Standard).

RFC 1828, IP Authentication using Keyed MD5. P. Metzger, and W. Simpson. August 1995. (Status: Proposed Standard).

RFC 1827, IP Encapsulating Security Payload (ESP). R. Atkinson. August 1995. (Status: Proposed Standard).

RFC 1826, IP Authentication Header. R. Atkinson. August 1995. (Status: Proposed Standard).

RFC 1825, Security Architecture for the Internet Protocol. R. Atkinson. August 1995. (Status: Proposed Standard).

RFC 1821, Integration of Real-time Services in an IP-ATM Network Architecture. Borden, Crawley, Davie, and Batsell. August 1995. (Status: Informational).

RFC 1819, Internet Stream Protocol Version 2 (ST2) Protocol Specification— Version ST2+. L. Delgrossi and L. Berger, eds. August 1995. (Status: Experimental).

RFC 1809, Using the Flow Label Field in IPv6. C. Partridge. June 1995. (Status: Informational).

RFC 1755, ATM Signaling Support for IP over ATM. M. Perez, F. Liaw, D. Grossman, A. Mankin, E. Hoffman, and A. Malis. February 1995. (Status: Proposed Standard).

RFC 1754, IP over ATM Working Group's Recommendations for the ATM Forum's Multiprotocol BOF version 1. M. Laubach. January 1995. (Status: Informational).

RFC 1633, Integrated Services in the Internet Architecture: An Overview. R. Braden, D. Clark, and S. Shenker. June 1994. (Status: Informational).

RFC 1585, MOSPF: Analysis and Experience. J. Moy. March 1994. (Status: Informational).

RFC 1584, Multicast Extensions to OSPF. J. Moy. March 1994. (Status: Proposed Standard).

RFC 1577, Classical IP and ARP over ATM. M. Laubach. January 1994. (Status: Proposed Standard).

RFC 1469, IP Multicast over Token-Ring Local Area Networks. T. Pusateri. June 1993. (Status: Proposed Standard).

RFC 1458, Requirements for Multicast Protocols. R. Braudes and S. Zabele. May 1993. (Status: Informational).

RFC 1301, Multicast Transport Protocol. S. Armstrong, A. Freier, and K. Marzullo. February 1992. (Status: Informational).

RFC 1136, Administrative Domains and Routing Domains: A model for routing in the Internet. S. Hares, and D. Katz. December 1989. (Status: Informational).

RFC 1112, Host extensions for IP multicasting. S.E. Deering. August 1989. (Status: Standard).

RFC 1075, Distance Vector Multicast Routing Protocol. D. Waitzman, C. Partridge, and S. E. Deering. November 1988. (Status: Experimental).

IETF Documents—Internet-Drafts

IETF Internet-Drafts are usually circulated and stored for six months after publication. At the end of that period, they are either replaced with a new version, replaced with an entirely new internet-draft, converted to an RFC, or removed. The names and dates of the drafts that follow were accurate as of November 1997.

Bagnall, P. and B. Briscoe. "Taxonomy of Communication Requirements for Large-scale Multicast Applications." draft-ietf-lsma-requirements-00.txt, 07/30/1997.

Ballardie, T. "Core Based Tree (CBT) Multicast Border Router Specification." draft-ietf-idmr-cbt-br-spec-00.txt, 10/27/1997.

Ballardie, T. ""shared-mtrace": A Multicast 'traceroute' facility for Shared Trees." draft-ballardie-shared-mtrace-00.txt, 10/27/1997.

Ballardie, T. and D. Thaler. "Core Based Trees (CBT) Multicast Routing MIB." draft-ietf-idmr-cbt-mib-00.txt, 07/21/1997.

Borden, M., J. Krawczyk, L. Berger, and E. Crawley. "A Framework for Integrated Services and RSVP over ATM." draft-ietf-issll-atm-framework-00.txt, 07/24/1997.

Briscoe, R. and P. Bagnall. "Taxonomy of Communication Requirements for Large-scale Multicast Applications." draft-ietf-lsma-requirements-00.txt, 07/29/1997.

Crowcroft, J., M. Handley, J. Ott, and C. Bormann. "The Internet Multimedia Conferencing Architecture." draft-ietf-mmusic-confarch-00.txt, 09/09/1997.

Crowcroft, J., Z. Wang, A. Ghosh, and C. Diot. "RMFP: A Reliable Multicast Framing Protocol." draft-crowcroft-rmfp-01.txt, 03/20/1997.

Dang, W. and J. Macker. "The Multicast Dissemination Protocol (MDP) Framework." draft-macker-mdp-framework-02.txt, 06/06/1997.

Estrin, D., D. Farinacci, S. Deering, D. Thaler, and A. Helmy. "Protocol Independent Multicast-Sparse Mode (PIM-SM): Protocol Specification." draft-ietf-idmr-pim-sm-specv2-00.txt, 09/11/1997.

Estrin, D., A. Helmy, and D. Thaler. "PIM Multicast Border Router (PMBR) specification for connecting PIM-SM domains to a DVMRP Backbone." draft-ietf-mboned-pmbr-spec-00.txt, 02/03/97.

Estrin, D., D. Meyer, and D. Thaler. "Border Gateway Multicast Protocol (BGMP): Protocol Specification." draft-ietf-idmr-gum-01.txt, 10/31/1997.

Estrin, D., S. Shenker, R. Braden, and D. Zappala. "Interdomain Multicast Routing Support for Integrated Services Networks." draft-zappala-multicast-routing-ar-00.txt, 03/27/1997.

Estrin, D., D. Thaler, and A. Helmy. "PIM Multicast Border Router (PMBR) specification for connecting PIM-SM domains to a DVMRP Backbone." draft-ietf-moboned-pmbr-spec-00.txt, 02/24/1997.

Farinacci, D., David Meyer, and Y. Rekhter. "Intra-LIS IP multicast among routers over ATM using Sparse Mode PIM." draft-ietf-ion-intralis-multicast-01.txt, 08/22/1997.

Fenner, W. "Internet Group Management Protocol, Version 2." draft-ietf-idmr-igmp-v2-08.txt, 11/03/1997.

Finlayson, R. "The Multicast Attribute Framing Protocol." draft-finlayson-mafp-00.txt, 01/17/1997.

Hay, K. "Multicast Chat (MCC) Protocol." draft-hay-mcc-00.txt, 03/26/1997.

Helmy, A. "Protocol Independent Multicast-Sparse Mode (PIM-SM): Implementation Document." draft-helmy-pim-sm-implem-00.txt, 01/20/1997.

Hinden, R., and S. Deering. "IPv6 Addressing Architecture." draft-ietf-ipngwg-addr-arch-v2-00.txt, 05/16/1997.

Hinden, R., and S. Deering. "IPv6 Multicast Address Assignments." draft-ietf-ipngwg-multicast-assgn-04.txt, 07/16/1997.

Jacobson, V., D. Farinacci, L. Wei, Steve Deering, and A. Helmy. "Protocol Independent Multicast Version 2, Dense Mode Specification." draft-ietf-idmr-pim-dm-spec-05.txt, 05/28/1997.

Jacobson, V., and M. Handley. "SDP: Session Description Protocol." draft-ietf-mmusic-sdp-04.txt, 09/09/1997.

Junkins, D. "Guidelines for Rate Limits on the MBONE." draft-ietf-mboned-limit-rate-guide-00.txt, 02/19/1997.

Katz, D., Y. Rekhter, T. Bates, and R. Chandra. "Multiprotocol Extensions for BGP-4." draft-bates-bgp4-multiprotocol-03.txt, 07/09/1997.

Kirstein, P., G. Montasser-Kohsari, and E. Whelan. "Specification of Security in SAP Using Public Key Algorithms." draft-ietf-mmusic-sap-sec-03.txt, 10/28/1997.

McCloghrie, K., D. Farinacci, and D. Thaler, "Internet Group Management Protocol MIB." draft-ietf-idmr-igmp-mib-05.txt, 07/21/1997.

McCloghrie, K., D. Farinacci, and D. Thaler. "IP Multicast Routing MIB." draft-ietf-idmr-multicast-routmib-05.txt, 03/26/1997.

McCloghrie, K., D. Farinacci, and D. Thaler. "Protocol Independent Multicast MIB." draft-ietf-idmr-pim-mib-03.txt, 03/26/1997.

Maufer, T., and C. Semeria. "Introduction to IP Multicast Routing." draft-ietf-mboned-intro-multicast-03.txt. 10/28/1997.

Meyer, D. "Administratively Scoped IP Multicast." draft-ietf-mboned-admin-ip-space-03.txt, 06/10/1997.

Meyer, D. "Some Issues for an Inter-domain Multicast Routing Protocol." draft-ietf-mboned-imrp-some-issues-02.txt, 06/10/1997.

Myjak, M., W. Smith, and S. Seidensticker. "Scenarios and Appropriate Protocols for Distributed Interactive Simulation." draft-ietf-lsma-scenarios-01.txt, 07/21/1997.

Patel, B. and M. Shah. "Multicast address allocation extensions to the Dynamic Host Configuration Protocol." draft-ietf-dhc-mdhcp-02.txt, 08/18/1997.

Pullen, M., M. Myjak, and C. Bouwens. "Limitations of Internet Protocol Suite for Distributed Simulation in the Large Multicast Environment." draft-ietf-lsma-limitations-01.txt, 03/26/1997.

Pusateri, T. "Distance Vector Multicast Routing Protocol." draft-ietf-idmr-dvmrp-v3-05.txt, 10/30/1997.

Robertson, K., K. Miller, M. White, and A. Tweedly. "StarBurst Multicast File Transfer Protocol (MFTP) Specification." draft-miller-mftp-spec-02.txt, 02/13/1997.

Schooler, E., H. Schulzrinne, and M. Handley. "SIP: Session Initiation Protocol." draft-ietf-mmusic-sip-04.txt, 11/13/1997.

Schulzrinne, H. "SIP URL Scheme." draft-ietf-mmusic-sip-url-00.txt, 05/14/1997.

Schulzrinne, H., A. Rao, and R. Lanphier. "Real Time Streaming Protocol (RTSP)." draft-ietf-mmusic-rtsp-05.txt, 10/29/1997.

Suzuki, M. "Architecture of the Resource Reservation Service for the Commercial Internet." draft-suzuki-res-resv-svc-arch-02.txt, 10/14/97.

Thaler, D. "Interoperability Rules for Multicast Routing Protocols." draft-thaler-multicast-interop-01.txt, 03/26/1997.

Thaler, D. and B. Aboba. "Multicast Debugging Handbook." draft-ietf-mboned-mdh-00.txt, 03/25/97.

Thaler, D., D. Estrin, and D. Meyer. "Grand Unified Multicast (GUM): Protocol Specification." draft-ietf-idmr-gum-00.txt, 07/30/97.

Wallner, D., E. Harder, and R. Agee. "Key Management for Multicast: Issues and Architectures." draft-wallner-key-arch-00.txt, 07/11/97.

Yamanouchi, N., T. Shiroshita, and T. O. Takahashi. "Reliable Multicast Transport Protocol." draft-shiroshita-rmtp-spec-01.txt, 09/03/1997.

Yamanouchi, N., T. Shiroshita, T. Sano, and O. Takahashi. "Reliable Multicast Transport Protocol Version 2." draft-shiroshita-rmtpv2-00.txt 08/29/1997.

Zappala, D. "A Route Setup Mechanism For Multicast Routing." draft-zappala-multicast-routing-me-00.txt, 03/27/1997.

Web Sites

This is a sampling of the more important Web sites related to IP multicasting and the MBone.

MBone Sites

MBone Information Site	www.mbone.com
Mbone Tools for Windows95	www.tascmad.mcg.gla.ac .uk/install.html
MBone-related mailing list archives	www.mbone.com/lists/
Index of MBone Binaries by Platform	www.merit.edu/net-research/ mbone/index/platforms.html
MBone Deployment Working Group	antc.uoregon.edu/ MBONED/
MSRI MBone Information	www.msri.org/computing/ mbone/
University College, London Archive (multicasting software)	mice.ed.ac.uk/mice/archive/

IP Multicasting

IP Multicast Routing Links	www.ipmulticast.com/ community/links-routing.html
IP Multicast Initiative	www.ipmulticast.com/

Reliable Multicasting

Comparing Multicast protocols	www.tascnets.com/mist/ doc/mcpCompare.html

MTP/SO: Self-Organizing Multicast	user.cs.tu-berlin.de/~nilss/ som/som.html
Reliable Multicast Links	research.ivv.nasa.gov/RMP/ links.html
XTP Home Page	www.ca.sandia.gov/xtp/

Others

IPSec Papers, RFCs	www.ietf.cnri.reston.va.us/ ids.by.wg/ipsec.html
RealNetwork	www.realnetwork.com/
RSVP Project	www.isi.edu/div7/rsvp/rsvp.html
RTP	www.cs.columbia.edu/~hgs/rtp
RTSP	www.cs.columbia.edu/~hgs/rtsp/
SIP:Session Initiation Protocol	www.cs.columbia.edu/~hgs/ sip/sip.html

I N D E X

Page references in *italic* type indicate illustrations. Page references followed by *table* indicate material in tables. Protocols and many other terms are indexed by acronym. For example, look for "DVMRP" rather than "Distance-Vector Multicast Routing Protocol".